The Solent

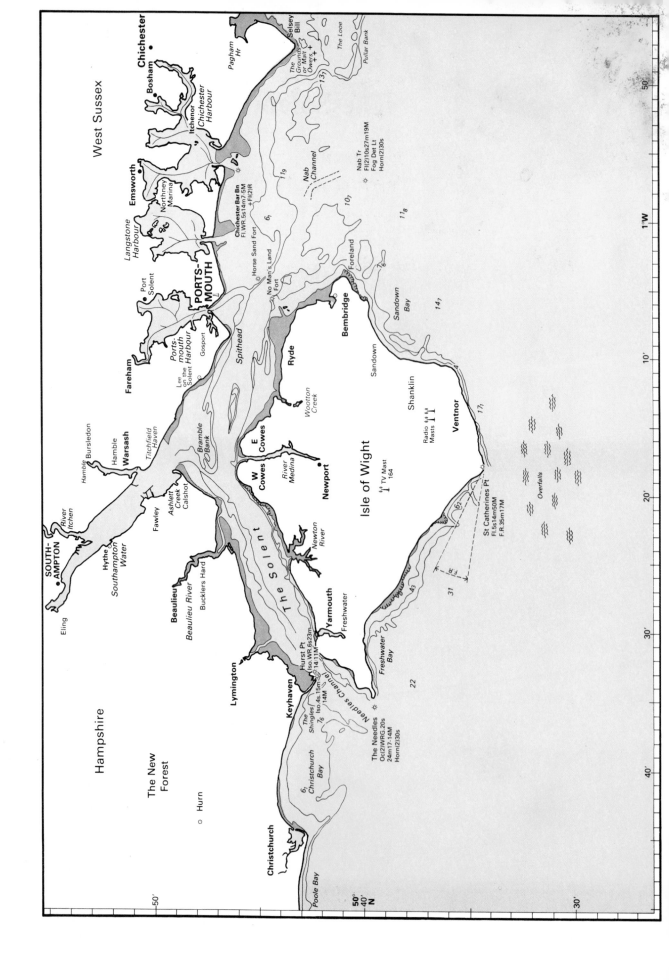

The Solent

A cruising-guide from Selsey Bill to the Needles including the Isle of Wight

Derek Bowskill

Imray Laurie Norie & Wilson Ltd
St Ives Cambridgeshire England

Published by
Imray, Laurie, Norie & Wilson Ltd
Wych House, St Ives, Huntingdon,
Cambridgeshire, PE17 4BT, England.

1990

British Library Cataloguing in Publication Data

Bowskill, Derek, 1928–
    The Solent.
    1. England. Solent. Pilots' guides
    I. Title
    623.89'22336

    ISBN 0 85288 140 1

CAUTION
Whilst every care has been taken to ensure accuracy, neither the Publishers nor the Author will hold themselves responsible for errors, omissions or alterations in this publication. They will at all times be grateful to receive information which tends to the improvement of the work.

PLANS
The plans in this guide are not to be used for navigation. They are designed to support the text and should at all times be used with navigational charts.

The last input of technical information was April 1990.

Printed in Great Britain at Tabro Litho Ltd,
Ramsey Forty-Foot, Huntingdon, Cambridgeshire

Contents

Evening
at Chichester
Harbour

On the Isle of Wight at the head of Wootton's navigation, there is a small pontoon permitting access to Wootton Bridge shopping precinct, a quarter of excellence.

Foreword

'Sunset and evening star
And one clear call for me!
And may there be no moaning of the bar,
When I put out to sea.'
Crossing the Bar Alfred, Lord Tennyson.

When I said I was going to the Broads, friends and colleagues alike set up the cry: 'Not the Broads; you'll never get a moment's peace.' They went on to wax eloquent regarding the faults, failing and general sins of omission and commission that infested the area. In the event, my visits proved them wrong, for a man can find there all kinds of cruising experiences: cowboys are not everywhere, choosing the boozing is a personal decision.

I got the same response for the Solent, except more so; not only was it packed marinas and speeding cowboys that got the thumbs down, but also flash boats, floating palaces and money, money, money all the way. I was more than happy to find they were wrong all over again.

There is no wonder that the Solent is popular. Its cruising variety is almost infinite; for you can always find some lively stretch to extend your sailing experience or some quiet backwater to stretch your muscles and relax. There are still places where you will be visited only by (nature's) wild life, but for those who like socialising, opportunities abound; for on the mainland and island alike, not only are the hostelries many and various but the people in general tend to be open, friendly and ready to be helpful. In addition, there is never any need to be far away from spare parts, a boatyard or an engineer; and since all boats bring their own kinds of bovver, that in itself is of major significance.

I spent three happy years working in the Solent. I hope that others find as much to treasure as I did in a domain in which I found little to fault and much to favour.

Acknowledgments

During the research for this pilot guide, the author has constantly referred to and made use of the following volumes:

The Shell Pilot to the English Channel; Ramsgate to the Scillies, Captain John Coote/K. Adlard
  Coles, Faber and Faber Ltd
Channel Pilot (NP 27), Hydrographer of the Navy
Creeks and Harbours of The Solent, Col. Sylvester Bradley/K. Adlard Coles, Nautical Books
Solent Hazards, Peter Bruce, Boldre Marine
Wight Hazards, Peter Bruce, Boldre Marine
Channel West and Solent Nautical Almanac for Yachtsmen, Adlard Coles Ltd
The Solent Way, Barry Shurlock, Hampshire County Council
Solent Shores, John Glasspool, Nautical Books
The Solent, R. L. P. and D. M. Jowitt, Terence Dalton Ltd
The Solent and Southern Waters, H. Alker Tripp, Conway Maritime Press
Portrait of the Solent, Barry Shurlock, Robert Hale
The Companion Guide to the Coast of South-East England, John Seymour, Collins

A full chart list is given in Appendix I.

The plans in this guide are based upon Admiralty charts with the permission of the Hydrographer of the Navy. The index has been compiled by Mrs Elizabeth Cook. The publishers also thank *Motorboats Monthly* for the loan of film for some of the photographs. The author wishes particularly to acknowledge the pleasure, the learning, the solace, the entertainment and general advantage he has gained from the following two works: *The Solent and Southern Waters*, H. Alker Tripp, Conway Maritime Press. *Sailing Tours, Part Two: From The Nore and Swin Middle Lightships to Tresco, Isles of Scilly*, Frank Cowper, Ashford Press Publishing. Sadly, both are now out of print, and neither can be obtained without the expenditure of some diligence; all of which will, however, be more than amply repaid by the joys to be found within their covers.

Dedication

In grateful thanks for their willing, generous and affectionate help during my sojourn in the Solent, this book is warmly dedicated to Tony Howarth and Pauline Maliphant.

Derek Bowskill
Pool-in-Wharfedale
April 1990

Introduction

Frank Cowper recalled the almost total lack of yachts in the South Coast havens when he started cruising in 1878. There was one small yacht at Bembridge, another at Keyhaven, Yarmouth and Lymington held three small yachts each, but there were none at Newtown, Bosham, Itchenor, Emsworth or Wootton.

Weather

Coast weather forecasts

Weather information is broadcast by the MRSC via Boniface and Newhaven every 4 hours from 0040 UT. When gale or strong wind warnings are in force they are broadcast at 2-hourly intervals from 0040 UT. Broadcasts are on VHF Ch 67.

Solent Coastguard uses two aerials for separate reports: Newhaven for Area 6 – Channel East: Selsey Bill to North Foreland and the French coast from Le Havre to Calais; Ventnor for Area 7 – Mid-Channel: Lyme Regis to Selsey Bill, the Channel Islands and the Cherbourg peninsula. In addition, remote radio stations are at Needles, St Catherine's, Newhaven and local conditions at Lee-on-the-Solent.

London Weather Centre ☎ 01-836 4311
Southampton Weather Centre, Southampton ☎ (0703) 28844
Marineline Channel East ☎ (0898) 500456
Mid-Channel ☎ (0898) 500457
Channel West ☎ (0898) 500458

Prevailing local conditions

St Catherine's lighthouse, Isle of Wight ☎ (0983) 730284
Calshot Coastguard, Southampton ☎ (0703) 893574
Solent Coastguard, Southampton ☎ (0705) 552100
Anvil Point lighthouse, Swanage ☎ (09292) 2146

Navigation

Decca waypoints

Off Dunnose	50°35'·00N 1°10'·00W	Beaulieu Spit Bn	50°46'·83N 1°21'·67W
Nab Tower	50°40'·05N 0°57'·07W	Salt Mead	50°44'·49N 1°22'·95W
St Catherine's Pt, 1M S	50°33'·04N 1°18'·00W	West Lepe	50°45'·20N 1°24'·00W
St Helen's Fort	50°42'·27N 1°04'·95W	Hamstead Ledge	50°43'·83N 1°26'·10W
Bembridge Ledge	50°41'·12N 1°02'·74W	Jack in the Basket	50°44'·25N 1°30'·50W
Chichester Bar Bn	50°45'·88N 0°56'·37W	Sconce	50°42'·50N 1°31'·35W
Dean Tail	50°43'·02N 0°59'·03W	NE Shingles	50°41'·93N 1°33'·32W
Dean Elbow	50°43'·55N 1°01'·83W	Mid Shingles	50°41'·19N 1°34'·59W
Horse Elbow	50°44'·23N 1°03'·80W	Shingles Elbow	50°40'·31N 1°35'·92W
Langstone Fairway	50°46'·28N 1°01'·27W	Bridge	50°39'·59N 1°36'·80W
No Mans Land Fort	50°44'·37N 1°05'·61W	Needles Fairway	50°38'·20N 1°38'·90W
Horse Sand Fort	50°44'·97N 1°04'·25W		
Outer Spit	50°45'·55N 1°05'·41W		
Spit Sand Fort	50°46'·20N 1°05'·85W		
SE Ryde Middle	50°45'·90N 1°12'·00W		
NE Ryde Middle	50°46'·18N 1°11'·80W		
E Bramble	50°47'·20N 1°13'·55W		
W Ryde Middle	50°46'·45N 1°15'·70W		
Hill Head	50°48'·12N 1°15'·91W		
Calshot	50°48'·38N 1°16'·95W		
Prince Consort	50°46'·38N 1°17'·48W		
Calshot Spit LtF	50°48'·32N 1°17'·55W		
W Bramble	50°47'·15N 1°18'·55W		
S Bramble	50°46'·95N 1°17'·65W		
Gurnard	50°46'·18N 1°18'·76W		
East Lepe	50°46'·09N 1°20'·81W		

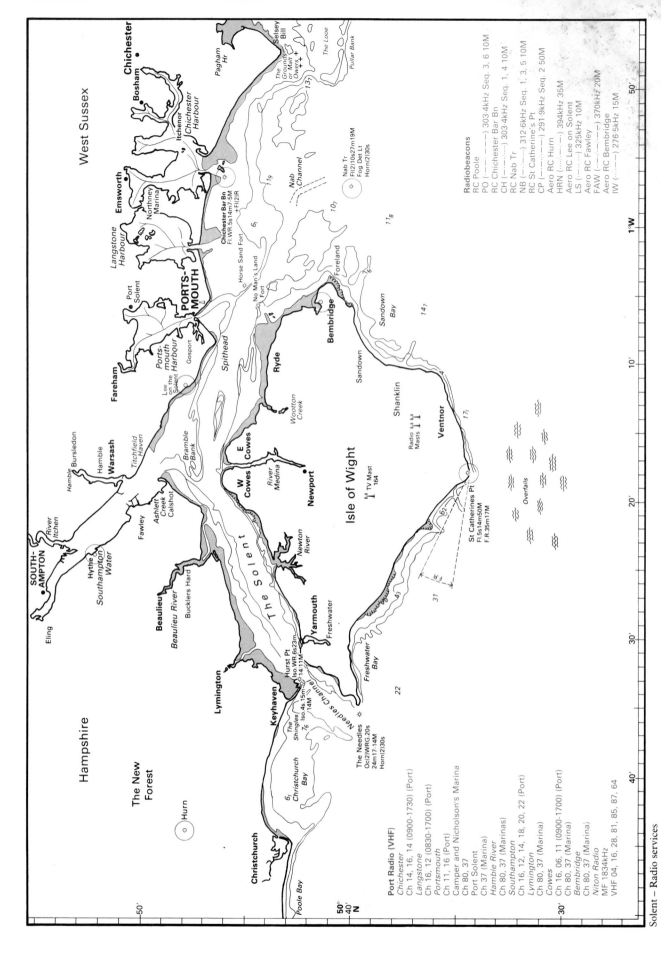

Solent – Radio services

Safety

SSO – SOLENT SAFETY ORGANISATION

Captain C. J. Nicholl, Harbour Master's Office, Shore Road, Warsash, Hampshire SO3 6FR. ☎ Locks Heath (04895) 6387. The following details on the SSO are from their pamphlet. It is an organisation established to preserve or assist in the preservation of life, and prevention of injury at sea, on the foreshore of the Solent and on the beaches of the counties of Hampshire and the Isle of Wight.

The SSO is a registered charity set up in 1977 to coordinate the inshore rescue services which provide safety cover for the people and craft in the Solent area. There are nine voluntary units.

Although the SSO units are manned by volunteers, there are considerable running expenses particularly for fuel, maintenance and insurance for the high-speed rescue craft. Also there is a continuous need to build up reserve funds for the replacement of the craft and engines which are increasingly more expensive. Funding for the SSO is primarily from Hampshire and Isle of Wight County Councils, River Authorities and Maritime Districts, the balance being made up by individual units' local fund raising.

Freshwater Inshore Rescue

Freshwater are based at the promenade in Freshwater Bay, operating a 6m Avon Searider with twin outboards. They cover an area between the Needles and St Catherine's Point on a 24-hour callout, 365 days a year.

Gosport and Fareham Inshore Rescue[1]

'Gafirs' are based at Gilkicker Point in Stokes Bay. They use 6m and 4m Avon Seariders, canoes and lifeguards to cover an area from Portsmouth Harbour mouth west to Titchfield Haven and Ryde Middle Bank. They too are on 24-hour callout all year round.

Hamble Rescue

This group is based at the Hard at Hamble and uses a 9m Atlantis Eagle with inboard diesel for callout in the Solent and Southampton Water. They are operational 24 hours a day, 365 days a year.

Lepe Rescue

They are based at Lepe Beach by the coastguard cottages and work in the Solent as required with a 7m Watercraft and a 4m Searider. They are operational summer weekends.

Portsmouth and Southsea Voluntary Lifeguards[1]

The lifeguards are based halfway between South Parade Pier and Southsea Castle on Southsea Promenade and cover the area off Southsea seafront from Eastney to Portsmouth Harbour using a 4m Searider, a 3·6m Commando and canoes. They are available from April to September during the day on weekends and bank holidays and also every day of the school holidays.

Ryde Voluntary Lifeguards[1]

Ryde are on a 24-hour callout, 365 days a year to cover the area between Osborne Bay and Seaview St Helens, out into the mid-Solent. They have a 5·5m Dory, a 4m Searider, a 3·6m Commando and canoes and are based at Appleby Esplanade on Ryde.

Solent Rescue[1]

Solent Rescue are based at Lepe Country Park during the daytime hours of weekends and bank holidays between Easter and the end of September. They use a 5·4m Searider and a 4m Searider to provide cover in the Solent area as required.

Stanswood Rescue[1]

The lifeguards work from Calshot beach to cover the inshore area between Calshot Activity Centre and Eaglehurst Castle. They operate during the day on summer weekends and bank holidays using a 3·6m inflatable.

South Wight Rescue

They are based at Western Shore at Sandown using a 6m Flatacraft to cover the area between Bembridge and St Catherine's Point during the daytime hours of weekends and bank holidays between April and September.

Communications

The coastguards coordinate all rescue operations within the Solent area using an amalgamation of SSO units, RNLI services and the search and rescue helicopters based at HMS Daedalus. All these units have been granted permission to operate on the coastguards private radio frequency (VHF Channel 0). In addition the SSO has its own private frequency issued by the Home Office to allow for close coordination during combined operations.

Training

The SSO provides centralised training facilities to support that given within individual units. This ensures a constantly high standard of performance and parity of experience. Courses include boat handling, use of radios, fire fighting and first aid seminars. Also the helicopter crews are always prepared to make themselves available for training exercises when operational requirements permit.

The units are recognised as a valuable element of the rescue services available and are deployed by HM Coastguard in the Solent area and around the coast of the Isle of Wight. Since its inception SSO units have been called out on numerous occasions to give assistance to craft ranging from rubber inflatables to large yachts and in addition there are beach patrols and rescue teams along the foreshore.

1. These stations are first-aid bases when operational

HM COASTGUARD

The District Controller, MRSC Solent, Whytecroft House, Marine Parade, West Lee-on-the-Solent, PO13 9NR. ☎ Lee-on-the-Solent (0705) 551775.

The area from Hengistbury Head to the Anglo-French median line, thence eastward to the Greenwich buoy and then to land at Belle Tout (west of Beachy Head) is now a single coastguard district entitled Solent District. There is Auxiliary Coastguard Rescue Equipment at Bembridge, Eastney, Hayling Island and Selsey; Sector Bases are at Calshot, West Wight (Needles), East Wight (Bembridge) and Hayling (Hayling Island). MRSC Solent is manned 24 hours a day; ☎ Portsmouth (0705) 552100 and monitors VHF Channel 16 and MF 2182 kHz as well as telex (869194) and the 999 emergency service.

RNLI

Craft are maintained as follows:

Selsey (inflatable)
Hayling Island (Atlantic 21)
Langstone Harbour (Atlantic 21 and inflatable)
Bembridge (Solent and inflatable)
Calshot (Brede)
Lymington (Atlantic 21)
Yarmouth (Arun)

HM CUSTOMS AND EXCISE

Norman House, Kettering Terrace, Portsmouth PO2 7AE. ☎ (0705) 862511. Yachts report to Albert Johnson Quay.

Radio

NITON RADIO

British Telecom International Radio Station, Dean, Whitwell Road, Ventnor, Isle of Wight, PO38 2AB. ☎ Isle of Wight (0983) 730496.

For RT booking of calls, centralised at Portishead Radio, dial 100 and request Ships' Service Portishead; or call direct on ☎ (0278) 781424. For general enquiries call ☎ Isle of Wight (0983) 730496 (no bookings).

2MHz radiotelephony service

Niton maintains a watch on 2182 kHz and answers ships on the same frequency. Once contact is made the station will normally transfer to 1834, 2628 or 2810 kHz. The station manager reports that the range of this service is about 200 miles but could be much less for a yacht depending upon her aerial arrangement.

VHF radiotelephony service

Niton has the following channels available for use: 4, 16, 28, 81 and 85. Channel 4 has a directional aerial pointing towards Brighton. Weymouth Bay Radio operates on Channel 5 and is controlled by Niton Radio.

Broadcast service

Niton broadcasts navigational warnings, gale warnings and weather forecasts to shipping on 1834 kHz after an initial announcement on 2182 kHz and on VHF Channels 28 and 5 after Channel 16. The areas are Dover, Wight and Portland. Broadcast times (UT) are as follows:

Traffic lists Every odd H+33 (except 0333)
Navigation warnings 0233, 0633, 1033, 1433, 1833, 2233
Weather bulletins 0733, 1933
Gale warnings 0303, 0903, 1503, 2103

Navtex service

This relatively new service, providing a printed copy of all the broadcast information, is becoming increasingly popular with small-boat owners.

Navigational warnings originated by the Hydrographic Office, gale warnings and weather bulletins issued by the Meteorological Office will be broadcast by Niton at 0018, 0418, 0818, 1218, 1618 and 2018.

VHF USERS

Bembridge Harbour Launch Ch 16, 10, 08
Chichester Harbour Radio Ch 16, 14
Langstone Harbour Radio Ch 16, 12
Portsmouth Harbour Radio Ch 11
Portsmouth Naval Base Ch 13
Southampton Port Radio Ch 16, 12, 14

VHF radiotelephony

VHF ship/shore radiotelephone service – direct calling. All British Telecom coast stations are now using direct calling on working channels. The procedure for calling direct on working channels is as follows:

1. Listen to one of the traffic channels to ensure it is free; a free channel is indicated by:
   a. no carrier noise
   b. no speech
   c. no channel engaged 'pips'
2. Call the required station on the selected free channel. Keep the carrier switched on for at least 4 seconds whilst calling.
3. If you are within range of the selected station your transmission will have started the shore station's transmitter which will then emit a carrier and a channel engaged signal, i.e. a series of 'pips'.
4. Wait until the coast station operator challenges or acknowledges your call before proceeding further.
5. If you do not manage to 'switch-on' the coast station's transmitter and receive the engaged signal after a few attempts, you may well be out of range of that station. Try another channel or station, or call when closer.
6. Avoid using the broadcast channel when possible particularly around scheduled broadcast times.

Solent tides

The tides in the Solent have been a source of special interest ever since Canute was supposed to have commanded them to turn or not to turn as he sat enthroned on the beach at Southampton, where Canute's Palace and Pub are there to prove it. (The original Canute's palace was supposed to be the Long House built around 1200 AD, nearly 200 years after Canute died.)

The 'double tides', 'double high waters' and the 'two hour stand of the young flood' at about mean tide level cause there to be little flow movement during this period, except for some local variations: for example, there is a tendency to ebb for a short time well before the end of the flood in Chichester Harbour, and there is a similar feeling up the Medina. Then, this rising tide of nearly seven hours is followed by an ebb of under four; and it is this powerful ebb that helps prevent silting up in many of the channels. If the Solent had the range of the Bristol Channel, then the tidal waters would indeed be something to behold – and something even more difficult to contend with.

The Romans, the Saxons and the Danes are all said to have benefited from these particularly helpful tidal phenomena. The Venerable Bede wrote, 'In this sea comes a double tide out of the seas which spring from the infinite ocean of the Arctic which surrounds all Britain.' And today, even as I write, the Cunard *Queen Elizabeth II* and her attendant tugs are exploiting the long stand of high water just across the road, as it were, at the QE terminal.

In quite dramatic terms, Drayton referred to them as, 'those prodigious signes ... which the Britans fore-ran'; and again, 'The Seas against their course with double Tides returne, And oft were seene by night like boyling pitch to burne.'

And yet again, regarding the Isle of Wight: 'And to the Northe, betwixte the foreland and the firme, She hath that narrow Sea, which we the Solent tearme: Where those rough irefull Tides, as in her Straits they meet, With boysterous shocks and rores each the other rudely greet. Which fierclie when they charge, and sadlie make retreat, Upon the bulwarkt Forts of Hurst and Cal-sheot beat.'

But for a more objective and scientifically determined view of this unique effect, here is an extract from ABP Southampton's *Tide Tables* as promulgated by the dock and harbourmaster, Captain M. J. Ridge:

'The unusual phenomenon of the 'Double High Water' in the Solent and Southampton area is well known, but is not caused by the existence of the two entrances to the Solent or the Isle of Wight as is popularly supposed. However, the two entrances to the Solent do cause other effects to the tide which are not so well known, namely, the 'Young Flood Stand' and the short duration of the ebb tide which are both valuable assets to the mariner.

Young flood stand
The 'young flood stand' occurs two hours after Low Water and is particularly pronounced over spring tides, although this is evident only from the shape of the curve of the tidal trace marks on tide gauge records. During the period of spring tides following Low Water there is a pronounced rise in tides; and two hours after Low Water the stream slackens off quite considerably for a further two hours before the final accelerated rise to High Water, which takes a further three hours. This slackening effect two hours after Low Water is known as the 'young flood stand'.

Short duration of ebb tide
A full tidal cycle lasts approximately 12½ hours and therefore if the flood and the Double High Water period lasts 9 hours, it is evident that the ebb tide runs for 3¾ hours. This short duration of the ebb tide creates a greater velocity of flow and is an uncommon feature as compared with other ports in the United Kingdom.

Double High Water
To try to understand the reasoning behind the description 'Double High Water', one has to look first at the tidal flow throughout the English Channel. When it is High Water at Dover it is Low Water at Land's End and vice versa. Imagine the English Channel as a rectangular tank 300 nautical miles in length and having a uniform depth of 36 fathoms pivoted at its mid-length. If inclined in either direction the water flows towards the lower end, thus giving the effect of High and Low Water at opposite ends. At the point of pivot, however, the level remains constant. Of course, the English Channel does not tip, but external forces created by the position of the moon and sun relative to the earth create the same effect, originating from the Atlantic Pulse which keeps the English Channel alternating between High and Low Water with the times of High Water at one end coinciding approximately with the time of Low Water at the other. This effect is called an oscillation and occurs twice daily.

If the actual physical features conformed to this ideal pattern there would be no rise and fall at mid-length, but though the tides at each end of the Channel do conform approximately to this pattern, the friction, irregular depths and restrictions in width of the Channel between the Isle of Wight and the Cherbourg Peninsula result in a further four oscillations daily within an area bounded by Portland, Cherbourg, Littlehampton and Le Havre. Combined with the natural twice daily oscillation, this produces the 'Double High Water' curve as experienced in the Port of Southampton. In the shallower waters within the Isle of Wight and in the Port of Southampton up to 30 further oscillations of varying magnitude again vary the 'Double High Water' curve to produce the ultimate Southampton tidal curve embodying the local tidal features, namely, the short duration of the ebb tide, the 'young flood stand', and the pronounced fall between first and second High Water stands.

Additional feature

One further tidal feature inside the Isle of Wight waters occurs because the western end of the Solent is nearest to the mid-length or axis of the English Channel, so that the tidal range is only about half that at the eastern end. The times of High Water and Low Water in the two places differ by only an hour or so, however, and the rising tide in the eastern end has to rise further in about the same time as the western end. It therefore overtakes it in height about an hour or so before High Water, though in both places the tide is still rising. This difference in level causes the Solent tidal stream to turn to the westward between one and two hours before High Water, and to continue in that direction near the following Low Water, when it again turns to the eastward.

General

This explanation and theory has come to light through continuous tidal observations since the early 1900s and although past hydrographers and research scientists have tried to discover a firm reason for the 'Double High Water' effect the remarkable tidal features shown in this tidal curve are undoubtedly due to modifications which brought about the existence of the two entrances to the Solent.'

When planning a cruise of the Solent, particularly if you want to stop off at as many ports and havens as possible, it is most economical of time, fuel and/or effort, to move from west to east. The flood tides from the westward will take you into the creeks with them; while the 'foul' tides from the east will stem and balk you as the water drops away at the very time you want to make your way in.

What Grenville Collins wrote, in 1692, is still true today: 'The Tyde of Ebb setteth on the Shingles, which are hard stones. The Flood setteth on the Needles.' He also noted the care that was needed when approaching Wight from the west, 'There is a strong Indraught that sets in at the Needles and into Pool; which Indraught hath hauld many Ships into Fresh-water Bay. But I think it, and I am sure, that no Ship can run ashoar in Fresh-water Bay if they did but mind the Lead; the neglect of which hath been the loss of many Ships. Keep a five and twenty and thirty fathom water, and you need not fear the Indraught of the Wight.'

Tidal stream diagrams

Rates of flow are given in knots, the first figure referring to spring tides, the second to neaps.

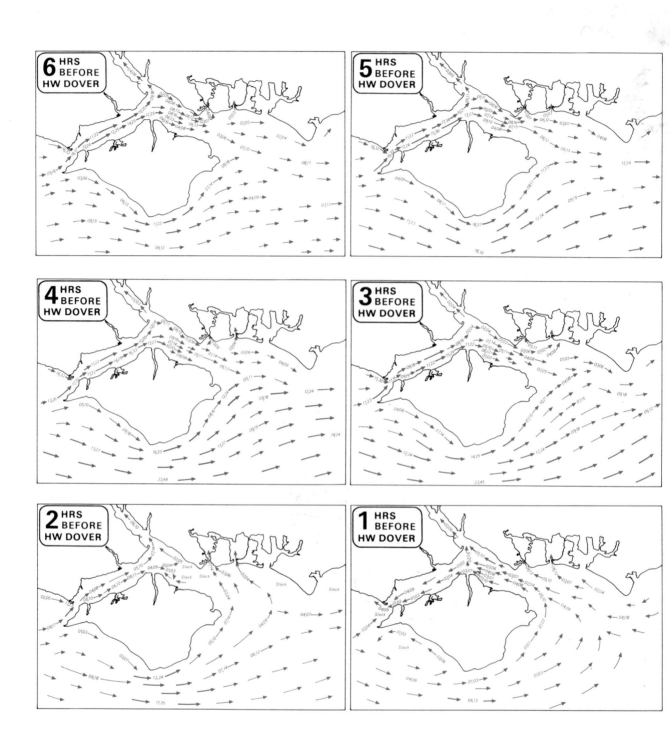

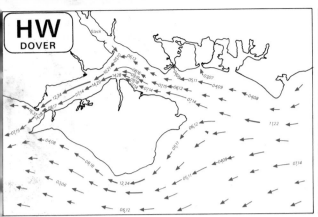

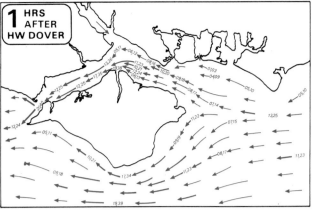

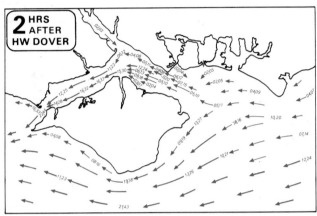

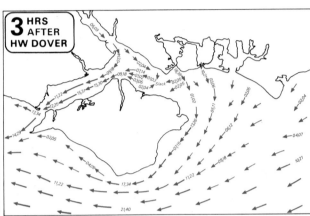

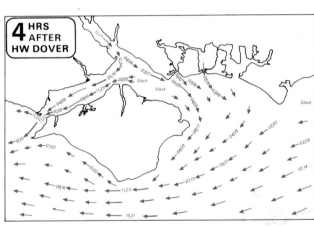

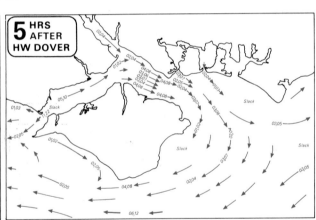

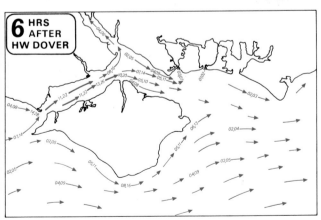

9

I. The north side of the Solent

Approaches: Selsey Bill and the Looe

If you are making for the Solent from France, the way is clear and plain: the Nab Tower (RC NB —·/—···) with the Owers left well to starboard. However, from the east along our own south coast, there is a choice: outside the Owers; or the 'overland' route through the Looe.

On a course from Beachy Head, there is little to choose so far as distance is concerned; but if you are coming from one of the Sussex ports or marinas (Newhaven, Brighton, Shoreham-by-Sea and Littlehampton) going outside the Owers is a considerable diversion that can frequently be a long, boring slog. So why the debate?

The answer lies in the tide race off Selsey Bill. It is neither as big nor far-reaching as Portland's; nor does it carry a swell like those to be encountered off Beachy or Flamborough Heads. In fact, by comparison, it is small beer or water; but therein lies the very cause for concern. The Looe tide race occurs between Boulder Bank and the Malt Owers (or the Grounds or the Dries as they are sometimes known) and it has no sea room for manoeuvre: nowhere to go but up and down. It progresses with much dash, verve and panache, apparently in all directions and all at the same time; creating the same sort of short, sharp wave formation that is the bane of the Thames Estuary and much of the east coast. The fast moving short choppy breakers can always beat you to the draw; and while they are no threat to life, I find them very demanding on limbs, for the motion they create is distinctly uncomfortable.

The Looe is marked by the red and green *Street* and *Boulder*; *Street* taking its name no doubt from the Streets (the NW end of the Owers) just off Selsey, and *Boulder* from the Bank. The Admiralty *Pilot* reads: 'It should be borne in mind that the buoys cannot be relied on implicitly, and they may give a poor response.' The drying Mixon rocks to the east are well marked by a beacon.

I have never run the Looe when it has been less than lively, and on occasions huge waves have piled up like bristling walls of water with the buoys swinging on their chains as if driven by crazed roller-coaster engines. Cowper had this to say:

'DANGERS LYING OFF SELSEY BILL. I am always glad when I have passed Selsey Bill. It is the nearest equivalent to the dreaded Penmarch Rocks, on the Breton coast, that I know, only it has no such lofty tower as now warns the mariner off those dangers.

This part of the Channel is considered the most dangerous from the Goodwins to the Wolf Rock. Not only is the coast very low and difficult to see, even when near, but the shoals lie out over five miles from the land and cover a large extent of ground. And the sea is nearly always broken, owing to the strength of the tides.

On the N. side of the Loose are the Mixon – beyond which N.E. lies the Park – the Pagham Flats, the Streets, the Dries, and a continuation of these last in a S.W. direction called the Brake or Cross Ledge, which connects with the Pullar and Boulder Banks, having from 6ft. to 19ft. only at low water, thus forming a rocky obstruction across the W. entrance of the Looe Channel. The Streets Buoy marks the passage through in the best water, being moored in the 16ft. off the S. extreme of the northern part of the ledge. The Streets starts from about three-quarters of a mile westward of Selsey Bill, extending in two parallel ledges, awash at the lowest tides, for one mile S.W. by W. from high-water mark, bending abruptly S.E. by S. for another mile. The N.W. part is called the Grounds or Malt Owers, the S.E. part the Dries, all drying at low water springs. The Mixon is an extension of these dangers, one mile to the E.

The coast from Selsey Bill to the entrance of Chichester Harbour is very low, with various buildings, such as the hotel, near the shore W. of Selsey Street; Bracklesham Farm, near the bay of that name. All this bay is shoal, and as Chichester Haven is approached great care must be taken to avoid E. Pole Sands, which dry out a long way.'

Back in 1928, Sir Alker Tripp described his experiences of the Looe with a companion in his 'exploration' entitled *The Solent & The Southern Waters*.

'"We've got to mend our pace if we're going to save our tide through the tide-race in the Looe. It's useless attempting it, on a wind, unless the tide will take us through."

PORTSMOUTH

Chichester Harbour

Hayling Island

Langstone Harbour

Hill Head Harbour

Lee-on-the-Solent

Gosport

Southsea

Spithead

Ryde

Ryde Sand

Sandown Bay

Bembridge

Foreland

Fishbourne

Wootton Bridge

Wootton Creek

NEWPORT

WEST COWES

EAST COWES

Old Castle Pt

River Medina

Isle of Wight

Nettlestone Point

Sandown

The wind had steadied a little since the return of the sunshine; so we took the risk and shook out the reef. With foam streaking away from us, we were soon slashing down in great style past the shingly shore and flat landscape of Selsey Bill, headed for the Mixon Beacon. If we missed our tide we should have to sail right round the Owers, seven miles offshore. I watched the clock. Yes, she could do it.

The Bill and the shoal-system seaward of it, was sheltering us considerably at present, and the sea was not rough in the Looe. But the overfalls were a different matter – a regular system of shoal-breakers, a turmoil of foam.

"We'll get a dusting!" I grinned, with a cheerfulness that was partly simulated; for, like most other people, I hate a tide-race.

The Mixon Beacon was astern; we were there.

Thud! Into the first wave Growler drove, and we were drenched in spray; but the first wave had killed her speed. If I had fluffed more I should have kept her drier. Almost a-shake, she was quite manageable; one could gauge progress by the buoys – the tide was taking her through.

But it was a curious progress, as such progress in a tide-race always is. The waves simply pounded on her, and the lift and tumble were steep and very sudden. The waves beat on her hollow hull like on a drum.

"Ever hear such a row?" my companion chirped, as an extra big one hit its solid blow. "Bang!"

The passage through the overfalls was brief, and, from a steadier well now, we were able to take pleasant stock of the landfall which had first opened at Selsey Bill. Twelve miles distant, the cliff reared itself nobly in the sunlight – the white face of Culver. There lay the Isle of Wight.

There it lay. We had rounded our last headland, and had reached the Waters of the Wight. It was only a minor nuisance that the wind took off to such an extent that we were persistently swept by the tide to leeward of our true course for Bembridge. This meant patient work to windward on a lee-going tide; but as soon as we had closed the shore, and were out of the full run of the tidal stream, we were able to make it good. Not that the delay was of any real consequence. We were able to reach the Drumhead buoy by the time that there was sufficient water to enter. Before eight o'clock that evening Growler had crept up the narrow tideway, and was comfortably moored in Bembridge Harbour. We looked about us with contented eyes as we tied the gaskets to the mainsail. Before ten we had turned in, and were deep in that comfortable sleep which follows when a passage, however small, is a thing accomplished.'

And indeed, his comments are fair and fine answers to the question posed by that famous Isle of White rhymester, that mariner *manqué*, Alfred, Lord Tennyson: 'Is there any peace In ever climbing up the climbing wave?'

Pagham Harbour is close by Selsey Bill, and forms, as it were, its shoresides' soft underbelly. It used to be bleakly open to the elements, but is now well protected from the sea. At one time it was called Andering or Undering and contained the very active Sidlesham Quay and its associated ferry. The sea breached it in the 14th century and flooded nearly 3,000 acres. 700 acres were reclaimed in 1876, but on 16th December 1910, the sea once more broke through at Church Norton and overwhelmed the area. It has been a tidal estuary ever since.

The harbour is, of course, no longer a harbour, and has become a Site of Special Scientific Interest (SSSI): a dedicated nature reserve comprising over 1,000 acres of tidal mud flats, shingle beach and farmland. Birds, from avocets to wrens, are to be seen throughout the year in their thousands.

Cowper says: 'Pagham Harbour no longer exists. It was reclaimed some years ago, and the shingle beach has since formed all along its mouth. There is an anchorage in the Park in three fathoms, with the Mixon bearing S.W. by W. ½ W. and Chichester spire N. ½ W. The holding ground is good, but with the wind eastward of S. it is a bad place to be caught in. It is, however, a favourite berth for coasters and barges waiting the tide through the Looe.'

At Sidlesham Quay coal and grain were shipped by 25-tonners. The nearby mill was left high, dry and impotent when the reclamation took place. In days gone by, the Sidlesham ferry used to ply from the peninsula to the 'mainland', when the tides covered the Wadeway, which is the present raised causeway. The ferryman was paid 4 bushels of barley a year.

At Pagham itself, St Wilfrid landed in 665 AD to spread Christianity to the wild men of the north. He built a cathedral. It is now beneath the waves, but there are those locals who claim to hear its bells; either from a none too secure berth in the famous Crab and Lobster at Sidlesham, or from an anchorage in the offshore roads known as the Parks (being a now-submerged deer park of the Tudor kings). Those selfsame locals also claim to hear the mermaids singing; but sadly they never seem to sing for me.

The Venerable Bede records that Wilfrid also did a useful thing: he taught the Selsey men to fish at sea by utilising the nets they knew of only to catch eels. The very first time they were thrown into the sea off the Bill, they netted over 300 of various kinds. No mention is made of any loaves or of water being turned into wine.

Selsey itself is a small village on the promontory doing its best to hang on to its style and character in the face of invasion by landlubbing foreigners. There is still hard professional fishing undertaken from Selsey and many of the boats are launched from the beach in a tradition that goes back centuries. Thanks to the protection afforded to the beach and the roads by the land mass and the Owers, there are also sea moorings for larger vessels; but bad southeasterlies can take their toll of moorings and beach alike. Fresh crabs and lobsters abound; but sadly there is nothing left of the old Selsey smacks except their fame.

Just a word about the massive structure of the Nab Tower, which must be praised for its function and efficiency, if not for its shape or style. It was one of two towers built about 1917 for antisubmarine defence, and was towed out to its present location and sunk to replace the previous lightship that had pride of place since 1812. It is the main marker for all commercial shipping as well as those cross-Channel yachts that are making for the East Solent. Local yachts use it little, since there is nothing to stand in the way of inshore passages.

Chichester Harbour

Chichester Harbour is an amazing phenomenon: a tidal inland lake or near-lagoon, well in excess of 4,000 acres, that is home to thousands of the boating fraternity and a haven to millions of birds. The Admiralty *Pilot* describes it as: '... a large area of low-lying land, marsh and drying banks, with 17 miles of navigable channels suitable for vessels drawing up to 2·7m and 30m in length. During the summer more than 3,000 yachts and pleasure craft are moored in its various branches and in the marinas and yacht harbours.'

As usual the Admiralty is pedestrian in its prosaic appraisal of its charms; but, unusually, its facts are in need of correction. In fact, there are nearly 9,000 vessels moored in the 11 square miles of tidal water in the harbour (not counting the 2,500 under 3m); and that figure is increased in season by the hundreds of visitors who flock to all its favourite stations, be they pontoons, buoys or hostelries. The 17 miles of well marked and lighted channels are contained in 11 square miles of land and 11 square miles of water.

What is less well known is that waders and wildfowl abound, with tern, shellduck, widgeon, dunlin, redshank and godwit all visiting in their season too. Importantly, up to 7,000 Brent Geese (around 10% of the world's population) have been known to winter there. Indeed, the harbour is managed by the Chichester Harbour Conservancy; and all the staff from the new harbourmaster, Captain Whitney, to the oldest hand are jealous of the purity of their refuge. As they say, there is within the harbour a veritable 'mosaic of varied habitats'.

Once inside, you are protected at most states of the tide from most winds in most places; but before that blessed state can be achieved, there is the well known bar and its associated sandbanks at the entrance: all famous or infamous according to your experiences and perceptions. Cowper described Chichester:

'People from the eastward, as a rule, know very little of Chichester Harbour. I discovered it for myself as far back as 1872, and have liked it more and more ever since, although the entrance is certainly worse than it used to be. I think the fact that I took Zayda, drawing over 6ft. and heavy to handle, in and out of this place, and up to Emsworth, Bosham, and Itchenor, without local assistance of any sort, and without ever touching even at low neap tides, is proof that it cannot be so difficult a place as it is thought to be.

To me it is a delightful change from the busy stress of such crowded anchorages as Southampton, Cowes in Regatta Week, and Portsmouth, to slip smoothly in here over the rolling waves as they break on either hand along the treacherous sands, to turn hard to starboard between the too obtrusive Pilsey Sands and the southern sand heads, and so, rippling peacefully on between stunted trees and oozy banks round the low spit of Cobnor, to anchor below that ancient church where sleeps the great sea king's daughter, in the soil, maybe in the very basilica, where trod, Titus, Wilfrid, Canute, Harold – a goodly array of great names to be associated with this tranquil and lowly fane. Bosham is even depicted in the Bayeux tapestry – at least Harold leaving it is, for hence he sailed to help Duke William to besiege Dinan up the Rance past St Malo. It is these old-world memories in these old-world nooks that make cruising so delightful to me. A lady has lately written an intolerant letter to a magazine, calling the people who like cruising "crustacea". I am sure I don't mind. Shellfish are very good.'

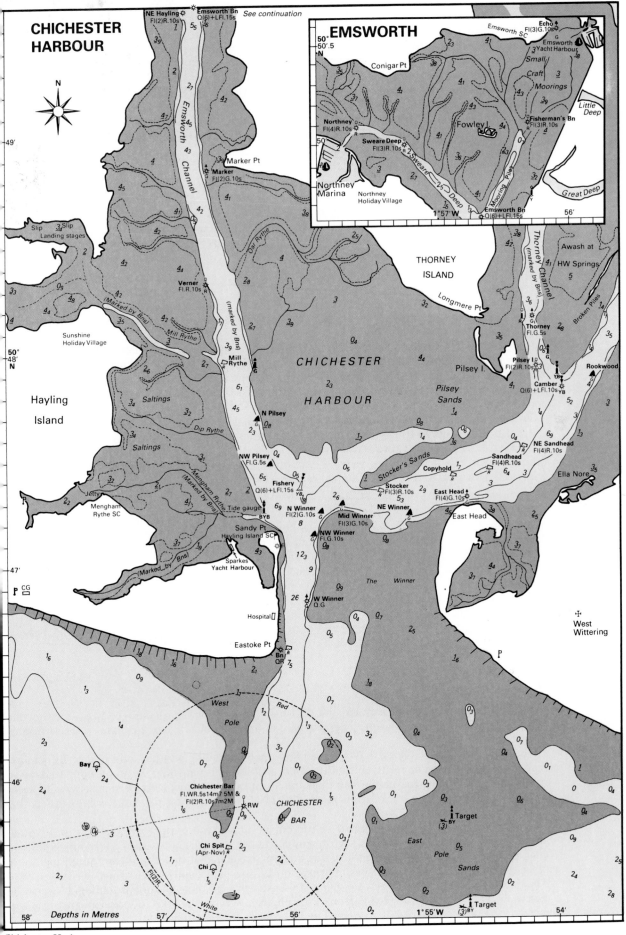

CHICHESTER HARBOUR

EMSWORTH

Directions

The Pole Sands are the hazards, and there are three of them: East Pole Sands, which spread from East Head and the Winner round towards East Wittering, and reach out for well over a mile; West Pole, a spit extending from Eastoke Point, for nearly a mile to the SSW; and, poised between the two as a trap for the unwary, Middle Pole, a collection of drying sandbanks, to the SSE. Standing as if portents at the gates, are the two wrecks on East Pole sands.

Coming from the S or SE (Nab Tower or Selsey Bill) you should stand well out in Bracklesham Bay so that you will be a good mile or so S of Chichester *Bar* beacon before turning N to make your approach into the Eastoke/Winner Channel. The Harbour Conservancy notes that:

'Chichester Bar is dredged to approximately 1·5m below datum giving a depth of 2m at MLWS. However, after severe gales, the bottom can vary up to +/− 0·75m. With a falling tide and strong winds from a southerly sector a dangerous sea may be encountered; it is advisable to exercise caution and cross the bar at slack water or between three hours before and one hour after HW springs. When approaching from the westward remain on the 5m line or with the Target Beacon in transit with Cakeham Tower bearing 064° until Eastoke Beacon opens up to the east of the Bar Beacon. Then alter course to pass between Eastoke and West Winner Beacons leaving Chichester Bar Beacon close to the west. Reverse this procedure when leaving.'

From the SW, the two yellow buoys, *Hard* and *Chi*, should keep you a safe distance from West Pole; and, in addition, there is a red can buoy *Chi Spit* in the vicinity of 50°45'·68N 0°56'·47W from April to November. A sand spit is now building up on the seaward-to-westward side of the beacon and the red can is laid to warn of the hazard. Its exact position depends on soundings taken at the beginning of the season.

It is declared possible to bring Cakeham tower into line with the north *Target* beacon on a bearing of 064°, but I have found the confusion of background detail such that I have never been able to do so. In fact, whether from S, SE or SW, it is not until you are quite close to the beacon itself that it stands out in any manner suited to its significance, in spite of its actual size and colour.

True to form, on my first encounter with the area, I actually mistook one of the *Targets* for the *Bar* beacon. Just to add to the confusion, the *Target* was not only being serviced at the time, but had also been pressed into service by a local trawler as a mooring buoy. My inveterate caution, however, meant that I was arriving on rising springs, so there was no shortage of water and I was able to retreat and reform without trouble. Cowper felt that:

'This large lagoon (Chichester Haven), which offers nearly as good cruising ground for small boats as Poole, is difficult of access, as it is quite unmarked by buoys, and the bar has scarcely more than 2ft. at low water spring tides, although at neap tides I have in Zayda, drawing 6ft. 3in., worked out on the last of the ebb, and entered with a fair wind at about a quarter of an hour after the flood had commenced. Personally I have a great liking for this neglected and rather dreaded harbour, although both these aspects are beginning to be modified, mainly, I am glad to think, owing to my repeated representations of mistaken impressions. I have never once got ashore, either coming in or going out, nor in any of the mazy creeks of this sinuous inlet, either up to Emsworth, or Bosham, or Itchenor, in Zayda (6ft 3in.), while in Undine II (5ft 3in.) I sailed right up to Dell Quay, where the bottom dries out, distant two miles from Chichester. Dell Quay I do not recommend except for barges or boats that take the ground easily.'

The entrance

For the last approach from seaward, the port-hand *Eastoke* beacon should be kept open to the east of the *Chichester Bar* beacon. The *Bar* beacon itself should be left a couple of ships' beams to port.

The bar nearly dries at some LWS, depending upon prevailing weather, and it also shifts more than somewhat. Even in relatively undisturbed conditions it can offer an unpleasant rock-and-roll experience; but whenever the wind has much south in it – and most particularly when such a wind is against the ebb – it is wiser not to be anywhere near it, for the short, steep seas can be dangerous.

It is important to have a sound and sturdy engine unless you are prepared always to leave on an ebb and return on a flood; but such planning cannot be entirely wise since it is impossible to guarantee the routine. The strength of the streams is such that many craft are quite unable to make headway at all in the narrows between the Winner and Sandy Point when the ebb is full. The Admiralty puts the strongest outgoing streams at over 6 knots and the incoming at nearly 3. *Valcon*, with 33ft and two 56hp Parsons Pike engines, was barely able to make progress against one spring tide, nor was a 45ft trawler. The facts speak for themselves.

The *Chichester Bar* beacon: one
of the most famous landmarks
in the world.

Eastoke Point has groynes all round, with those to its east being marked by red beacons. After the 1987 winter, the one with the infamous October gale, the actual easterly spit off the Point moved dramatically enough to justify a special notice to mariners, noting the growing challenge of its eddies.

From here on, it is important for strangers to read the chart and keep a careful watch for the channel buoys: the Winner is so extensive that it is easy to overlook the long trek round the greens and find yourself making for the wrong one. There is a most useful tide gauge on the *West Winner* starboard beacon.

The Chichester Winner is a drying bank of sand and shingle. Just like its Langstone sisters, it is well known for the number of 'incidents' it claims each year. Indeed, a favourite pastime during the season is for folk to visit Sparkes Yacht Harbour on a Sunday afternoon just to survey the strandings.

Hayling Island, in company with many other parts of our coastline, is being eroded at a fair rate of knots. Centuries ago, it stretched far out to sea. In 1798, HMS *Impregnable* hit the Winners (once known as the Wolsinars) with much cause for grief; and a few years later a vessel from Gibraltar (in the grip of the plague) having been driven away from all other havens tried for sanctuary. She went aground on the Pole Sand and coastguards were ordered to shoot anyone who tried to leave. Sadly, in the event, death claimed them all swiftly, for a southwesterly wind blew and all were lost.

Eastoke Point: the regular line of beacons on the shore mark
what can be a bleak spot with a speedy tide rip.

The headquarters of the Hayling Island Sailing Club: since the
closure of the Treloar Hospital, now the main architectural feature on the west bank.

Sandy Point

The HQ of the Hayling Island Sailing Club on Sandy Point itself appears first on the port shore; showing signs of the bleakness of its position. Sandy Point brings decision time: east, north or west? To the west is Sparkes Yacht Harbour and Mengham Rythe; to the north the channel to Emsworth and Thorney; and to the east the Chichester Channel for the rest of the harbour.

The charts give little idea of the confusion of mooring buoys, and channel markers in the form of cardinals, rods, poles and perches that abound just off the point. In most channels, you can count on the bigger craft at their moorings plainly indicating the deep-water channel; but here, their profusion and proximity do nothing but confuse the stranger. I recall at one high water, so controversial and various were the currents, eddies and counter eddies, that the boats were ferociously pulling at their moorings every which way, giving no indication of any kind as to the run of the channel. Had I not been conversant with the channel by that time, I would have almost certainly turned back and waited for more clement conditions.

The entrance channel to Sparkes Yacht Harbour is found by leaving the yellow buoy off the point to port, and proceeding midway between the two scrubbing posts to port and the tide gauge to starboard on a course of 277°. This will lead you towards the starboard side of the four substantial wooden piles, and on to the recently established leading marks. You will then see the red and green posts marking the close channel into the marina itself. The channel has 2m at lowest water spring tides, so most yachts can get in and out without let or hindrance. (However, a recent report from friends indicates that in autumn '88 they ran aground in mid-channel at low water in a 5ft draught Contessa. One can never be too careful!)

Sparkes is an intimate business project run by Basil Rizzi and his family; not forgetting their two dogs, one of which, the major guardian, while possessed of only three legs, does better than many of its kin with a full complement.

It is a recent project, and is working hard to keep up with the demand that their fast, friendly and efficient service has created. One of the noticeable developments has been the opening of the Mariner's Wine Bar & Restaurant, where home cooking is supported by a well selected drinks menu. In terms of simple, straightforward, whiter-than-white efficiency, their laundrette facility is one of the best on the south coast.

I can find nothing wrong with their self-portrait: 'The position of Sparkes Yacht Harbour on Hayling Island and inside Chichester Harbour offers a wide range of sailing opportunities. It has a large area of well protected waters, abundant places of interest nearby, windsurfing and sailing schools. Visitors are welcome ....'

While more improvements and expansions are proposed, the very situation of the place and the natural charm of those who run it must guarantee a long waiting list for some time to come.

Just before the October hurricane, I was there for a predicted tide of 4·9m that actually exceeded 7·0m, taking all present by surprise. Had we known, we might have read it as a sign of even more unusual things to come. On the night of the October hurricane, the predicted tide was 3·4m and the actual tide was 5·1m. Had the catastrophe occurred during the exceptionally big spring tides I witnessed at Sparkes and at Bosham (where three cars became salty write-offs), the damage would have been even more disastrous than it was, with more vessels driven further ashore and deposited in the middle of fields.

My experience was middling. Fortunately I was housed at a well placed berth and so spared some of the worst elements and some of the engendered fear. Nevertheless, being at almost 90 degrees for some two to three hours in the small hours of the morning (3 a.m. is notorious as the hour of the wolf) knocked the stuffing out of me, as did hearing the distress VHF traffic and thinking of the Yarmouth lifeboat crew preparing to quit the harbour. Happily, neither *Valcon* nor I sustained any serious physical damage, but the shock to my psyche was such that I terminated my cruising season in November that year – at least a month earlier than I had ever done. In Chichester Harbour alone, more than 250 vessels were sunk or driven ashore.

Perhaps one of the unhappiest postscripts must be the fact that vandals were at work almost before the storm had abated.

Once out of the marina, it is a tortuous trip by water via the drying channel to the head of Mengham Rythe, where Wilsons of Hayling have a boatyard on Marine Walk. Situated on the eastern edge of South Hayling, there is a real inland waterways feel about the place; a quiet, characterful spot, where folk tend to work on their boats perhaps more than sail them. The boatyard and moorings have access 2 hours each side of high water. Mengham Rythe and its pretty environs form an excellent anchorage when the wind is in the west.

Access is also tortuous by road; but well worth the journey for it enables you to taste to the full some of the more garish and outlandish aspects of Hayling Island. The island separates the waters of the two harbours of Chichester and Langstone, which meet, mix and mingle at the northern tip of the island by the grace and favour of Langstone Bridge, which could at one time have been converted into a solid barrier to protect the rights of some of the more riparian and territorially minded inhabitants.

19

Mengham Rythe is not far from the shopping centre at Eastoke, where you can buy all the things you expect to find at a two-horse holiday resort. In addition, there is a butchers of note: Stenning's in Creek Road, where you can get excellent T-bone steaks. Of particular interest to boat provisioners is the fact that they specialise in vacuum-packing them, and will also deliver.

An overview of Hayling Island reveals it to be a conglomerate of contrasts: from mad merry-go-rounds to saltings, gorse, and coarse grasses; from costly if uncouth holiday homes that gaze out from their ribbon development over Hayling Bay, to primitive arks on the Kench at the back of Gunner Point. Then from the over-busy mainland road traffic bridge to those fierce streams (known locally as Runs) in both east and west channels; to the protected islands and isolated creeks with their secretive activities, slipways, groynes, landing stages and disused quays; and finally to all the intriguingly named Rythes.

However, there have been other perceptions of Hayling. For example, in 1826, one promulgation called up such phrases as 'The Genius of Taste and Pleasure'; 'Sublime and Beautiful'; 'Pearl of the Ocean'; and 'Beautiful Sands, Equal to Velvet in Softness'. There are indeed, those who suggest that the island derives its name from the German *heilige* meaning 'holy'; and that should give pause for thought.

A final word about those creeks: the Ordnance Survey people have it as Rithe, whereas those at the Admiralty favour Rythe. Either way, one is tempted to ask, is this where the mock turtle first encountered reeling and writhing?

The Emsworth Channel

Mengham can claim, by a whisker, to be the first Rythe in the Emsworth Channel. The second, but really the first in the main channel, is Mill Rythe, about a mile to the north of Sandy Point. It is marked by a red can channel buoy *Mill Rythe*, and also by its own port and starboard beacons, as well as a cardinal mark. The sinuous channel, which is marked by beacon/withies, divides after a few cables; with the port-hand branch leading to the Hayling Island Yacht Company, and the starboard to the Yacht Haven. The area dries almost completely.

This part of the island is known as Middle Hayling, and is quite different from the south version. Car breakers and scrap dealers are the order of the day here, appearing from behind all kinds of covers and corners. To find the neighbourhood landings, quays and slips that litter the maps but are not sign-posted, you must persevere down tortuous lanes of private lands with legends telling of territorial rights. But after such a labyrinthine land navigation, threading your way through piles of carcasses or car cases will be no more than a minor obstacle.

You will finally arrive upon the Hayling Island Yacht Company. They make fishing boats, motor sailers and cruisers, and offer slipping and modest berths with all the usual boatyard facilities. While they are the main focus of maritime life in the area, they are neither exclusive nor unique for there is in addition the remote spot known as the Yacht Haven, with the appealing address of Copse Lane. It is a no-man's-land of skeletal constructions, and a no-man's-water of lost pontoons. One sadly distressed boat, once someone's dream, remains like an ageing sentinel to guard the yearning spirits of times past.

Back in the Emsworth Channel, Marker Point is a bleakish spot on the west side of Thorney Island. There is little to tempt you to stay – and even less reason to land for the whole stretch is given over to the army (see page 00).

The channel is quite busy in the season, so it is not a good idea to anchor anywhere but well out of the fairway. While this can safely be done in a number of places, traditional anchorages are on the starboard hand just before Mill Rythe (near the *N Pilsey* green buoy) and, also on the starboard hand, between Marker Point and the Fowley Island fork.

In the *Harbour Conservancy News*, anchorages are referred to as follows: 'West of Fairway Buoy on the southern side of the channel; East of Pilsey Island; North of East Head, but do not anchor in the main channel which is very crowded at the weekend.' But in addition, there are of course the five southern pile berths towards the top of the Emsworth Channel which may be used as double berths.

However, most skippers tend to be impatient to make for the *NE Hayling* and *Emsworth* beacons marking the Fowley Island fork: to port is Sweare Deep for Northney Marina and to starboard is Emsworth's own channel.

Photograph above

The *West Winner* beacon and tide gauge: on good days, you may see some speedy locals leaving it to port – a really risky manoeuvre.

Sweare Deep to Northney Marina

In Sweare Deep, there are two shoal patches between the *NE Hayling* and the *Northney* beacons. They tend to the port hand, but cause no problem unless you are navigating with 6ft at low water springs. Otherwise the approach is clear and plain both for markers and depth of water. Northney Marina itself lies to port and you make a ninety degree turn to enter. The final approach is via a dredged channel that allows access to craft of 6ft at all states of the tide.

The site is dominated by the Post House hotel. Physically and aesthetically the enclave tends to a kind of socio-clinical isolation in the midst of nature – otherwise mainly untamed. It reminded me of the five-star air-conditioned hotel in Nigeria's Kano, where, within yards of that shrine of cosmopolitan luxuries, there was nothing but scrub, bush and wild northern life. For years, the marina was part of the Rank empire, and while the phrase, 'Rank by Name and Rank by Nature' was never used in my presence, many clients protested at the lack of charm at the helm. Recently, the marina has been taken over by MDL (Marine Developments Ltd), and time will tell all.

Northney was the site of the first-ever holiday camp; and that is not out of keeping with the present atmosphere. The area is also the home of another first: sailboarding. This popular pastime was started by 12-year-old Peter Chilvers in Mengham back in 1958. Northney is now its acknowledged Mecca.

There is water up to the bridge; but the sailing and cruising is only for small shoal craft – although, in a suitable boat, there is great fun to be had searching out the very last inch of navigable alleys.

The Emsworth Channel presents a pretty sombre face to the stranger; discouraging all but true believers.

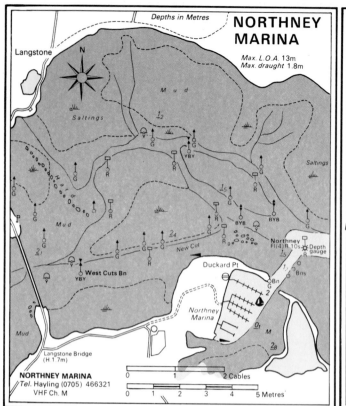

Northney Marina

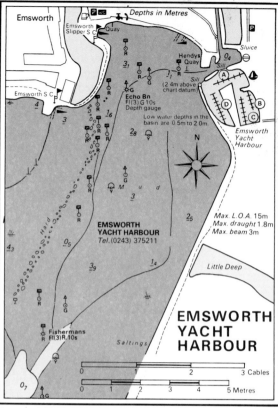

Emsworth Yacht Harbour

Wickor Point to Emsworth Yacht Harbour

The area surrounding Fowley Island forms what might be referred to as the Emsworth Basin. It is a mass of mini-buoys, withies and beacons, marking not only the main channels into Emsworth town port and the nearby Emsworth Yacht Harbour, but also Fowley and Nore Rythes; the back passage off Conigar Point; and the low water landing at the end of the ancient hard. Shoal craft and local knowledge are necessary ancillaries for those who wish to move into these secret waters.

Emsworth Yacht Harbour is in what used to be known as the New Slipper Mill Pond, and is now a fully dredged and berthed basin with a sill. It has most boating facilities that residents and visitors are likely to need, but does not go in for any sybaritic excesses. It is run by Jenny Duxbury; and it is perfectly logical that, in her hands, you will find a characterful place peopled by character-full folk. The whole tenor of the surroundings is one that tells, quite clearly, that boaters go there to get away from everything except water, boats and each other.

Under most circumstances 5ft is the maximum draught and skippers should only attempt entry at springs – there are a few 5ft deep-water berths. If you want to be able to get away at all states of the tide, you need to be moored about half a mile into the channel.

Central to the marina site, and not entirely separate from the clientele, is a select band of stilted-property owners with their cabin-like premises overlooking the moorings. They are coveted by many and afforded by some.

An experience not to be missed by enthusiasts of arts and crafts is to be found in the workshop of Trevor Ellis, the carver of almost anything in the wood, vendor of the handmade works of his postcard-painting wife.

The 'village' of Emsworth (it is in fact a town, but no-one refers to it as anything but a village) is a busy little bee of a place, with chandlers and pubs on every front. If it is service with that dash of added personal eccentricity that puts the stamp on a chandler, you will find Ostar in Queen Street and The Wheelhouse in High Street worth your perusal.

Emsworth is the proud possessor of a peaceful old world harbour by an equally peaceful old mill stream. In fact, Emsworth, deriving its name from the river Ems, grew up between two mill ponds that were used for tide mills. Barges came with corn and left with flour. By Slipper Mill, King's Quay (also known as Hendy's Quay after the man who built the mill) can be seen vestiges of the milling – which was still working up to the Second World War.

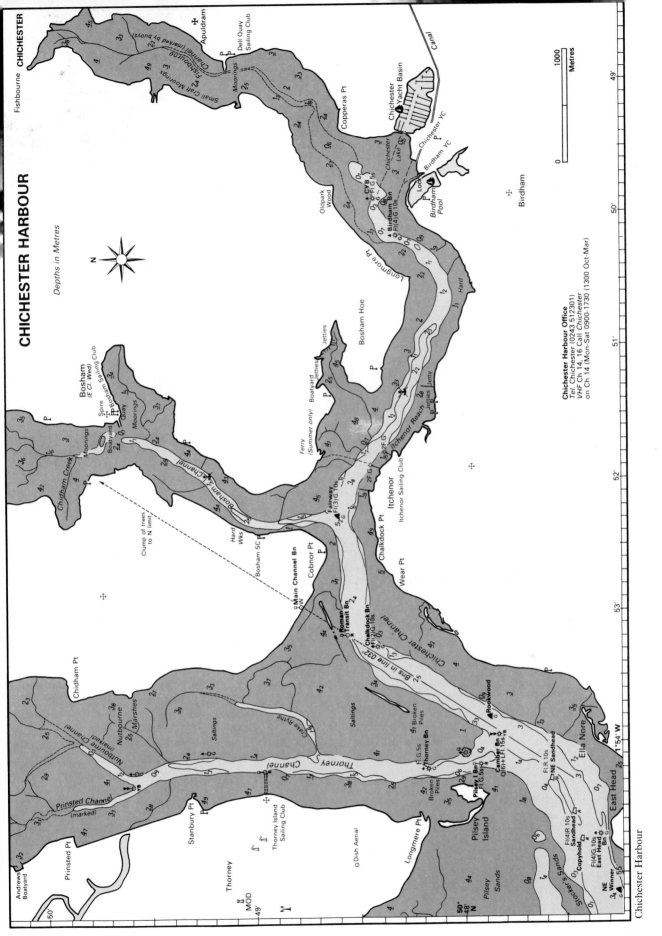

CHICHESTER HARBOUR

Depths in Metres

N

Chichester Harbour Office
Tel. Chichester (0243 512301)
VHF Ch 14, 16 Call *Chichester*
on Ch 14 (Mon-Sat 0900-1730 (1300 Oct-Mar)

Chichester Harbour

The town rose in prosperity as a port as Chichester declined. In particular, it became the preeminent centre for scallops and oysters. However, in 1902, when the Dean of Winchester and other local worthies came to a sad end after stuffing themselves with Emsworth oysters, the trade followed suit – with the banning of their sale. (Greens will want to know that it was not just a surfeit of seafood that killed off the godly and the virtuous, but typhoid, credited to the discharge of untreated sewage poisoning the oysters. *Plus ça change!*)

Chichester Channel

If you don't want Sparkes, Mengham Rythe or the Emsworth Channel, the alternative takes you to starboard, through Stocker's Lake, right round the Winner itself, between Stocker's Sands and East Head, and then between Ella Nore and Pilsey Island for the junction of Thorney and Chichester Channels.

Just off West Wittering, to the eastern side of the harbour entrance, is the excellent anchorage tucked in behind East Head. It offers easy access to the pleasant beach, and is sheltered and well protected except from easterlies, which occur in this area only infrequently. It is to be noted that swimming can be dangerous here because of the unexpectedly strong tides. Although the place is extremely popular, it is seldom crowded enough to make it unpleasant; and most of the time it feels much more remote than it actually is. Thanks to the keen efforts of local conservationists, the threat from erosion is no longer the force it was in the 16th to 18th centuries. However, there is no danger of erosion at Bracklesham and East Wittering where there are caravans, bungalows, and camping in abundance.

The manor of West Wittering, or Cakeham, used to possess by grace and favour the rights of wrecks; and it is mooted that there was frequently much confusion between goods obtained 'lawfully' this way and contraband that 'just happened' to float in on the tide. Indeed, so rampant was the trade, illicit or otherwise, that special watch and coastguard dwellings were built to staunch the flow or stem the flood.

According to the Anglo-Saxon Chronicle, West Wittering is where Aella and his sons Cymen, Wenceling and Cissa landed to march to Shoreham to fight Britons in AD 495. In the 16th century, a creek ran right past the church, and it is said there used to be rings for mooring in the wall. Before the 1939–45 war, there were still a few fishermen working West Wittering, but in the previous century, there was a fleet of nearly a hundred luggers. There was supposed to be a famous fig garden here in 1745, but I could find no-one to verify what is a sweet idea.

Thorney Channel

Pilsey Island stands at the entrance to the channel and should be left well to port on entering. The island, still referred to by some knowledgeable locals and foreign pedants as Pilsea Please, used to have nearly a dozen good acres of crop land, with a house and a garden. Now it is an SSSI (Site of Special Scientific Interest) where flourish such rarities as sea bindweed. It is an officially restricted area, and there is no picnicking above the MHW line.

Thorney is one of the quietest and most remote of the Chichester channels. It has good holding ground all through, with enough pleasing anchorages for all those who like this kind of sequestered ambience to be able to frequent it without threat. Moreover, Creek Rythe (or Crake if you are so inclined) and Nutbourne Channel offer shoal craft alternatives; and for those who really want to pierce the pastoral hinterland there are the Green and Cobner Rythes where you can rely on being utterly undisturbed except by fish, birds and their still and quiet watchers from nearby Cobnor Point. The main and traditional anchorage is to be found to the starboard hand, just off the northerly tip of Pilsey Island. It is wise to double check your position vis-à-vis the broken piles that are in evidence all round. These are all that remain of the attempt made, just before the end of the 19th century, to retain the main working channel. It failed, and the residual embankment at the southerly edge of the Thorney Saltings now serves as a miniature tern sanctuary.

Thorney Island

It is long since Thorney was an island: it was inexorably joined to the mainland over a hundred years ago. The one hundred and seventy acres of land that were once united are now divided by the awesomely named Great Deep, which itself was at one time the major route from Portsmouth to London.

Although Thorney Island itself is by no means unfrequented, there is little to be seen from the water except the hard and the modest headquarters of the sailing club shared, not between town and gown but between mun. and gun; for this is the territory of the 26th Regiment Field Artillery.

Having served in the field artillery forty years back I decided to do the right thing and approach the C.O. ashore for permission to go alongside. Once my bona fides were established to the near satisfaction of an officer, incredulous to a degree at my appearance and my mission, I was accompanied by a gunner to inspect the delights of Thorney Island Camp.

Away from the army barracks, the officers' mess, the NAAFI and other such military diversions, the location is remote and bereft. The church and vicarage were both very much in need of care and attention. Charity begins at home? The gunner, who was remarkably well informed on the life and times of Thorney, spoke somewhat enviously of the possession and exploitation by the RAF in 1935; commented dispassionately that the graveyard was made up of corners that are forever foreign – and, moreover, German; and then waxed lyrical about the site that was once the refuge of the Vietnamese boat people.

The channel has its points, four of them in fact: Longmere, Stanbury, Chidham and Prinsted Points are all, it must be said, distinguished by the fact that they look nothing like points at all, no matter from which position you perceive them. However, the last named is important since it is the significant landfall for the channel that leads up to Thornham and Prinsted. (The points are so unsharp that they should be called blunts; and their span is so well shared by the two of them that there is doubt as to which is Prinsted and which is Thornham. Or whether, in fact, there are or ever have been two of them. Perhaps they were mariners' follies or smugglers' ploys.)

Prinsted moorings; where life is real and life is earnest, where nature is reddish in tooth and claw, and where a man can fend for himself.

Prinsted Channel

Things are now really moving in this neck of the withies. One Jim Conwell has invested his family and part of his all in a marina development on the port hand of the drying channel. (Just to prove how close everything is around here, the address is Thornham Lane, Prinsted, Emsworth). New alongside and swinging berths are being established, together with a large expansion shoresides both on the boating and the social/domestic front.

Next door is Paynes Old Boatyard, where the remaining few ('We few, we happy few ...') keep the place in proper fashion according to centuries of tradition. 'Fings' here are indeed still what they used to be.

At the head of the many miniature creeks is the small village settlement of Prinsted. Most people say that Bosham is the jewel in the crown of Chichester; but for my money (and when it comes to the price of property, we are speaking millions here) Prinsted must be the prime contender for prettiest village of the harbour. It has a splendid claim to fame: no church, no pub, no corner shop; but is blessed by its manor house, with its legend 'I&SG 1663'.

Chichester Channel

Back in the Chichester Channel, moving northeast after the *Camber* beacon and the *Rookwood* green buoy, the remains of walls and the stumps of broken piles lead towards an historic point: one from where you can still line up the old Roman transit. Here you can see beacons in line on 032°, and note the Admiralty's comment: 'Clump of trees lies beyond N limit of chart'. I have yet to see a clump so blessed with such abundant growth yet denied the status of even thicket or copse. Once observed, it tends to dominate the horizon.

At sea level, on Cobnor Point, just after the Roman transit, is a bird watchers' hut in the style of a Second World War German POW camp guards' hut: small, unpretentious and not quite ugly. Outside, on the forecourt and all around, you can join in the fun by spotting assemblies of persons, most with binoculars, some with telescopes, and a few with tripods on which are perched cameras that are dwarfed by their extruding lenses.

A vantage berth for this is offered by the main anchorage in the Chichester Channel itself; that is opposite Cobnor Point on the southerly side between Chaldock Point and Wear Point.

Bosham Channel

Just round Cobnor Point, roughly in a northerly direction, Bosham Channel opens up. The channel is not as bleak as Thorney, and feels more homely almost straight away. No doubt the influence of the famous village casts a spell all the way down its channel.

The church, which is easily identifiable at the head of the creek, indicates where the navigation divides: the channels of Chidham, Cutmill and Colner tend to the northerly ahead. They are locations that appeal to the drying-out-pipe-at-anchor brigade; every natural prospect pleases – and not even man is all that vile if he has got this far away from it all.

Chidham village, bay and miniature harbour, are all isolated parts, redolent of a history that goes back over 4,000 years. At one time, there was an effort to reclaim land for farming by building a dam/embankment from Chidham to Bosham. However, autumnal gales nearly as furious as those in 1987 brought tides no dam could withstand, the sea has had its way ever since.

The final approach channels into Bosham are to starboard: the first, between the green beacon and the YBY cardinal, takes you through the moorings into the main bay, the Emsworth Sound as it were; while the second, by the YB cardinal, takes you to Bosham Quay with the substantial jetty to port and equally substantial stakes to starboard. The intriguing building on the jetty front, looking much like a barn, used to hold ships' gear. It is affectionately known as the Raptackle. The harbour village of Bosham is a hundred of the Lord of the Manor of Bosham and as such launching fees are payable to his agent on the one hand and harbour dues to the Conservancy on the other. It is not a place for deep draughted vessels since it dries out completely; but there are deep pools both below and above the entrance in the main channel with least depths of 2m and 4m, respectively.

By tradition, the Roman Emperor Vespasian had a holiday residence here, and there were certainly parts of a Roman basilica found in the Saxon church which was once itself a royal chapel. Bosham is probably the oldest Christian community around: after the Romans, according to the Venerable Bede, a monk, Dicul, founded a cell there 200 years before St Augustine. This cell is supposed to be the present vault under the present church. Today the creek is still in the ownership of the Lord of the Manor of Bosham (a miniature Montague you might say); so continuing the tradition of history and patronage that bought Bosham a place in the Bayeux tapestry as Harold's point of departure for Normandy.

Bosham Creek leads to a vast foreshore and hard; with little enough water to float a metre boat for the most part, but with enough on big springs to wreak havoc with carelessly parked cars.

Above
The miniature harbour of Bosham: the entrance is quite as well guarded and protected as it looks.

As if all that were not enough to gild the lily, it is claimed by some that the coffined bones dug up near the chancel arch of the church of the Holy Trinity (itself in Bayeux too) were those of the eight-year-old daughter of Canute. This is taken to be proof that the king committed his famous watery deed here.

Bosham must be deemed to be something of a tourist trap, in so far as it has everything to entice a visitor to stay well past the allotted span. And this becomes especially significant when the said tourist may have arrived by car and left it in front of the well known and heavily patronised pub, the Anchor Bleu, from which there is a splendid view of the harbour. One of the views only too often seen from its balcony, however, is a forlorn one. As the Chichester Conservancy Board puts it: 'Cars parking on the foreshore road are liable to be submerged by the tide.' Although car gazing has become a local pastime at big spring tides, it must be said that the natives are not hostile. Bosham is pronounced, by those in the know, as Bozz'm; so if you want to be in the swim, drop your aitches like a man.

There is a regular water ferry from Bosham to Itchenor in the season, so if your own craft is not best suited to such an outing, there is no need to be denied the pleasure of a channel passage.

Itchenor Reach

Back in the main channel, after the YB cardinal *Deep End* and the green fairway buoy, the Chichester Channel becomes known as the Itchenor Reach. Although there appears to be plenty of good water in this area, it is fool's gold. It is not wise to cut any of the shallow shoal corners.

However, the main drag itself certainly is deep enough, and the fairway is marked all along by moorings that if not exactly to be described as congested, must come near to qualifying as such.

Itchenor is the heart of Chichester Harbour, being the HQ of the Conservancy Board, and proud host to the many who come from far and near, by water for its excellent visitors' moorings, and by land for the benefit of its splendid free tidal hard.

There are six visitors' moorings off Itchenor Jetty which are capable of taking up to six vessels each dependent upon size. (The nearby Emsworth pile berths may be used by only two vessels.) Craft may not be left unmanned overnight when on these moorings. It may be possible to be allocated a single mooring by the harbour office, the launch *Regnum* or one of the boatyards. The scrubbing piles at Itchenor and Emsworth should also be booked at the harbourmaster's office here. The harbourmaster's call sign is *Chichester*, working VHF Channel 14 ashore or in the launch.

Even near Itchenor, Chichester Harbour's most favoured port of call, it is still possible to get away from it all.

Itchenor offers almost anything the visiting skipper may need; and
much is to be found on the foreshore.

During the 18th century, it possessed huge shipbuilding and dockyards and was a thriving
centre of commerce. For example, in 1816, nearly 20,000 tons of coal and 2,000 tons of other
goods were put into lighters there to be taken to Dell Quay for Chichester – and other such foreign parts.

A different historical aspect emerges with the tale of Charles II and the lady he had installed
in Itchenor House. He had strange tastes in mistresses, and this one he called Fubs, the current
slang for a chubby 'pretty boy' the likes of whom he fancied and she resembled. He named one
of his yachts the same for her amusement. The name of the village is also of interest, being
derived from the Olde patronymic Icca and the Old English 'ora' meaning a bank or margin.

Itchenor is also the place for inflatables of another kind: together with all manner of outboards
they are to be found at the emporium of Ted Bailey. It is interesting to find that Ted (near-
crowned king of such craft) should himself work a small traditional wooden dinghy; and, what is
more, that he should propel it by equally wooden oars.

Entertainment and distraction are not hard to find. You can take a trip on one of the two
pleasure cruisers that ply their trade from the public jetty. The *Wingate II* is a 70-seater traditional passenger boat, and, in the words of the idiosyncratic operator, Peter Adams, is 'identical
to the famous *African Queen*.'

Alternatively, you can use the services of the ferry men. Based at the Conservancy workshop,
by the harbourmaster's office, and also operating from the jetty, they are almost all things to all
persons. For yachtsmen, they provide the traditional to-and-fro job for skippers and crew. They
also do a cross river run to Smugglers Lane Hard on the northerly bank for those who fancy the
short walk into Furzefield Creek, or the longer haul up to Bosham. However, for those who
want to go to Bosham the lazy way, they even do a regular run there in the season.

I had cause to be grateful for that milk run when a swiftish wind against tide got up and caused me to be isolated at Bosham Quay, my Avon and Seagull not being man enough for a sensible trip. My dinghy was taken in tow and I got a ride in company with two ladies who thought that was the only way to get from Itchenor to Bosham. I was not the only one to benefit from the water boatmen's enthusiasm which takes them well beyond any summons of duty or the call of lucre. For example, at spring tides I saw them piggyback clients from the boat to dry land, and to carry the bicycles of three young female souls who could not manage on their own.

In the miniature village (which is no more than one long street) there is the Ship Inn, a pub which actually manages to provide drinkable coffee, and makes you an interesting offer on Sunday papers. It also houses a goodly spectrum of local wines; and for those who go in for interior star gazing, there are ornaments galore in the form of chamber pots.

On the one long street near the hard is a chandlery, and, nearer still, is the harbourmaster's office overlooking the public jetty. Just round the corner you will find Haines Boatyard; specialists in marrying efficient contemporary service with the charm and friendliness of traditional craftsmanship – a happy knack. See Chris Hammock, he will put you right and your boat to rights if that is what you want.

If you take a visitors' mooring and have time to spare, the movement of the tidal streams are worth some study. The flow of flood and ebb at about two hours after high and low waters is not exactly what you expect. The still stand and near back flow are intriguing phenomena.

Across the way at Furzefield Creek, there is an entirely different kind of community to be found; quite dominated by the presence and ethos of Combes Boatyard. The entrance to the creek is a little tortuous, but well marked by withies and beacons with noticeable 2m marks. On the starboard hand by the entrance are two of the most desirable of the many mansions that are to seen overlooking Chichester Harbour.

The locked entrance into Birdham Pool – where there is always time to stand and stare.

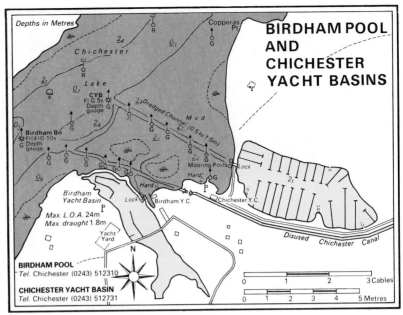

Chichester Yacht Basin

Inside the creek is an enclave of the last, past century in an area that is mainly well into the acquisitive eighties. It is a haven for those who have, in the style of Gerard Manley Hopkins, a mind to spend, sir, life upon thy cause of wooden boats. At the head of the creek, there are half a dozen pretty, if pretty unsubstantial, private jetties.

To Birdham

Past Bosham Hoe and Longmore Point, the previous crowding begins to ease just a little, and allows you full views of the scenery which on this stretch excels itself. Whether cruising or walking along the banks, it soon becomes obvious why this part of Chichester Harbour is so popular with indigens, Johnnies-come-lately and tourists alike. For once, even the most expensive of motor cruisers or yachts are put into the shade by the design, execution and opulence of the dwellings that litter the scene.

Boat people have two choices: Birdham Pool or Chichester Yacht Basin. They are both on the starboard hand and Birdham Pool comes first. It has an entrance channel marked by the lit green beacon *Birdham* Fl(4)G.10s. It is important to keep about 10ft from the rest of the starboard-hand channel markers as there are steep-to edges and a dogleg to be negotiated. However, it is all clear and plain. Access is through a lock that is operated for three hours before and after high water, and locking hours are 0700–2200. Limiting dimensions are 55ft x 16ft x 6·5ft.

In the July 16th edition of *The Motor Boat* in the year 1937, the following appeared: 'Five years ago there were no yachts at Birdham, on Chichester Harbour, except two or three small locally owned craft, and the place was unheard of as a centre. Since then it has become known through the opening up of the old Chichester Canal as a non-tidal fresh-water yacht basin, and nearly 100 owners now keep their boats there, a club and yacht yard being provided. The attraction of this spot is that the adjacent property, including Court Barn Farm, an ancient water mill, two large mill pools, and a village green on the harbour edge are entirely unspoiled.'

Apart from the fact that the marina now holds more than two hundred craft, little appears to have changed since the article was written over 50 years ago. Although the mainland 'village' of Birdham may have changed more than somewhat due to expansion over the recent decades, in fact, not all that much has changed at the coal face of the waterfront since the days of Nelson when ships of the line were built here. You can still see the in-use residuals of the 1939–45 war: launching and recovery rails for assault craft. The area was, like many of the Solent sites, a source of salt, hence the local name, 'Salterns'. The lagoons in which sea water was entrapped and allowed to evaporate for the creation of salt, were known as salterns. Moreover, there is still the edifice of the tide mill, and indeed, an old mill was mentioned in Domesday. The tide mill has not worked for many a day, and its pound now forms the marina.

The nature of the place is still in keeping with its heritage; and while there is no shortage of modern facilities and service, there is no pressure on berth holders or visitors to pay'n'display or indeed to do anything at all other than enjoy the peace and quiet of the setting.

Nevertheless, Birdham Yacht Club is quite up to date and 'visitors from the sea' are made freely welcome in what they call their 'unique ambience, and friendly nautical flavour'.

Birdham Pool

This area is a particularly good one for shopping from the boat. Between Birdham Pool and the next door Chichester Yacht Basin is the aptly named Lock Stores, a licensed miniature supermarket and home-made food purveyor (which, in addition, serves yachtsmen's breakfasts). Just across the canal, in the Chichester Yacht Basin there are general stores, chandlery, clothes, food and drink. And on the not far away main road known as Birdham Strait there is a first-rate well stocked store (butcher, baker, candlestick factor and the lot).

For all spirituous liquors, you cannot do better than make a trip up river to Pallant Wines at Apuldram Manor Farm, Appledram Lane (not far from Dell Quay) where you will find booze in abundance, new wines and regular special offers. They offer decent discounts for bulk buys (and a bulk is no more than a box).

As you would expect, the town Chichester could fill a book, but here is a quick word: the place is a miracle of easy navigation, for the (conspic) clock tower presides at the crossroads of North, South, East and West Streets, and nothing could be easier. There are also names for the homesick city slickers, such as Little London and St Pancras. Of course, there are all the shops you would expect, but there is also a specialist treat for fish lovers. At Hoopers, they will not only sell you the goods, but will advise regarding the best ways of cooking them – even if it means rescuing well thumbed and scaly recipe books from the deeps to do so. They don't stock all the world's most unusual fish, but you will be hard pressed to find a serious request that defeats them.

Meanwhile, back at Birdham, we move on to Chichester Yacht Basin, just up the river from the Pool. The straight entrance channel is also marked by a lit green beacon, *CYB* Fl.G.5s. There is a yellow buoy opposite the floating pontoons near the lock pit, and when that buoy is just afloat, the channel carries two metres. The lock operates on a 24-hour basis.

With its 1,000-odd berths, Chichester Yacht Basin is a really large-scale operation. At one time, it was the biggest marina in Europe. Even now it is in the process of massive upgrading of

The old Chichester Canal, now habited by birds and other songsters seeking harmony, and suitable for navigating nothing but one's self *solus*.

Another day draws to a close at Birdham Pool

all its facilities. There are all services to hand, and Vernon's Shipyard Ltd is on the harbour side of the site, near the lock control tower.

Also near the lock pit is the Chichester Yacht Club, with a splendid (food at all times) restaurant, bar and laundrette. It is an extremely busy (but efficient) and friendly place, with hard grafting secretaries who are apparently open all hours. Members put much time and effort into organising club and family cruising; although, of course, the racing and regatta type programmes are not overlooked.

The Chichester Canal lock gates have now been refurbished and are in working order. If you wish to avail yourself of an opportunity to proceed into that minor sea of tranquility, you need to know that a month's notice is required before opening of the gates can take place. Not only do you need to get the timing right, but you also need to be psychologically prepared for such a passage. Houseboats, in the form of floating homes and land-bound little ships, cling to the south bank, leaving only a narrow channel hardly wide enough for the many kinds of ducks and cross-bred waterbirds (many of which look as if they are moulded in plastic) as well as an ancient goose with riparian rights. In addition, there is a great and grand growth of lily-to-weed. Perhaps, the wisest course is to appreciate it from the non-threatening aspect of the towpath, along which you can walk (on the Chichester Yacht Basin side) to Hunston and on to Chichester along the only surviving stretch of the Portsmouth and Arun Canal.

It is not the only place that calls to the walking instinct. From the lock, along the foreshore, tending northeasterly through the Copse of Apuldram Salterns and the fields, you reach the delights of Dell Quay. Not far away is Apuldram, of the famous roses; and also of the recently opened D-day Aviation Museum. An extra lure must be the presence of Pallant Wines.

Alternatively, a general westerly drift first along the public footpath, private roads and the foreshore, will finally get you to Itchenor. But not until you have passed through an estate of estates with domestic architecture that in very truth would have left Ibsen's master builder looking with a wild surmise. The spectrum runs from manors and minars to mansions, with only one Corbusier *manqué*.

Dell Quay

At one time, Dell Quay was the seventh most important port in the land. It seems to have started life around 1500 AD as a private quay much devoted to smuggling, and got its name after the field on which it stood: one called Dell. Until the 19th century it was busy with commerce; now it thrives even more on the backs of tourists.

It is still possible to get to Dell Quay by water. However, you must work the tides, for the river virtually dries after Copperas Point, marked by the blind, green *Copperas*; and the channel becomes, if not exactly tortuous, certainly less obviously straight, although perfectly well marked. Apart from the shoal residents, most yachtsmen take a trip up on the tide to enjoy the hospitality of the pub that has been a centre for centuries: the Crown and Anchor, from whose balcony there is a magnificent vista of Chichester Water. Get there as early as you can, tide and licensing hours permitting, for the place is so popular that it is often impossible to gain access to the bar. Dell Quay is still quite busy with maritime affairs: the eponymous sailing club; a chandlery and boatyards, one being the outflyer of Ted Bailey; a sailmakers; and a fish and seafood factory.

For those with an eye to the aesthetics of size, shape and colour, there is an amazing property on the landscape, or mud cum waterscape. It is a floating habitation in the form of a junk heap; and, according to taste, it is an offensive eyesore or a charming tribute to the British genius for thick skinned determination and eccentricity.

Fishbourne Channel

After Dell Quay, the waterway changes its name for the last time, taking its title this time from the village that was once a Roman port. Landing there is now virtually impossible, except in flat-bottomed inflatables – and then you need oars. For those who enjoy exploring the last inch of navigable water, and doing so without benefit of beacon, withy or buoy, it will be a challenge to get to Fishbourne. The rest of us will no doubt walk from Dell Quay, or drive down from the recently bypassed A27.

The name Fishbourne means 'River of Fish', but its main contemporary claim to fame is that of the Roman palace and museum. It consists of the remains of the largest Roman residence yet found in Britain. It is believed to be the palace of that reprobate old atrebate 'King of the British', Tiberius Claudius Cogidubnus.

The head of Fishbourne Creek is an intriguing spot. There is no embankment at this stage, and the result is a fine example of plant succession from saltmarsh to fresh marsh. It is tricky to get to by water or by land, but is well worth the effort of exploring its almost hidden delights; but do take boots or waders. Every time I visited, I was welcomed by a positive crowd of intriguing, Heinz 57-type ducks. They are so friendly that you will kick yourselves if you do not carry a goodly supply of bread. It is as good a place as any within the harbour for the sounds of, if not exactly the wind in the willows, then at least the whispers in the wispy grasses.

Langstone Harbour

Langstone Harbour has frequently been described as 'the same as Chichester, but smaller'. True, at 5,000 acres, it is smaller, being only a third of its neighbour's size, but otherwise I disagree. Chichester is in general sheltered, sophisticated and urbane; while Langstone tends to be exposed, elemental and rural. Chichester is domesticated, Langstone is still wild.

Cowper disliked it: 'I dislike Langstone quite as much as I like Chichester Harbour. The tide sets in very strongly, and the banks are awkward and dangerous in S. or S.E. winds, while there are no snug nooks to get into. The small bight called Sinah Lake on the Hayling Island side is very shallow and limited in space, while the vast extent of mud flats are very soft, the anchor dragging in them like pins in butter.'

Directions

The East and West Winner

The Admiralty *Pilot* says: 'The approach to Langstone Harbour lies between West Winner, a gravel bank, and East Winner, a sand bank, both of which dry, and which extend offshore for 6 cables from Eastney Point, and 11 cables from Gunner Point, respectively; locally these banks are known as The Woolseners. The W side of East Winner is steep-to and can usually be distinguished by broken water. *E. Winner* buoy (S cardinal) is moored about 1 mile SSE of East Winner. These banks frequently shift and are subject to alteration in height after gales; in rough weather, if there is any swell, there is generally one sheet of broken water over them, with heavy rollers.'

My own experience has been mainly of flat calms, and the entrance under such circumstances is a pure delight, provided you have enough energy of one kind or another (arms, sails or engine) to be able to cope with the power of the stream. However, on two occasions I was unfortunate enough to have to proceed with a briskish southerly wind against a strong ebb tide, and this creates really nasty turbulence. Threats of grounding on the East and West Winner did nothing but make the matter (and me) worse. Between them, the stream and the Winners can be a serious hazard when the weather is indifferent to bad.

From the east

This is the trickier of the two approaches, for the East Winner reaches out seaward twice as far the West. A course that keeps you 1½ miles off East Wittering and Eastoke Point (about a mile from the *Chichester Bar* Beacon), tending westerly, will take you seaward of the East Winner to a position where you can pick up the *Langstone Fairway*, the *Rowan* isolated danger beacon and associated yellow buoys. After which, you can proceed into the entrance accordingly. The conspicuous chimney onshore to the west of the entrance, near Fort Cumberland, is impossible to disregard.

The entrance to Langstone Harbour is easily recognised by the conspicuous chimney, the refurbished jetty works and dolphin near Eastney Point.

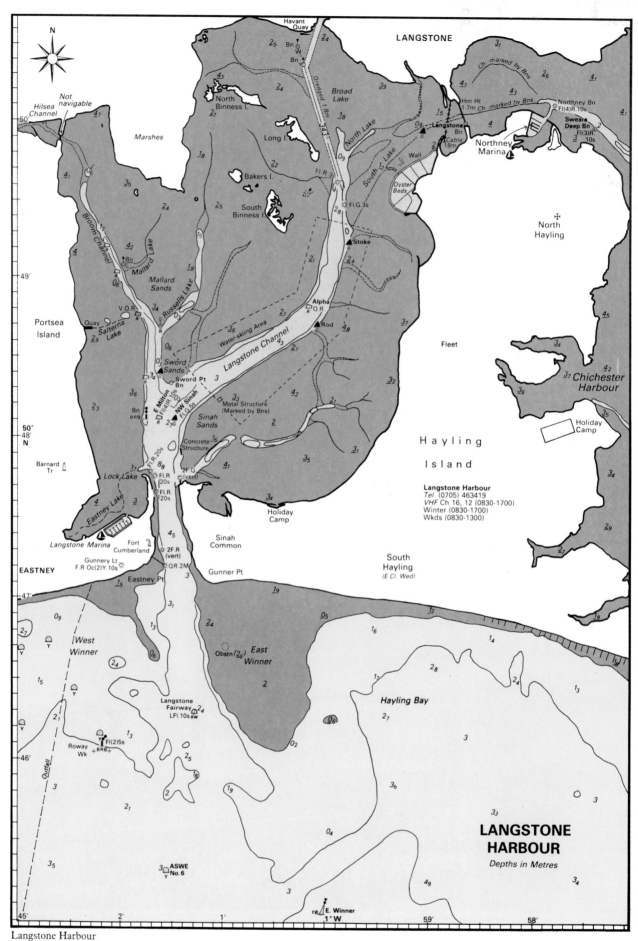

Picking up the *Rowan* wreck and the *E Winner* buoy is still the key. The approach from the south is completely open. A vessel from Portsmouth, having rounded the Horse Sand Fort, will be able safely to head straight for the *Fairway*. However, those who have used the well marked gate that indicates the channel through the submerged/submarine barrier will need to make sure they stand out again far enough (on a course better than 090°, and tending to the southeast) not to be caught by the wily witch finger of the West Winner. There are those, with shoal-draught craft, who enter close inshore on the top of the tide, but I am not of their number; and having seen the Winner's winning ways at work, I have no wish to be.

The entrance – Eastney and Gunner Points

The final approach from the *Langstone Fairway* buoy is straightforward: when it bears almost due north, you will be clear of both Winners and straight on course for the dolphins that serve as your stand-off mark for Eastney Point. After that the entrance is straight and straightforward. Since the shallow inshore banks are steep-to in places, it is best for strangers to tend towards the centre of the channel.

The main concern in settled weather is the matter of power. The Admiralty *Pilot* says the tidal streams in the harbour entrance are strong, with a maximum of 3·5 knots. The Harbour Board promulgates a notice that suggests they reach 7 knots. In my opinion, the Harbour Board has got it right. For example, I saw powerful motor cruisers making no headway at all in some patches when faced with some local eddying eccentricities of the ebb. Not only did I experience their regular energy and force, but I also came bows-on to some of their more powerful idiosyncrasies. Even so, from what I heard, I was spared their worst excesses.

Langstone Marina and Eastney Point, Gunner Point beyond.

The inner entrance to Langstone Harbour is marked by the refurbished jetty works and dolphin near Eastney Point, and the English Heritage military developments.

I was told of the puissance of the Hayling Whirling while browsing in a MIND shop in South-sea. My informant was a lady who had had personal experience of the lighting up of the truly amazing Portsmouth Harbour replica, built to deceive the Nazis during the bombing days of the 1939–45 war. She said that Sicily's Scylla and Charybdis were pretty good harbingers for the waters and banks of Langstone. Indeed, so many and various are the strong eddies in the entrance that they will allow progress to be made against an ebb tide – without power of any kind. I found them to be at their most confusing and most vigorous off the ferry landing stages by the harbour offices; the stretch of water between Sinah Common on the mainland and Sinah Sands out in Sinah Lake. There are moorings near the fairway, and the unoccupied ones frequently get pulled right under.

With regard to the power of the regular ebb, it is to be particularly experienced, predictably enough, in the bottleneck section between the two inward-growing promontories to the east and west.

I also heard of the famous Langstone languishers, the notorious sinking sands that take the unwary to their clammy bosoms. Eventually, I concluded that, no matter how mysterious and deadly they were purported to be, they were in fact more mystical, and, if anything, would prove to be entirely mythical.

Once past the dolphins and walkway, Fort Cumberland, the tall chimney, and the head-quarters of the Eastney Cruising Association attract the eyes to port. To starboard, those with keen eyes will be able to pick out the gaps in the bush, the slim masts behind, and the reminder of a hard that gives away the position of the Solatron Sailing Club. Then, the long line of beach leads on to the cluster of buildings containing the harbourmaster's office and the local pub, the Ferry Boat Inn.

There are six visitors' moorings to the east controlled by the harbourmaster and six more to the west leased from the Harbour Board by the ECA for their visitors. They are restricted to craft not exceeding 35ft since the moorings are laid in shingle on the very edge of the Deeps. Even slight dragging could involve the loss of the tackle because of the strength of the stream.

Larger vessels may anchor subject to the prior approval of the harbourmaster. Once through the entrance channel, past the headlands and well into the body of the harbour, the anchorages are to the starboard side of the channel. Masters must show an anchor ball or light, and keep a watch on board at all times.

All visitors must report to the harbourmaster's office. Not that this is any ordeal, for it is staffed by folk who are completely in tune with the natural charms of Langstone Harbour; a realm whose honour they guard jealously – and they do so seven days a week except for two days at Christmas and New Year's Day.

The harbour manager and the harbourmaster make a splendid pair, working together in all kinds of contrapuntal harmonies that combine the best of lilting Welsh and West Country. They are always willing to give of their time and knowledge: 'We would much prefer that visitors should trouble us with their questions or problems rather than get the wrong information from other sources – especially those informal ones that are supported by the unwarranted optimism that often inhabits pubs late in a session.'

The call signs of the harbour launches are *Sampson* and *Pilot*. They listen on VHF Channels 12 and 16 as does Langstone Harbour Radio.

There is a deep-water landing pontoon at Ferry Point on Hayling Island. Priority must be given to ferry and charter vessels picking up and landing passengers and to vessels fuelling (petrol and diesel). There is also a landing pontoon on the Eastney side. Water and toilets are available on both sides, but discerning patrons are advised to favour the facilities on Hayling.

The cross-channel (Langstone) ferry runs regularly throughout the year: peak times every 20 minutes, otherwise every hour. Weekends and bank holidays it is every 30 minutes early in the morning, otherwise every hour. (Children under 3 years, prams, pushchairs, etc. no charge; parcels 30p!)

Lock Lake and Eastney Lake

Lock Lake does not get its title as the result of any capricious or fanciful notion; it is well and plainly named since at one time there was a scheme to connect the harbour with an inland waterway route to London. From its basin in the middle of Portsmouth, the canal entered Eastney Lake by the premises of the local Fishermen's Association. It was to serve the rivers Arun, Wey and Thames, and was opened in 1823, but like so many others was put out of business by the railways.

Lock Lake gives access to the western shores (within the jurisdiction of Portsmouth, not the Langstone Harbour Board, logical as that may appear) for the few amateurs (and even fewer professionals) who work from this remote shoreline. There are boating, domestic and social services here, but only the dedicated make the pilgrimage. If you are of a mind to find a second-hand bit of this or that, or to exchange a small boat, then this is your territory.

There are small-craft moorings in Lock and Eastney Lakes, but not many of them are visited all that often; and it is not uncommon to witness the sad sight of one of them going down as the sun goes down and the tide rises up to seep into its opening sides.

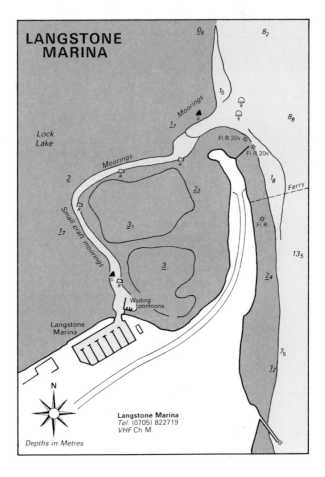

The conspicuous BRB wreck marker near the main channel separation by Sinah Sands and Milton Lake.

There is a hairpin bend round the headland that leads into Lock Lake and Langstone Marina.

Langstone Harbour proper

Out in the harbour again, the 'concrete structure', situate on Sinah Sands (and noted as a wreck on some charts) is one of the 'mulberry' harbour caissons that broke its back before leaving for Normandy. The 'metal structure' (which is a wreck) is a leftover piece of wartime work that was sunk when a ship collided with it. They are not the only wrecks or results of wrecking that are to be found in the area. In addition, there are the rusting but not wilting navy barges that are currently in use as testing stations for paints and other anti-climatic treatments.

Oyster Island is supposed to be amongst them; a quaint affair, being a man-made job of stone and gravel. Its famous Oyster House was built nearly 200 years ago supposedly for a man to inhabit as guardian of the bedded oysters. Sited three miles from anywhere, as it were, and completely surrounded by water, mud and marshes, the place was remote enough to be a hermit's paradise. Approached by a causeway at lowest water, it seems more likely that it was headquarters for well organised smuggling; and what a good cover it must have furnished.

There are quite a few low-lying islands in the harbour, mainly called Binnesses, and legend has it that in its death and glory days, Furse Bush Binness was a favourite rendezvous for prize fights. Then, they were as much sought after as are dog fights today. Now the area is a reserve of the RSPB, with grounds for ringed plovers, terns, mallard, oystercatchers and redshanks. Even I, pretty incompetent bird-watcher that I am, poodling in the dinghy, have been able to observe and recognise some.

Sword Point and Sword Sand create the diversionary fork between the main Langstone Channel and the Broom Channel for Kendall's Wharf. Great Salterns Quay was the site of a large salt workings and continued in use till well into the 19th century. They were in fact Crown property until 1830. Mallards Sand and Russell's Lake offer a detour for those who want to remove themselves from the roar of the traffic on the close by A2030. It affords an alternative shoal route to Binness Rithe that bisects the islands; meeting the Deeps in the main channel at Round Nap Island.

The smaller channels in the harbour are now being marked with buoys, replacing the previous withies. In particular, Sinah with its old railway line is being re-marked in this manner.

The islands and lakes

Elsewhere in the Solent, the name 'lake' is given to quite small waters and creeks, but here, 'lake' is reserved for larger waters and the name Rithe (or Rythe) is preferred for the smaller cousins.

There are excellent opportunities for observing wildlife of many kinds in the harbour. The Royal Society for the Protection of Birds has put a lot of effort into the area and their following notes indicate what has come about in recent years.

'A BETTER PLACE FOR BIRDS AND PEOPLE.

Thanks to the co-operation of harbour users, the RSPB islands in Langstone are rapidly becoming one of the most important sea bird breeding sites in southern England. We are pleased to announce that since the introduction of restricted island landing following the RSPB's purchase of this large reserve, several new breeding species including the common tern and black headed gull are now well established. Other species which have benefitted are the oyster catcher, ringed plover and sandwich tern, but the most impressive success story is one of Britain's rarest sea birds, the little tern. This very attractive bird first bred in Langstone Harbour in 1976 and by 1987 one of Britain's largest and most successful colonies had been established with nearly 150 pairs.

Restricted island access is also vital outside the breeding season, for the undisturbed islands are the major roosting sites for Langstone Harbour's internationally important numbers of wintering waders and wildfowl.'

Restricted island details are as follows:

North Binness Closed at all times.
Long Island Northern end closed.
Long Island Southern end open at all times.
Round Nap Open outside breeding season; signs advise.
Baker's Island Closed at all times.
South Binness Closed at all times.
Sword Sands To the south is always available at low tide.

The Eastney Hards offer accommodation to a variety of craft: from Noah-type house vessels to genuine workboats.

Dredging quays

There is still considerable commercial traffic in gravel and aggregates to Havant Quay with the coasters of the Chichester Line. The Broom Channel to Kendals Wharf is also similarly busy with dredgers. Nevertheless, in spite of perhaps as many as half a dozen dredger movements on a tide, both the Broom and Langstone Channels (together with their tributaries) feel open and remote.

While civilisation in large doses is to be encountered at their heads of navigation (the Tudor Sailing Club at the top of Broom being one) there is little or no sign of such activity in the channel leading to them, and it is possible to put the rest of the world out of sight and out of mind with the greatest of ease in this often starkly bleak but always appealing cruising ground.

Shoresides

It is interesting to note that Langstone town was once the eastern limit of the Port of Southampton; the western limit being Lymington. It was the original port for Havant at the head of the ancient wadeway to Hayling Island. It is difficult to realise, looking today at the tiny community with all the surrounding silt, that it was a coasting port as late as the last century. In time past, there was a ferry for pedestrians, while those with wheels used to wait for low tide before risking their axles to the waterline. With the onset of barge business, a deeper channel was needed, and so a bridge became an imperative. In 1824 one was completed with a central swinging section. This enabled the passage of water traffic from Portsmouth to London, thus avoiding the open seaway and its consequent risks. In 1956, the old toll bridge was seen to be suffering timber fatigue (it was actually shuddering quite violently at the passage of every vehicle) and so the present structure was erected. It is still possible for small craft with masts down to negotiate (a good word for a tricky manoeuvre!) a passage through to Chichester Harbour at the right state of tide and bridge height.

That connection with the mainland is a far cry from the entrance, where another attempt was recently made to bridge the gap between mainland and main waterway. This was the star-bright project that failed to realise the dreams of locals and visitors alike: Langstone Marina. In the event, it got off to a ropey start; failed to attract support from locals, foreigners and visitors alike; and got into financial difficulties (in an area where marina projects seemed to be licences to print money) and was taken over by Arlington Securities as a Port Solent type development. As from 1988, the marina was completely closed to visiting yachts.

In the beginning there were all kinds of dredging problems. The channel was not only steep-banked but nearly vertical and the mooring buoys swung too far out, restricting space. The harbourmaster advised leading marks, but beacons in the form of withies were installed. They also restricted access to the channel and the moorings. When I was last there, according to the direction of the wind, boats would lie at all angles to the channel making safe navigation difficult.

In order to overcome the problems, there should be a freshly dredged channel, about 50ft wide, with banks that are not near-vertical but that slope at a 1 to 5 ratio. Yet all of this would once more restrict mooring space, and initially all mooring holders were promised their tidal access would remain the same or be improved after dredging. In any case, some of the boat people firmly believe themselves to have ancient rights. Nothing is as yet finalised. To quote the harbourmaster: 'It is all a grey area. The channel to the marina is not the province of the Harbour Board, yet nor is it a private passage; and in any event the marina is now closed!'

However, 'in any event' transpired to be the unexpected event, with Langstone (still a subsidiary of Arlington Securities) operational once more, and fully open to visiting yachts. There are 300 berths, with those for visitors being sited immediately inside the entrance. The marina is open 7 days a week with 24-hour security. The stated depth in the approach channel (which is to be provided with much needed new pile markers for the 1990 season) is never less than 1·5m. Access over the sill is advertised at a minimum of 3 hours either side of high water, with pontoons just outside for waiting.

Across the other side of the entrance, in the secluded bay known as the Kench, there are some unique and truly intriguing houseboats. For once they are exactly what their name suggests, in so far as they are 'houses built on boats'. They can be found on the shores of the bay and on the point.

Over at Eastney, there are similar arks, but a better 'ole is the one provided by the Eastney Cruising Association, known locally as Echo Charlie Alpha. The spirit of welcome that pervades this club that still glories in the renowned exploits of its hero and commodore, Sir Alec Rose, does a lot to compensate for the lack of services or facilities elsewhere. In the main, they are open all hours.

For some time, ECA members have had plans for expansion, one of which includes a marina development – much needed now that the original Langstone Marina project is defunct, with the intention that it should be converted into boat accommodation exclusively for those who have shoreside property.

Further inland, the scene becomes varied, as you move away from the marine environment into that of the Marines. Housing looms large, and you escape the expensive depressions of the ineptly designed private estates, only to be engulfed by the inexpensive dejections of the unfit tenement-like lots that are euphemistically known as flats. Big business and small government have a lot to answer for in the spoilation of this neighbourhood.

After all, it was not long ago that close to these Eastney Barracks there used to be snipe shooting laid on for the gentry on vacation in Southsea; and just to hammer in the insult, nearby Fort Cumberland, now English Heritage, goes back to the 18th century. Built in the shape of a five point star, it housed eight 24-pounder guns (and much more) to protect Portsea Island from the east.

But in spite of a mainly unbecoming environment, there are attractions and services shoresides. For those in need of boating assistance, there are the two experts: Ron Hale for outboards and inflatables in Highland Road, with a first rate, speedy and inexpensive cycle repair shop almost next door; and the well stocked chandlery of Chris Hornsey in Eastney. Chris is well sited, for he is in the middle of a modest (but, let it be said, inexpensive) shopping centre. There is a regular bus service into Eastney and into Southsea and Portsmouth, from the modest shopping centre up the junction.

Fort Cumberland is not the only piece of heritage to be accessible. Just down the road from the shops, there is an historic beam pump at Eastney Pumping Station. The present engines, by James Watt in 1886, can be seen not only in working order, but, from time to time in the holiday season, in full blown action. At their acme, they shifted a quarter of a million gallons of sewage an hour into tanks that were emptied into Langstone Harbour on the ebb. The nearby Royal Marines Museum is in what once used to be the officers' mess. It is said to have been built on such a lavish scale because one civil servant carelessly placed an extra nought on the estimates. One wonders how really careless he was.

Langstone harbour is indeed fortunate in being on the very edge of civilisation: on the one hand it offers you all the benefits of organised contemporary life, and, on the other, it reveals how, in its quiet settings, you can avoid the excesses of the worst aspects of that society.

Portsmouth Harbour

'This fortress built by Nature for herself against infection and the hand of war'; this must surely apply to Saxon-named Portsmouth, self-styled flagship of maritime England, first home of the Royal Navy, and one of the world's greatest naval bases.

'It pleased the Lord King Richard to build the town of Portsmouth.' (Curia Rolls 1194); and its first surviving charter goes back to that date when it was no more than a hamlet on the southwest corner of Portsea Island.

This naturally formed and well protected harbour comes under the jurisdiction of the Captain of the Port and Queen's Harbour Master. He is responsible not only for the harbour itself, but also for a considerable part of the eastern Solent. Not many people realise that his net comprises a fine meshed web that is as wide-spreading as to reach from Old Castle Point, just to the east of Cowes and light years away in ethos, to Nettlestone Point, just to the west of Bembridge, and equally removed from both. In addition, so efficient is the Computer Aided Radar Scanning organisation and system in Semaphore Tower that for miles and miles QHM may be watching you.

Indeed, Portsmouth, or Pompey as the lower deck have always called it, was for so long the greatest naval base in the world that it must find it difficult to adapt to being anything else. In spite of the incontrovertibility of this aspect to the waters, it has to be said that the QHM considers his prime task as one of ensuring that all his customers have safe and free passage throughout his area. Indeed, both the QHM and Portsmouth City Council believe the present rapid growth of the commercial and ferry port together with the development of Port Solent and other marinas indicates a high degree of adaptation on the part of both of them.

Portsmouth Harbour forms a tidal basin of approximately 3,800 acres with a shoreline of 33 miles. It resembles a large, almost land-locked lake at high water but at low water about 60% of the harbour is exposed as mud flats. Its physical shape has been altered over the years by reclamations, the largest and most recent having been those at North Harbour for the construction of the M27 and M275, IBM's UK headquarters, and for refuse disposal. More recently, Port Solent has become the latest project to exploit the area.

Shoresides, you will meet a redoubtable attitude in City Hall that is tantamount to a good dose of pride, power and glory administered in one shot: 'Variety, contrast, surprise, excitement and, perhaps, a little awe: this is Portsmouth, the first home of the Royal Navy and for centuries one of the world's greatest naval bases.' Thus sprach the Zarathustra of the city's publicity department, going on to remind all present of the lives and times of Lord Nelson, of Anson, Rodney, Jervis and Hawke; HMS *Victory* and HMS *Warrior*; Portchester Castle and fort after fort; together with the ghosts of hulk-imprisoned convicts. 'All these conspire to make it a land of legend.'

Semaphore Tower and its associated quays; home to the QHM and staff.

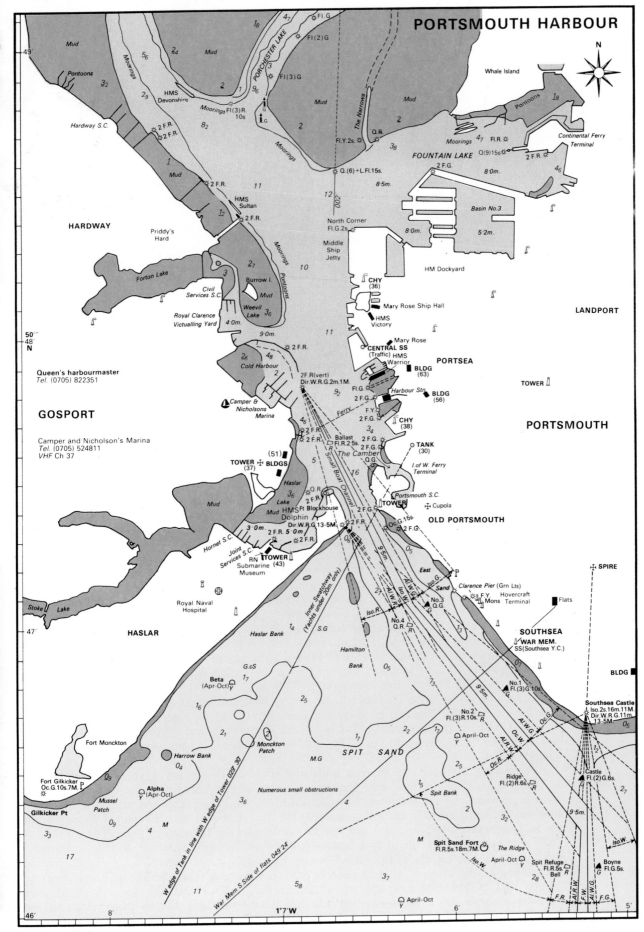

N

Mud

Porchester Lake

1.8

4.7

Fl.G

Fl(2)G

Mud

2.4

Mud

5.6

Moorings

Pontoons

3.2

Fl(3)G

9.6

Mud

Whale Island

1.8

Pontoons

2.9

HMS Devonshire

2

1

Mud

The Narrows

2

Q.R.

Moorings

4.7

Fl.R

Continental Ferry Terminal

Hardway S.C.

Moorings Fl(3)R 10s.

8.2

G

Fl.Y.2s

Q.R.

3.8

Moorings

Q(9)15s

2 F.R.

4.6

2 F.R.

Mud

2 F.R.

1

FOUNTAIN LAKE

2 F.G.

8.0m.

2 F.R.

Q.(6)+L.Fl.15s.

8.5m.

Basin No.3

HARDWAY

11

2 F.R.

North Corner Fl.G.2s

5.2m.

12

200'

Priddy's Hard

1.2

HMS Sultan

2 F.R.

Middle Ship Jetty

8.0m.

LANDPORT

Forton Lake

3

2.7

Burrow I.

10

HM Dockyard

CHY (36)

Civil Services S.C.

Mud

Weevil Lake

3.6

Mary Rose Ship Hall

Royal Clarence Victualling Yard

4.0m.

11

HMS Victory

9.0m.

50'
48'
N

2 F.R.

Cold Harbour

2.6

4.8

2.7

Mary Rose

CENTRAL SS (Traffic)

HMS Warrior

PORTSEA

BLDG (63)

TOWER

Queen's harbourmaster
Tel. (0705) 822351

2 F.R(vert)
Dir.W.R.G.2m.1M.

9.2

Fl.G.

Harbour Stn

BLDG (56)

2 F.G.

GOSPORT

Camper & Nicholsons Marina

4.6

F.Y.

2 F.G.

CHY (38)

PORTSMOUTH

Camper and Nicholson's Marina
Tel. (0705) 524811
VHF Ch 37

2 F.R.

Ballast Fl.R.2.5s.

3.4

2 F.G.

2 F.G.

TANK (30)

TOWER (37)

BLDGS (51)

5

Haslar Lake

3.6

Q.R.

Small Boat Channel

16

Q.G.

TOWER

I.of W. Ferry Terminal

Portsmouth S.C.

2 F.G.

Cupola

OLD PORTSMOUTH

Mud

2 F.R.

Ft Blockhouse Dir.W.R.G.13.5M.

HMS Dolphin

Oc.G.15s

2 F.G

3.0m.

2 F.R.

5.0m.

2 F.R.

Hornet S.C.

Joint Services S.C.

RN Submarine Museum

TOWER (43)

0.6

9.5m.

0.5

SPIRE

Royal Naval Hospital

1.4

Haslar Bank

Inner Swatchway (Yachts under 20m. only)

East Sand

Iso.G.

Clarence Pier (Grn Lts)

F.Y.

Hovercraft Terminal

Mons

Flats

47'

Stoke Lake

HASLAR

Hamilton Bank

S.G

No.3 Q.G.

No.4 Q.R.

0.5

SOUTHSEA

WAR MEM.
SS(Southsea Y.C.)

BLDG

G.cS

1.7

0.5

0.7

Beta (Apr-Oct)

2.5

No.1 Fl.(3)G.10s.

Fort Monckton

1.6

2.1

Monckton Patch

1.7

1.3

No.2 Fl.(3)R.10s.

9.5m.

Southsea Castle Iso.2s.16m.11M.
Dir.W.R.G.11m 13.5M.

Harrow Bank

0.4

M.G

SPIT SAND

2.2

1.7

April-Oct

2.5

Castle Fl.(2)G.6s.

0.5

Fort Gilkicker Oc.G.10s.7M.

0.9

Alpha (Apr-Oct)

3.6

Ridge Fl.(2)R.6s.

2.7

Gilkicker Pt

Mussel Patch

0.9

M

4

Numerous small obstructions

1.5

Spit Bank

2

3.2

9.5m.

3.3

17

W edge of Tank in line with W edge of Tower 027 30'

3.6

4

M

Spit Sand Fort Fl.R.5s.18m.7M.

The Ridge

April-Oct

Spit Refuge Fl.R.5s. Bell

Boyne Fl.G.5s.

11

War Mem. S.Side of flats 049 24'

5.8

3.7

2.8

F.R.

F.W.

F.G.

1°7'W

8'

6'

April-Oct

5'

46'

Portsmouth Harbour

45

Spit Sand Fort stands at the entrance to Portsmouth Harbour between Spithead and the notorious Hamilton Bank.

Ballast buoy: one of the markers of the official small-boat channel.

He could have spoken of Sir Alec Rose, the well renowned namesake of the uplifted *Mary*; reminding us that Sir A has never experienced the Lady Mary's need for painstaking and tangible restoration. Mention might also have been made of the Spithead Mutiny – but that might have brought to mind too soon too many telling images of that rebellious, egalitarian band of seagoing warlike brothers.

Portsmouth lies between two huge and natural harbours. To the east is Langstone, that still untamed thing of natural delights, while to the west is the highly disciplined and sophisticated experience that is the harbour itself.

The name of the new marina enterprise, consisting of the two words 'Port Solent', can be spellbinding, for, after voicing this near-shibboleth, I have been fixed, as with the steely stare of the Ancient Mariner's 'glittering eye', by enthusiasts eager for news.

So what is so gripping? Is it the Solent segment? In keeping with good, better, best, we have sole, solen, Solent: sole a suitable flat fish; solen an even more suitable razor fish; and Solent the most suitable possible strait between England and the Wight.

Or is it the Port part? If so it has competitors. To name but three: Port Royal, the 17th-century Jansenist convent, southwest of Versailles; Port Said, the 19th-century Suez HQ of exotic vice on the Suez Canal; and Port Salut, a flat round cheese.

According to Henry of Huntingdon, after the Romans left their naval base at Portchester, two Saxon ships, in the year 501, arrived, commanded by a man named Port, and his two sons Bieda and Maegla. The Saxons landed and routed the Britons, who fought bravely, and settled and named what is now Portsmouth, Portsun. Some think it is older, being Roman or Celtic. Either way, it could be true, but one idea seems obvious: the mouth of the port. But just to keep the ball rolling, Port is also Latin for 'door' or 'haven' or 'dark red wine', and, what is more, just happens to be an old word for any town or city.

All of which brings us to Portsmouth, famous as Britain's foremost naval base, and proud to describe itself as the flagship of maritime England. It has for centuries been affectionately known as Pompey, but must not be confused with Pompeii, buried by volcanic action in 79 AD and excavated, well preserved, in 1748; nor with the generic name for a black footman in London society.

To arrive at Port Solent, the mariner must first approach Portsmouth harbour from the Channel, thus coming face to face with features evocative of the past: firstly the Nelson memorial obelisk (conspic) and the Hamilton Sand Bank (dries). One is prompted to wonder if the noble lord and his sometime lady are still connected. Do they hear of wars and rumours of wars, from the many barriers, forts, fortresses and wrecks that inhabit the environs?

Do they mourn at the site of that famous Rose of all England, *Mary*, or do they 'spiritually' celebrate the other one, the *Lively Lady* Rose, at the Lonely Yachtsman.

Steaming in, the mariner can next observe relic after heritage relic: the Square Tower built by Henry VIII in 1494 for new artillery to defend the harbour entrance; then the Sally Port Gateway through which monarchs and admirals passed on their way to their vessels in the Solent.

After which comes the Australian Settlers' Memorial; a reminder of the traffic in human souls that occurred between 1788 and 1838, when two ships a year each 'transported' up to 300 convicts. On 13th May, 1787, eleven square-riggers left the harbour on a voyage that was to end with the founding of Australia.

On board for the 13,000-mile, 8-month endurance test were 1350 sailors, marines and convicts. All in all, nearly 30,000 went the way of the Tolpuddle Martyrs, many to face much sadder fates.

Perhaps appropriately, the next feature is the eighteen-gun battery and the infamous palisade next the seaman's 'liberty area', and Point Beach, from whence left convicts and pressed men.

Not to be missed is the splendidly towering dome of the office of the Queen's Harbour Master, after which comes the other Sally Port, the 'Common' through which passed convicts quitting England. Last is the Round Tower. Completed in 1415, in fact it was the port's first proper fortress against invasion. Henry V ordered it to be built after the sixth raid by the French during the Hundred Years' War.

The only hazard in the approaches, either just outside the harbour or well inside and on to Portchester Lake, is the large amount of traffic that can be afloat and on the move at any one time. In 1988, there were an estimated 100,000 recreational craft moves and an average of 65,000 commercial and naval moves, a total of 165,000.

You are sure to see all kinds of vessels: from Greenpeace to HM submarines; from deep-keeled but fast tugs to crawling men-of-war; and from ancient noble gaff rigs to speedy, flashing, Bullitalian jobs that would not disgrace a seagoing Michael Caine or Steve McQueen.

In the summer of 1988, I was being advised and instructed by the QHM (as well as being put right by most of his staff) when there was a kind of swarming movement towards the windows overlooking the sound. In spite of the stiff upper lip of the classic British service types, there were various intakes of breath and a kind of communal sigh to be heard as *Charybdis* came in from the Armilla patrol. The only phrase I caught was, 'She's been out there some time, and she looks like it as well.'

The one-time hulk, HMS *Warrior*; her guns never fired in angry warfare, and now at a kind of peace in Portsmouth Harbour.

Indeed, the only reason that stands in the way of Portsmouth Harbour claiming a veritable full house, *Jane's* and all, is the sin of omission of a Cunard *Queen*.

Just off the mainland is Spitbank Fort, a good example of Victorian engineering, built to defend against the threatened French invasion. 150 men lived inside the maze of passages and 'rooms' that were to be found within its walls that are 15 feet thick and finished with 26 inches of armour plating. You can take a boat trip to this now privately owned property: fully licensed, with food, 38-ton guns and its own freshwater well. The ferry boat leaves from Gosport Pontoon and Clarence Pier.

Directions

When making for Portsmouth from the east, it is almost impossible to avoid some contact with either the area known as Horse and Dean Sand or the well known Horse Sand Fort and its neighbour, the No Man's Land Fort.

Horse and Dean Sand extends more or less from the West Winner to Southsea Castle, and reaches out to seaward for a similar distance, thus occupying approximately 4 square miles in a 2-mile-square shape. They consist of coarse sand mixed with gravel and broken shells, thus should make the worst of crunching sounds upon bottoming. However, apart from their shallowness towards the beach and general suitability for shoal craft, they offer no hindrance other than the submerged barrier to which they play host.

Horse Sand and No Man's Land Forts are both conspicuous, and when making for Portsmouth, the former is left to starboard and the latter to port. However, in poor visibility, I have found that they both look so much alike that it is not difficult to fall into careless error and mistake one for another, leaving Horse Sand Fort to port and thus approaching the eccentric hazards of the remains of the wartime barrier which consists of concrete blocks that are partially uncovered at low water.

If you don't want to stand off the two miles to round Horse Sand Fort, you can search out one of the two 'windows' in this old submerged barrier. Known as the Main Passage and the Boat Passage the first allows you to pass through about 8 cables from the shore, while the second, the inner passage, takes you little more than a cable off, passing gloriously close to Southsea Castle. Both are suitable for small craft and have obvious starboard and port markers. The underground section is marked by yellow beacons and is irregular in size and shape; the Admiralty *Pilot* recommends that it should not be approached within 30m on either side.

Fishing and other local boats, of course, know their way in and out, and I have seen intrepid sailing yachts going through at a great rate of knots. However, having seen some of the hefty obstructions at low water, my trepidation has always made me deem it wiser to go round about.

The close entrance into the harbour from the east brings two choices: either crossing the main shipping channel and going on to use what is known as the Designated Boat Channel (see below) or keeping very close inshore to the east.

From the west, leaving Gilkicker to port, there is also a choice: the Main Shipping Channel, leading to the Designated Boat Channel; the Inner or the Outer Swashway, sandwiching, as it were, the Hamilton Bank; both channels leaving the Spit Sand Fort to starboard.

The Outer Swashway uses the long-established transit of the War Memorial and St Judes Church spire. This has been obscured by the construction of a block of flats. The recent *Notice to Mariners* issued by the Queen's Harbour Master designates the new transit as follows:

Dockyard Port of Portsmouth Local Notice to Mariners – Outer Swashway Transit
1. A new transit has been established to replace the transit lost by a new block of flats obscuring St Judes Church Spire.
2. This new transit is the War Memorial and the right hand edge (viewed from the sea) of the block of flats in transit bearing 049 degrees and 24 minutes.
3. The new transit gives a better lead through the Swashway and will appear on all new editions of the Admiralty charts covering the Swashway.

The Inner Channel (if that is what it can be called, for it nearly dries) is usable only on the top of a good tide and, in the main, only by shoal craft skippered by local knowledge. The transit here keeps the western edge of the Portsmouth Round Tower in line with the (conspicuous) tank a little further inland.

Those skippers intending to use either of the Swashways, or needing the information for any other reason, can check on VHF Ch 11 with QHM Portsmouth Control for the state of the tide.

For the Main Channel, Spit Sand Fort is the most important mark of delineation. Keeping to the westward on the final approach takes you into the Boat Channel which is a boon of a safeguard. (Please see below.)

All this is a much-needed discipline in a harbour near solid with crane-filled jetties and wharfs; ferries, warships, supply ships and submarines; yachts, cruisers and powerboats; as well as sailing clubs and other ancillaries, both afloat and ashore. Craft approach from nearly all angles and at varying speeds, so a good lookout is called for. The present number of recreational craft in Portsmouth is about 3,500. It is expected that it will rise to 6,000 in the next five years. Careful observance of the regulations laid down by the QHM is essential. Please see below for full details.

QHM'S NOTICES TO MARINERS

The following extracts from the QHM's *Notices to Mariners* are of relevance to all yachtsmen using the harbour.

PORTSMOUTH HARBOUR ENTRANCE AND APPROACHES (ANNEX A)

1. *The Main Channel*

   The Main Approach Channel to Portsmouth Harbour is considered to be a Narrow Channel. The limits of the channel from the Harbour entrance to Outer Spit Buoy are clearly marked by the Channel buoys (Admiralty Chart 2625). Within the harbour entrance the main channel is bounded on both sides by the 10 metre line (See Rule 2).

2. *Boat Channel*

   a. *General* A boat channel for vessels under 20 metres in length is deemed to exist off HMS DOLPHIN and extending 50 metres from the shore. The northern extremity of the channel is abreast the northern end of HMS DOLPHIN and the southern end at No 4 Bar Buoy. In practical terms yachts and small craft using this channel are to keep to the west of the western limits of the dredged area immediately south of the entrance and then a line from the NW corner of that dredged area to Ballast Buoy. It should also be noted that the red arc of the harbour entrance leading light (situated on the southern dolphin off Oil Fuel Jetty: characteristics ISO phase 1 sec on 1 sec off) coincides with the Boat Channel. The intention of this channel is twofold; to prevent vessels under 20 metres in length and vessels larger using the same water and to allow the smaller vessels, berthed on the Gosport side, direct access to their berths when entering harbour, without crossing the channel twice as required by the normal starboard hand rule. Vessels under 20 metres in length that have entered harbour in the Boat Channel are to keep to the west of the line from the NE corner of the Boat Channel to Ballast Buoy until clear to the north of the buoy. All vessels under 20 metres in length leaving harbour are to use the Boat Channel. The normal traffic rules apply across the entrance to Haslar Creek.

   b. *Entering and Leaving the Boat Channel* The Channel may only be entered or left at its northern or southern extremities or to the west. No vessel may enter or leave the channel by crossing the eastern limit of the channel. The effect of this rule is that vessels intending to use the channel when outbound must pass to the west of Ballast Buoy in order to enter the channel at its northern limit. Similarly vessels inbound must pass to the west of No 4 Bar Buoy to enter at the southern limit. The provisions of this rule also apply to vessels crossing the Harbour Entrance. Vessels crossing the entrance may only do so to the North of Ballast Buoy or to the South of No 4 Bar Buoy. Small vessels are reminded that they are extremely difficult to see and the Harbour Entrance is a 'blind bend' to larger vessels who cannot see clearly along the next stretch of the channel until they have negotiated the bend.

   c. *International Regulations for the Prevention of Collision at Sea 1972* Nothing in the regulations set out in a. and b. above amends or amplifies the International Regulations. The effect of b. is to create two separate channels such that the International Regulations apply to two individual traffic streams.

   d. *Exceptions* The following official vessels under 20 metres in length are authorised by QHM to use the main channel when their duties so require; Pilot boats, Police launches, Customs Craft, RN and RMAS craft flying official flags or discs.

   e. *Use of Portsmouth side of the Harbour Entrance* The existence of the boat channel does not prevent yachts that wish to enter harbour on the Portsmouth side from doing so, but they are to keep well to starboard clear of the main channel.

   f. *The Inner Swashway* The Inner Swashway is closed to vessels of 20 metres and over in length. Such vessels are to conform to the main channel between the Harbour Entrance and No 4 Bar Buoy.

3. *Entrance to Cold Harbour*

   The entrance to Cold Harbour, which lies between the Camper and Nicholson Marina to the West and Oil Fuel Jetty to the East, presents some difficulty in certain tidal conditions to tugs towing barges. All boat traffic in the vicinity, and particularly boats within Cold Harbour, are warned to proceed with caution and keep well clear of tugs towing barges. To ensure boats are aware of their presence, tugs with barges in tow will sound one prolonged blast before entering Cold Harbour.

4. *Haslar Creek – Reserved Area*

The hull of a submarine extends outwards below the waterline for some distance. This is particularly the case for the new class of submarine entering service in a few years time. In addition these new vessels have a low freeboard and, with their hatches open, are vulnerable to the wash of passing vessels. To protect both the submarines and the passing traffic a Reserved Area in Haslar Creek has been established in accordance with the Dockyard Port of Portsmouth Order 1978, Regulation No 12 and is shown on Charts 2625, 2629 and 2631. (Admiralty Notice to Mariners No 2690/83 refers). Masters of vessels and small craft not on Ministry of Defence service and navigating within Haslar Creek are warned that entry into the above Reserved Area is prohibited.

5. *Use of Engines*

All sailing vessels fitted with engines are to proceed under power through the Harbour Entrance and between Ballast Buoy and Southsea War Memorial.

6. *Vessels under Sail*

Vessels under sail not fitted with engines are expected to conform with the traffic rules for all vessels under 20 metres. If under 20 metres in length use the Boat Channel and keep clear of the main channel irrespective of length and size. If the wind or tide are such that a sailing vessel cannot enter or leave harbour in accordance with the rules then it either waits for a change in conditions or is towed through the entrance.

7. *Tide*

The tidal stream runs at up to 5¼ knots in the Harbour Entrance at certain states of the tide. The maximum flood makes between 3 hours and ½ hour before HW. The maximum ebb flows between 1½ and 3½ hours after HW. DO NOT GET CAUGHT IN THE HARBOUR ENTRANCE UNABLE TO MAKE HEADWAY, if you do, keep well clear of the main channel (i.e. in the boat channel or close in on the Portsmouth side) so that you do not block this vital stretch of water for shipping.

GENERAL RULES

8. *Crossing a Narrow Channel or Fairway*

A yacht shall *not* cross a narrow channel or fairway if it impedes the passage of a large vessel. When clear to do so the fairway should be crossed at right angles.

9. *Failure to Understand Intentions*

A large vessel that is in doubt whether sufficient action is being taken to avoid collision will indicate by giving 5 or more short blasts on the whistle. This may be supplemented by 5 or more short flashes on a light. You should move clear as rapidly as possible.

10. *Anchoring and Fishing*

Do not anchor or fish in the fairways, the main approach channel, within 100 metres of fixed naval installations (e.g. jetties) or 150 metres of naval moorings.

11. *Fog*

Remain at your moorings if there is fog.

12. *Speed Limits*

Within the Dockyard Port of Portsmouth the following speed limits apply.
Within Portsmouth Harbour: 10 knots
Within 1000 yards of the shore in any part of the Dockyard Port of Portsmouth: 10 knots
Within 1000 yards of any warship in any part of the Dockyard Port of Portsmouth: 12 knots
Within Wootton Creek to the west of 0°12′48″ W (the meridian at the mouth of the Creek): 5 knots
The limit in each case is taken as speed through the water. These limits do not apply to designated water skiing areas.

13. *Water Skiing*

No water skiing is permitted within Portsmouth Harbour or within 1000 yards of the shore in any part of the Dockyard Port of Portsmouth except in the two areas designated for water skiing: one off Lee On The Solent and a second to the north west of Wootton Creek. These areas are shown on Admiralty Chart 394. Other boats and swimmers should keep clear of the water ski areas and the entrance from the beach. Nevertheless, drivers of ski boats are to take due care to safeguard the lives and property of all other users of the sea and foreshore. All boats engaged in towing water skiers within the Dockyard Port of Portsmouth are to carry third party insurance.

14. *Underwater Swimming or Diving*

A licence from the Queen's Harbour Master is required by all persons who wish to dive or swim underwater within Portsmouth Harbour.

15. *Board Sailing*

Board sailing is not permitted in the Main Approach Channel to Portsmouth or within Portsmouth Harbour in the navigable channels south of latitude 50°49′N.

16. *Reporting Damage or Incidents*

Any incident that reflects on the safe operation of the Dockyard Port is to be reported immediately to the Queen's Harbour Master. Such incidents are considered to be those that involve:

a. Damage to vessels

b. Movement of or damage to navigation marks

c. Damage to shore facilities that could affect the use of such facilities by other vessels

d. Close quarters situations between two or more vessels, which results in emergency action on the part of the vessels involved. In these circumstances an immediate report is to be made to the Queen's Harbour Master preferably on VHF Channel 11 or 13 but otherwise by telephone and is to be followed by a written report if requested. In cases when damage is caused to commercial installations the Port Manager Portsmouth is also to be informed.

DOCKYARD PORT OF PORTSMOUTH – LOCAL NOTICES TO MARINERS

Spithead – Site of the Mary Rose wreck

1. The following information is promulgated on the status of the site of the wreck of the Tudor warship MARY ROSE and hazards affecting navigation:

a. The site of the Historic Wreck consisting of an area of radius 300 metres centred on position 50°45′·8N 01°06′·17W remains covered by The Protection of Wrecks Act 1973 against unauthorised interference until further notice.

b. The unlit MARY ROSE Buoy in position 50°45′·8N 01°06′·17W will remain on station.

c. A number of unlit mooring buoys within the area described above remain on station.

d. Some obstructions on the seabed remain.

e. Following disturbance of the seabed during recovery operations charted depths on the site should be treated with caution.

Danger Area – Small Arms Firing

1. A Small Arms Firing Danger Area exists in Portchester Lake, extending to 2500 metres from the Tipner Firing Range. The Danger Area limits are defined by the following points:

a. The 400 yard Firing Point Flagstaff (50°49′·43N 01°05′·55W)

b. Pile 84

c. Pile 78

d. Unnumbered Pile 60 metres North of SPIDER Survey Pile

e. Position 50°49′·55N 01°07′·83W (unmarked)

f. Pile 62

g. Pile 87

2. Piles 62, 64, 70, 78, 84, 87, 89 and the unnumbered Pile at 1(d) above carry DANGER AREA WARNING Notices.

3. When firings are taking place a Red Flag by day or a Red Light at night is exhibited from the Flagstaffs at Tipner Range.

4. Whilst firings are taking place all craft are, as far as is practicable, to keep clear of the danger area outlined in paragraph 1 above; alternatively, those navigating the Portchester Channel are to pass through the area as quickly as possible.

Movement of vessels during poor visibility

1. Portsmouth Harbour fog routine will be ordered by the Queen's Harbour Master when visibility is so low that normal shipping movements would be dangerous.

2. Notice of the introduction of the fog routine will be promulgated by:

a. Broadcasting "Harbour Fog Routine in force" on VHF Channels 11, 13 and 73.

b. Hoisting a red rectangular flag with white diagonal bar at the Central Signal Station, Fort Blockhouse and at Fort Gilkicker Signal Station by day and by displaying 3 all round lights, a red over 2 green in a vertical line by night.

3. The Gosport Ferries and naval cross-harbour ferry services may continue operations unless otherwise directed by the Queen's Harbour Master.

4. Small boat and yacht traffic may continue at the skipper's discretion, but such boats are warned that they must proceed with great caution, keeping well clear of the main channel and avoiding hampering ferries and seagoing vessels navigating in the channel with the use of radar. They are especially cautioned that in low visibility the presence of radar echoes from

small vessels within the main channel can cause much doubt and difficulty for the Master of a large vessel. For their own safety and that of major craft using the Harbour they are strongly advised not to move when fog routine is in force.

VHF – Use of Frequencies

Within that part of the Dockyard Port of Portsmouth covered by the Southampton Port Signal and Radar Station, that is from Nab Tower inwards but excluding the area north of the line from Fort Gilkicker to Outer Spit Buoy, vessels are to maintain a continuous watch on VHF R/T Channel 12 or 14 and report to Southampton Port Radio (SPR) as appropriate when passing the designated reporting points and in addition if embarking a pilot, when the pilot has boarded. To the north of the line Fort Gilkicker to Outer Spit Buoy vessels are to maintain a continuous watch on VHF R/T Channel 11 with the Queen's Harbour Master (QHM). Fort Gilkicker (Callsign Gilkicker) maintains a continuous listening watch on Channel 16 on behalf of the Queen's Harbour Master, Portsmouth.

Use of Channel 11

VHF Ch 11 is designated the Portsmouth Harbour Working Channel. It is controlled by the Queen's Harbour Master and is to be used by all vessels underway in Portsmouth Harbour north of Outer Spit Buoy. The Commercial Port Manager (c/s Portsmouth Harbour Radio) maintains a constant watch on this channel.

Use of Channel 13

VHF Ch 13 is designated Portsmouth Naval Port Operations. It is controlled by the Queen's Harbour Master and is mainly used by RN vessels to control tugs and by all vessels as an alternative to Ch 11. Vessels wishing to use Ch 13 are to request permission from the Queen's Harbour Master on Ch 11 before chopping to Ch 13. In time of high traffic density the Queen's Harbour Master may instruct vessels to maintain watch on Ch 13. In these circumstances it will be the responsibility of the Queen's Harbour Master to re-broadcast pertinent information on the alternative channel to ships maintaining watch on that channel.

Local Visual Signals

Notice is hereby given that the following signals affecting traffic are hoisted by HM Ships or at Signal Stations at Portsmouth. All other signals are of purely Naval interest.

Displayed on the Central Signal Station at Fort Blockhouse and at Gilkicker Point.

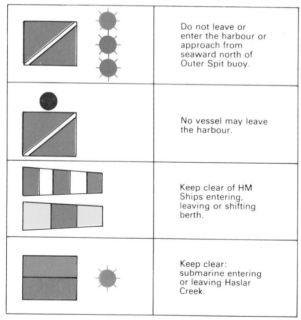
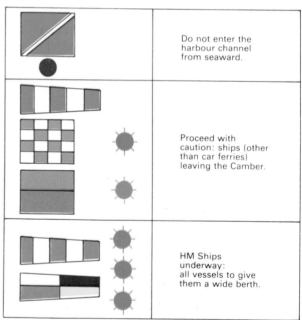

Portsmouth Harbour signals

Notes

1. Within the context of this Notice a large vessel is deemed to be one that is constrained by her length or draught to maintain the centreline of the Channel.
2. Instructions from QHM will be passed on VHF Channels 11 or 13 as appropriate.

Gosport

Before you arrive at this, the first port of call to port, the big marina for which most visitors are heading, you pass the buoys and the boards with the notices by Fort Blockhouse and HMS Dolphin. The fort was built in the reign of Queen Anne to protect the harbour entrance. Its guns were fired only twice, and the occasions were completely contrasted in style and purpose. First was during an episode in the civil war in 1642; second was in the 1939–45 war when a pom-pom gun shot down a marauding plane. HMS Dolphin is the base of the 1st Submarine Squadron.

Haslar Creek

Before going really upstream, there is Haslar Creek to be considered. Criminals were left in chains on a gibbet in Haslar Creek after they had been hung in Southsea Castle. The ethos is hardly improved today, since, sadly, the quality of its landscape is marred by its stark perimeter of industry and the lack of any pleasing landscape on the open space on the northern shore. Actually, the precinct has tremendous potential as an amenity and tourist attraction.

Found between Fort Blockhouse and the town of Gosport, it is famous on two counts: first it is headquarters water of Her Majesty's submarines, and the resting place of HMS *Alliance*, the Submarine Memorial; second, HMS *Hornet*, the wartime gunboat base next the bridge, is the home of the Joint Services Sailing Centre and Marina facility. The members will make you welcome (although not on an absolutely unconditional basis) but you will need to take care if you want to take photographs in the vicinity of the subs.

The QHM Portsmouth had suggested that I should not fail to visit the area while in the harbour. In spite of having my bona fides guaranteed I was stopped and detained by the Royal Naval personnel whilst I explained myself and they tried, in vain, to contact QHM. Inconvenient it was, but a graphic illustration that the security works, even if other boats passed me during this incident happily taking pictures right, left and centre.

There is a marina proposal for Haslar. It involves dredging the mudland area south of the Esplanade and northeast of Haslar Bridge to create a facility for 600 berths; with reclamation west of the Haslar Bridge for car parking and associated services.

After the open water that gives on to Haslar Creek come the public ferry pier heads, and just upstream of them, the marina entrance is marked by huge piles. The Admiralty *Pilot*, in its wisdom, refers to the marina, probably one of the best known in the world, as Cold Harbour Marina. True, it actually is situate within Cold Harbour, but there can hardly be a skipper in the land who would refer to this famous boatyard (all the British J-Class yachts and later *Gypsy*

Camber Quay: the place for the best and freshest fish in Portsmouth. Small yachts approach with caution for it is a busy, vulgar and Speedy Gonzales waterway.

Moth IV were built here) and yachtsmen's haven as anything other than Campers. The fact that it now has yet another title deed proper and owner is being ignored. They offer all the facilities you can possibly want boatwise at Campers, and their laundrette equipment, while no longer to be described as new, is one of the most efficient in the country. In particular, the driers are exceptionally good. Recent extensions have resulted in an increase of 90 berths, and it is possible there may be room for even further extensions in this general area if car parking and ancillary services problems can be solved shoresides.

The name Gosport is often claimed to be derived from 'God's Port', a title supposedly wished upon it by Bishop Henri de Blois of Winchester after a 'blow' in the Channel around 1140. I prefer the alternative, 'Gorse Port'; it seems much more pleasing, natural, appropriate and altogether more likely. However, Gosport's great crest portrays de Blois sailing into the harbour.

Known also as Little Village of Fisschar Men, it changed its character dramatically once it received Benefit of Navy. The fishermen left their nest to become fishers of men, manning and victualling their ships of the realm. Wandering around its somewhat unseemly architecture, it comes as something of a surprise to discover that Lee-on-the-Solent (established in 1884 as a health resort by one Mr C. E. Robinson while cruising the Solent) is the most western outreach of the borough.

Around the 1800s, there were just under seventy pubs, three coach houses, two theatres, one bridewell, three breweries, two flour mills, fourteen bakehouses, one iron foundry and many malthouses, warehouses and wharves. There were, of course, hundreds of boaties, who rowed people backwards and forwards in the harbour. The prisoner-of-war hulks, old wooden walls with the ugly addition of topsides excrescences, that lay out on the moorings became notorious.

In the 18th century, one Erasmus Carver, a merchant, created a massive fleet of ships for carrying captured French gear to West Africa to barter for slaves for America, to swap for sugar in England. By the middle of the 19th century there were supposed to be nearly 2,000 ships lying in the roads off Gosport.

Just upstream from Campers marina are Weevil and Forton, both somewhat euphemistically described as Lakes, next the Royal Clarence Victualling Yard (beef, pork, bread, biscuits, rum, wine and clothing since the 18th century) and the intriguingly named Priddy's Hard (ammunition and explosives, complete with gunpowder store). Situate in Weevil Lake is Burrow Island, also known as Rat Island. It is said to be the burial ground of those convicts (known as Rats) from the hulks in the harbour who were shot or drowned while trying to escape. It was also infested with the real things living in style on the Royal Clarence. If you want an entertaining couple of days jilling about in a dinghy when and where there is water, you will find numerous alcoves to divert you in what is an otherwise depressing and drab environment.

Portsmouth, Old Portsmouth and Portsea

Before proceeding upstream, let us cross the channel (at right angles, please) to the starboard side where the main measure of Portsmouth is to be found. The chances are that you will either do so in the company of one of the Gosport green ferries that ply regularly across the harbour, or that you will meet one face to face.

One of the reasons for using the close inshore passage on the east is to get a good view of the architectural and historical treasures that abound along the foreshore.

The Round Tower is the oldest fortification dating as far back as 1418. For some time it has been the traditional waving-off point for those who are committing their loved ones to the high seas as well as despatching horse and troop with warlike intent.

The Square Tower was built in 1494 and has been used in its time as a powder magazine, victualling store, semaphore station, Napoleonic prison and pilot house. True to the proper British respect for distinction, there is a special opening set aside for the elite class, the commissioned officers, to use when embarking. It is known as the Sally Port.

The Portsmouth forts started life in Palmerston's head around the late 1850s, when he had the bright idea of making the harbour impregnable. The plans (often called 'Palmerston's Follies') consisted of twenty shoreside forts with six more out at sea, but only four of which were built. Fort Gilkicker was brought up to strength at the time, being armed with twenty guns up to 12″ and seven 13″ mortars. Although disreputable in appearance, the fort is now owned by Hampshire County Council. The armaments of the other forts were impressive: at one time Horse Sand had one 12″ and twelve 10″ breechers and ten 12½″ muzzlers.

The most obvious of Palmerston's remains are the four sea forts which span the eastern entrance to Spithead and the Solent. Built in granite and Portland stone, the forts faced the possible enemy with sheets of armour on the walls. Fortress Portsmouth was also defended by

The obelisk on the Southsea waterfront: 'In memory of 48 officers and men who died during the epidemic of yellow fever on board HMS *Aboukir* at Jamaica in 1873/74.'

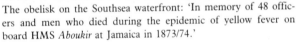

Opposite: The well known landmark of the famous war memorial on the Southsea waterfront.

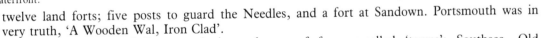

twelve land forts; five posts to guard the Needles, and a fort at Sandown. Portsmouth was in very truth, 'A Wooden Wal, Iron Clad'.

The present city of Portsmouth is made up of four so-called 'towns': Southsea, Old Portsmouth, Landport and Portsea. The parts that are of most interest to the cruising and sailing fraternity are Old Portsmouth and Southsea: the former because of its direct marine connections particularly in the Camber; and the latter because it is one of the best shopping quarters in the whole of the Solent region. In particular, not to be missed is the Oriental cuisine of the South Sea Chinese restaurant known somewhat beguilingly as Stranded at Lee's. The chefs are experts in their own esoteric lines. Pricewise, it reflects its excellence, but the saki is rated as dissolved gold dust. Be warned!

The 'town' of Southsea (for it must surely not be allowed to be swallowed up in the maw of the city as no more than a suburb) must offer solace and relief to any weather-beleaguered skipper with a family to distract and entertain. Southsea has fascinating architecture, is broadly and largely entertaining and can boast a good shopping precinct – with intriguing offshoots.

The Camber is the famous and busy miniature harbour; a safe and well protected natural haven used commercially since the 1300s. A maximum of 20 recreational moorings has received the go ahead as part of the redevelopment proposals for Vosper's former yard. The place is busy enough already, and you might not immediately stumble across the fresh-fish delights offered by Johnsons at Camber Quay, but no man should pass through the Solent without benefiting from their retail sales.

55

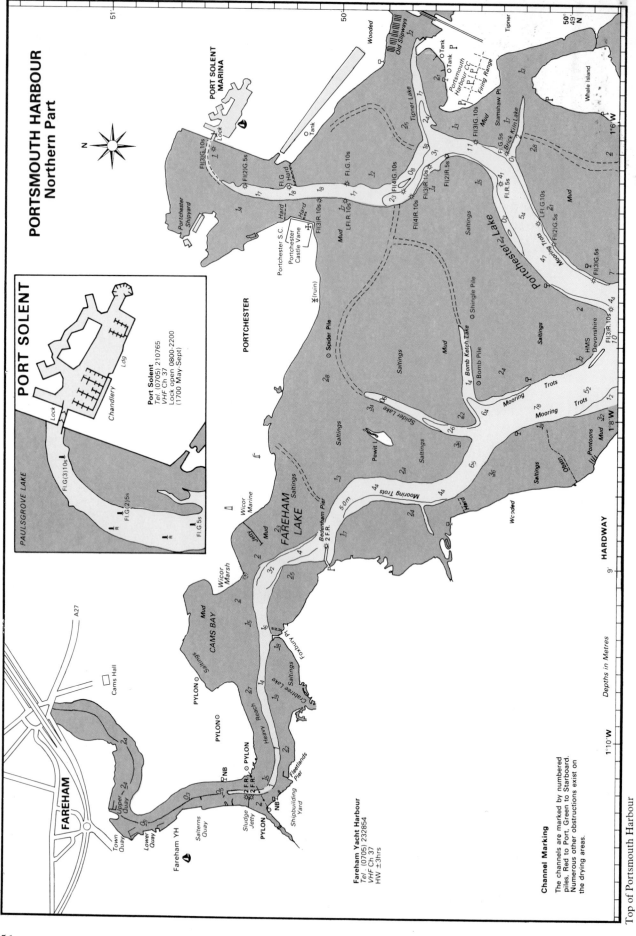

PORTSMOUTH HARBOUR
Northern Part

N

PORT SOLENT

Port Solent
Tel. (0705) 210765
VHF Ch 37
Lock open 0800-2200
(1700 May-Sept)

Chandlery

Log

Lock

PAULSGROVE LAKE

Fl.G.(3)10s

Fl.G.(2)5s

Fl.G.5s

R

R

PORT SOLENT MARINA

Lock

Fl(3)G.10s

Fl(2)G.5s

Fl.G.5s

Fl.G.

Hard

Portchester Shipyard

Portchester S.C.

Portchester Castle Vane

⚓ (ruin)

Hard

Hard

Fl(3)R.10s

Mud

L.Fl.R.10s

Fl(4)R.10s

Fl(3)R.10s

Fl(2)R.5s

Fl(4)G.10s

Fl.G.10s

Old Slipways

Wooded

Tipner

Tank

Tank

Portsmouth Harbour CC

Firing Range

P P P

Whale Island

Tipner Lake

Stamshaw Pt

Brick Kiln Lake

Fl(3)G.10s

Fl.G.5s

L.Fl.R.5s

Fl.R.5s

Fl.G.10s

Fl(2)G.5s

Fl.G.5s

Fl(3)G.10s

Mooring Trots

Mud

Fl(3)R.10s

HMS Devonshire

Portchester Lake

Saltings

Mud

Saltings

Spider Pile

Shingle Pile

Bomb Pile

Bomb Ketch Lake

Mud

Mooring Trots

Mooring

Mooring Trots

Saltings

Obstn

Pontoons

Mud

Saltings

Wooded

Hard

Mooring Trots

5.0m

PORTCHESTER

Spider Pile

Saltings

Pewit I.

Spider Lake

Saltings

2 F.R.

Bedenham Pier

FAREHAM LAKE

Saltings

Wicor Marine

Wicor Marsh

Mud

Wicor

CAMS BAY

Mud

Saltings

Cams Hall

A27

FAREHAM

Town Quay

Upper Quay

Salterns Quay

Lower Quay

Sludge Jetty

Fareham YH

2 F.R.

2 F.R.

NB

PYLON

PYLON

PYLON

PYLON

PYLON

PYLON

NB

NB

Heavy Reach

Foxbury Pt

Crabtree Lake

Saltings

Shipbuilding Yard

Fleetlands Pier

Fareham Yacht Harbour
Tel. (0705) 232854
VHF Ch 37
HW ±3hrs

HARDWAY

Depths in Metres

Channel Marking

The channels are marked by numbered
piles, Red to Port, Green to Starboard.
Numerous other obstructions exist on
the drying areas.

51'

50'

50
49

N

16' W

1·8' W

1·10' W

9'

Today, the Camber is the hub of fresh-fish life for the whole of the area, and in addition almost all yachtsmen's needs can be met in the vicinity. First among equals comes Ken Brown, a man of maritime affairs and of character. His premises and his staff should be able to offer all that you need. That is, provided you have the right attitude; he has a craftsman's approach to work and he does not expect you to challenge it. (There is no hustling a craftsman, and no skipper has ever managed to hurry a boatbuilder.) However, patience can be rewarded in more ways than one, for there are pubs aplenty; and one of special interest must be the Lone Sailor, with its tributes to the one and only Sir Alec Rose.

The main part of Portsmouth Harbour itself has always been a popular cruising ground with sail or power skippers. Frank Cowper had this to say about what he considered to be a Navy-dominated harbour:

'For mudlarks nothing could beat a cruise up Portchester Lake, but since those joyous old days finger-posts have been put up, which makes things much more clean, prosy and expeditious. The official directions sum up the situation in Portsmouth Harbour rather neatly, if a little grimly. They say: "The deep-water space in Portsmouth Harbour is occupied to a great extent by moorings for H. M. ships; Fareham Lake is also utilised for this purpose as far as space and depth permit. The lower part of Portchester Lake is occupied by the torpedo school ship and tenders."

Yachts are not wanted, nor idle people pleasure-seeking. I'm glad I did most of my cruising about here from 1872 to 1892. Matters were easier then, before we thought of having to fight any three other navies. However, there's no knowing what we may come to if certain politicians and the Labour Party have their way. Cruising in small yachts in Portsmouth Harbour may resume its former happy-go-lucky tranquility, and mudlarks may be even thicker than of yore. "Tis an ill wind that blows nobody any good", and I dare say the Germans, or whoever annex our harbours, won't interfere with our harmless eccentricities or sports, so long as we contribute a proper quota to swell the annexers' army, navy, and treasury: so, of course, it's ridiculous having so many ships when one looks at it in this way.

If obliged to anchor off Gosport, choose slack water and low tide if possible, otherwise there is every chance of a mess. I usually anchor between the coal hulks off Rat Island and the mud bank, as being most out of the way; but the authorities don't always approve of this, I am told, although I have never been interfered with.

On the whole, Portsmouth Harbour is the best place I know for trying one's seamanship, judgment, tact and good temper, if in a small or large sailing boat. For motors and steam vessels things are different.

Years ago I used to go in and out of Portsmouth as easily and unconcernedly as I did at Bembridge, or lately at St Malo or Burnham. But now it is different. I should hardly know where to bring up, and one enters with an uncomfortable feeling of not being wanted, which is exactly the case. Portsmouth is no place for yachts. Fortunately, there are Southampton, and, better still, Beaulieu River and the Hamble. But if obliged to go into Portsmouth, I should try to find a berth off Gosport, out of the way of the floating bridge and steam launches if possible, or else go right up Haslar Creek (no easy job now with a head wind), or else moor inside the coal hulks, if allowed. The fact is, there are so many "ifs" connected with this business that I had rather ride off Southsea Beach or in Stokes Bay – not at all a bad place, by the way, in moderate weather and with off-shore winds, even if strong.'

The harbour is not only packed with boats, ships and dories, but also with historical interest. You won't be able to miss the ferries and their green omniwaterbuses.

It was in Portsmouth that the case of Admiral Byng was heard. He was tried, on board the *Monarque*, of not having properly defended Minorca. Found guilty, he went on to the quarter-deck, bandaged his eyes and gave the execution signal to the marines himself. It was of this 'disturbyng' case that Voltaire said, 'Dans ce pays-ci, il est bon de tuer de temps en temps un amiral, pour encourager les autres.'

Another famed death was that of George Villiers, Duke of Buckingham; killed by the malcontent Felton in 1628 outside a house in the High Street known as the Spotted Dog. Yet another was the murder of Adam Moleyns, Bishop of Chichester, who tried to win the sailors over to the cause of Henry VI in not paying their wages. He came to his end at the bottom of the High Street; another churchman who got mixed up in politics.

The Point, opposite Blockhouse and by the entrance to the Camber, is celebrated in Portsmouth's history. A close community of fishermen, stevedores and wherrymen, it was familiarly known as Spice Island because of the busy landings of spices, tobacco and potatoes. It became legendary for high life or low life, entirely depending upon your point of view. In Nelson's time it was still highly insalubrious and beyond the jurisdiction of the town in every way.

Moving upstream on the starboard hand takes you past the naval establishment and all its good works, including Semaphore Tower, the centre of the nervous system of the Queen's Harbour Master. Nearby, is HMS *Warrior*, Britain's first iron-hulled, armoured battleship. She was launched in 1860 and was the largest, fastest and most formidable warship of those days. Fresh from her Hartlepool revamp: 'sleek, black and powerful, the ship that once ruled the waves is now restored to her former glory', and known as 'The Black Snake among the rabbits.'

The hull of Henry VIII's *Mary Rose*, that 'flower of all ships that ever sailed', was rescued from the deeps in 1982, and is now spectacularly housed, in company with her most valued 'treasures': the everyday objects that went with her to sea. These range from plant fragments, seeds and fleas; through tooled leather items and delicately carved pocket sundials; musical instruments, games, clothes and cutlery; all kinds of tools, the medical chest; to massive bronze guns. She was built in Portsmouth in 1509–10. Initially rated at 600 tons, she was a beamy vessel with a 32-metre keel. After her rebuild in 1536, she carried 91 guns. On July 19th, 1545 the ill-fated ship sailed out of Portsmouth Harbour to do battle with the French. However, before she even opened fire, she heeled over and sank. Legend has it that Henry, at the head of his army on Southsea Common, heard every single cry of the drowning men – and never got over the shock.

HMS *Victory* is the world's oldest surviving ship of the line of battle, and wore Nelson's flag at Trafalgar. Laid down in Chatham in 1759, she is now the flagship of the Commander in Chief, Naval Home Command. She has been in continuous use since 1778 and is still manned by the Royal Navy and Marines.

The Royal Naval Museum is housed in Georgian storehouses and presents the history of the Navy from Tudor to today. There is a collection of Nelson relics and an audiovisual treatment of Trafalgar.

For those who want to ferret out a relic of more recent times, and one somewhat closer to the dreams of cruising folk, *Lively Lady*, the ketch sailed round the world by Sir Alec Rose, will be an irresistible temptation.

The lakes

Well away from the charivari of shopping lanes, shipping lanes, wreckers' havens and artillery islands, Fareham and Portchester Lakes offer fishing, bird watching and calm anchorages. Set against a backdrop to rival any Greek amphitheatre, their extensive watery expanses, with all kinds of buoys, rods, poles and perches marking their drying acres, they own a plethora of delights.

Just past the Naval Dockyard, the traffic begins to thin and it soon becomes not-quite-clear among the many piles and moorings which way is which after the fork. Indeed, it is not even obvious where the fork is. I would urge any first time visitor to study the large Admiralty chart with some care before trying to make a passage up either of the arms of the fork. Theoretically, it is all plain sailing, but the clarity of the numbering on the piles leaves a lot to be desired, and there is by no means a straight one-to-one correlation between chart and actuality in this cluttered expanse.

Before the major fork, Fountain Lake is found to starboard, between the north end of the dockyard and Whale Island. It is a patch busy with commercial wharfing; that is, when it is not dressed overall in its best bib and tucker for a visitation or royal progress from *Britannia*. There is nothing there but fussy sightseeing for visiting yachtsmen; RoRo for passenger and vehicle ferries make all the going. In fact, it is a prohibited anchorage, and should be used only by yachtsmen proceeding to and from the Whale Island naval sailing centre.

Leaving Fountain Lake and Whale Island to starboard, the main channel leads on to Fareham Lake to port, and Portchester Lake to starboard. Whale Island, with its mainland occupied by the naval establishment, HMS Excellent, is, in the main, a vast spread of drying mud, with a particularly low-lying part known as Half Ebb Lake and split by the miniature channel called the Narrows (local knowledge and grace and favour only) marked by pile No. 99. It is possible to creep into the entrance at most states of the tide, and some find it a popular spot for fishing. The nearby firing range (marked by piles) may not disturb the fish, but it certainly put me off.

Portchester Lake

Once passed the hurly-burly of myriad craft (from small to large, from peaceful to warlike, from tug to tub, and from luxury palaces to green water boatmen) the route becomes quieter and Portchester Lake begins to open up as something of haven.

Although there are plenty of markers, all large posts in solid order, and all fairly well coloured, nevertheless it is not easy to find one's way about for they are not at all well numbered. Some are without numbers of any kind and some are almost impossible to read, tempting one to conclude that the channel is marked for those who already know their way – and not for strangers. A good number of trips need to have been made before it can be deemed advisable to try a night or foggy entry; not that there are any hazards much worse than the soft mud that spreads for acre upon acre. It is important to remember that the channel takes some big bends, and not to be misled by the first apparent marker to catch the eye.

In spring 1989, it was the intention of Port Solent to light a number of piles to 'assist' with night passage. In that very same season I heard from Lieutenant Commander John Whitehead, Captain of HMS *Victory* and recently Assistant QHM: 'You may wish to know that I still get confused when finding my way to Port Solent!'

Basically, Portchester Lake is in the form of a dogleg. The first stretch tends to the northeast, leaving Whale Island to starboard and going on to Tipner where there is another firing area, well marked by boards with directions and instructions. (Please see QHM *Notices to Mariners* page 49.)

Next it tends northwest and north, past Tipner Lake and Horsea Island on a course straight for the old Roman fort at Portchester Point. By this time the channel markers are no longer confused or confusing, but clear and plain all the way to Port Solent. The mainland and its shore to starboard are not things of beauty. There are occasional vistas of nature, but on the whole the scene is one of wrecks, wreckers, breakers, refuse and debris crisscrossed by arterial roads and bridges.

From the yachtsman's point of view, Whale, Tipner and Horsea Islands do offer some minor boatyards, but they are overshadowed by major scrapyards. Their approaches tend to be desolate, shoal-water affairs, choppy and inhospitable in the extreme with the slightest wind against tide – especially when coming straight across the Great Lake. There are some swing moorings, and while they do not present themselves as being very substantial they do have the undeniable air of belonging to hardened sea dog mariners possessed of ancient rights.

Finally, the channel moves northerly between the hard by Portchester Castle and the slipway at the south west tip of Horsea Island.

Dutch-style land reclamation, in a flurry of publicity, brought the IBM UK HQ here, to what had previously been wastelands in a sea of scrap metal. The area is still the resting place of numerous leviathans, and, moreover, is immediately next the Tipner firing range, where things go bump, not just in the night, but at all hours. Not to be outdone, Port Solent is creating its own flat monolith across the way, where leisure cruising fantasies of Thatcherite proportions and origins can be indulged.

However, neither the 'Vermuyden' essay in reclamation, nor the recent excavation (delving, burrowing and building by the digger daddy of them all, McAlpine) can claim to be anything more than a pale reflection of the Romans' achievement at Portchester Castle.

The gateway to gratification; the locked entrance to the smooth lifestyle of the area's most recent acquisition, Port Solent.

Portchester Castle

Carausias is believed to have built it either in 285 AD against barbarian pirates or in 286 AD as an act of defiance against the central authorities. The Romans had a major naval base here.

Then in turn, the Saxons, Alfred the Great, the Danes by default and finally the Normans all had a hand in the creation of the conglomerate that is now host to a Roman fort, a Norman castle and a church. The most dramatic feature of the place, then and now, must be the massive defence wall, 10ft thick and originally 20ft high, enclosing 9 acres. It required some 24,000 cubic yards of flint and mortar in the superstructure alone, all of which had to be manhandled to the site.

Across the way, Port Solent's 84 acres have all mod cons to get hard and soft core on site; a sobering comparison, but the Romans were not opposed to slaves, and that must have helped.

Its system of defence was as up to date as it could be: massive and thought to be impregnable. Port Solent also lays great emphasis on up-to-date security.

Inside the Roman Principia were the usual offices: a bath suite for those in charge, an abattoir, well equipped kitchens, and modestly comfortable sleeping and lavatorial facilities. However, the latrines were of the most basic: cesspits (emptied from time to time) with timber seating above. Over the centuries, the castle's fortifications were improved and its domestics enhanced: first, to provide a permanently manned fortress and a secure haven for the king whenever he wanted to enter or leave his kingdom; second, to accommodate, in the style to which they were accustomed, those royal parties which had to be entertained while they pursued birds and game of all kind in the surrounding villages, pastures and forests.

Port Solent

Port Solent does not possess the ability to despatch kings or armies, but it does provide most of the other facilities. Although there will not be an abattoir on site, all other requisites of gracious if not indeed luxurious living will be present and no one will have to rely on an infrequently emptied cesspit.

Modern Port Solent is next mud flats, marshes, shingle banks, saltings and dunes where the sometime plaintive cries of the birds of the air inform of a nature still reddish in tooth and claw; unspoilt and untamed. The stilt-legged heron and the anchored mariner can peruse each other in peace.

This modern man-made creation could well be renamed Port Solvent, for its over-riding ambience is POSH: Port Out Solent Home. For those who like their life afloat to be land based, it is unlikely that there will be a contender for front runner for years to come. It is lush and lotus-like, possessing everything that any marina-eater could drool over.

But for those who are keenly dedicated to a life on the Solent waves, it represents something of a long haul to open waters; and for those with a draught of more than 6ft, low water springs will keep them in their bunks for a time. The regular free flow that was expected has not been obtained with any regularity.

Fareham Lake

Back at the fork again, once well into the port-hand channel for Fareham Lake, the way ahead is clearly marked with piles, and there is none of the previous confusion. For a time, the shoreline is an industrial scene, with jetty after jetty prominent, Vosper's and Powder being of note. To starboard are massive cranes and small-boat moorings, while to port is the welcoming sight (in an otherwise inhospitable stretch) of Hardway, with its sailing club mooring buoys, pontoons and jetty; close by the site of the exotically named Sultan Jetty. It is worth noting that there are plenty of facilities ashore at this point, but no further up until you reach Fareham.

Up the channel, there comes another fork, whereabouts three miniature lakes more or less conjoin. They are known as Bomb Ketch, Spider and Frater. Bomb Ketch Lake gets its name from the fact that the vessels that were frequently moored there were the actual warlike 'bombarding ketches'. This lake and Spider, make serious inroads into the mud flats to the south of Portchester Castle, and provide good grounds for shoal craft and fishermen. Each has an entrance marked by posts and its channel illustrated by small-craft moorings. Frater Lake, on the other hand, is little more than a creek with a small wharf.

Pewit Island sits in state (complete with tripod as if in readiness for Neptune) in the middle of the Portchester Flats, where it constitutes a sort of rest home for birds, shellfish and an anchorage for retiring Ancient Mariners. For those wanting a short cut from Port Solent to Fareham, it is possible in dinghies and shoal craft to disregard the main channel and cross the flats, skirting Portchester Castle, on the top of the tide.

Next on the port hand comes Bedenham Pier. Unauthorised vessels are not permitted within 12 metres of the pier, not that it presents an attractive facade.

The channel then closes in so that it clearly can be seen to have banks on both sides. Foxbury Point and Wicor Hard mark the first closing, before it opens again for Cams Bay to starboard. As well as a Wicor Hard, there is a Wicor Jetty, Wicor Marsh, Wicor Lake, Wicor Path, and, useful for the yachtsman to know, Wicor Marine, who tend to run the patch, and who have a special affection for wooden and classic boats.

From Cams Bay to Fareham is a slow business, with plenty to look at, but not all that much that is worth seeing. True, in the memorable words of W. Elmsly Phillip, 'everything is interesting', but the haul up to the virtual head of navigation has little to recommend it, and it is symbolised by the appellation of its first stretch: Heavy Reach. Shoresides there is little to inspire until you come to Salterns Quay and Fareham itself. What is by now a creek, leads to the old bridge in the town, and there is no great depth of water even at the top of the tide. At low water there is very little – if any.

The shopping centre is not far enough away to be a serious problem unless you have to victual for a long weekend for six people – and then the walk could be tiring. There are the usual boatyard and chandlery facilities. There is also a specialist dealer in outboards of all shapes, sizes and strengths. After a few very tiring dinghy trips with my failing under-powered Johnson all the way from Portchester Castle and Campers up to Fareham, in wet, wind-over-tide conditions, I fell for a larger Mariner. The dealer brought it over to *Valcon* at Port Solent where it was tried and tested. I paid by cheque (Barclaycard number on the back; thank you, Sir!) and left early the following morning for Beaulieu. Now, not many folk bother to call me when I am on a sea leg, so it came as a surprise to be shouted up by Niton. I had neglected to sign the cheque. Happily, he was not without a sense of humour, but he confessed to breathing a little easier two days later when the replacement cheque was cleared.

For those who make the pilgrimage to Fareham, there is a decent reward. The Castle in the Air pub, on the Lower Quay at Fareham, has a good atmosphere and is proud of its even better grub: classic doorstep sandwiches made with real bread and real taste, washed down with real ale.

It is no more than a couple of miles west of Fareham to Titchfield Haven, by road that is, but as the boat floats it is quite a long turn. We shall be looking at Titchfield and Hill Head next.

Southampton Water

Southampton Water is well known as the home of the last of the *Queens*, the *QE2*. She still comes and goes in the same way as the first lady of that royal ilk used so often to enter a room: 'like a galleon in full sail'. For yachts, there are two main approaches to Southampton: the North Channel from the east, and the Thorn Channel from the west via the Western Approach Channel.

Directions

From the east, the North Channel is approached from the direction of Gilkicker Point to reach the *East Bramble* (BYB) off Lee-on-the-Solent, and then on to *Hill Head* (red can) off Titchfield Haven and River Meon. The whole area is well marked by buoys and the only eccentric hazard is the foul ground off Lee Point and upstream of the Elmore outfall.

From the west, the mark to identify is the *West Bramble* (YBY) standing by the Western Approach Channel at the entrance to the Thorn Channel, the through route past Calshot Spit. At one time, the main marker in the area was the renowned Calshot Spit light vessel, but it has gone the way of most classic light ships, and it has been replaced by a much less romantic object.

As the Admiralty *Pilot* says, 'Bramble Bank is the principal danger in the approach to Southampton Water....'; but since it is so well marked it should not interfere in any way with a competent skipper's progress. From Cowes, of course, it stands directly in line with the centre of the Water, so there is no straight course across. The recommended route for leisure craft crosses the big ship channel just to the east of the *Prince Consort* cardinal marker (BY) and then just to the south of *Bourne Gap* lit red can buoy.

There is a restricted area off Calshot Spit. The following caution is in effect: ABP *Notice to Mariners: Restricted Area of use by yachts and other craft under 20m LOA.* 'The transit and movement of small craft under 20m (66 feet) LOA through the area shown on this Yachting Guide (published by ABP Southampton and available free of charge to yachtsmen) when vessels of over 100m (320 feet) LOA are navigating the Western Approach Channel (including the Thorn Channel and Calshot Reach) between West Bramble Buoy and Hook Buoy will not be permitted.'

Calshot Spit extends out from the narrow Calshot isthmus that runs in a northerly direction up Southampton Water. It is almost impossible to disregard Calshot because of its many eye-catching features: Luttrell Castle, with its flagstaff, is just north of the onshore Bourne Gap beacon and just before the well marked sewer beacon and lit outfall, the conspicuous radar tower and Calshot Castle itself. However, surpassing and diminishing all of these is the dominating landmark of the Fawley power station chimney, which, at its 198 metres height, can be seen for miles.

Once inside Southampton Water, navigation could not be simpler. All the features are well marked and lit. The only hazard is the quantity and quality of the traffic that abounds.

Associated British Ports Southampton publish an excellent brochure: *The Yachtsman's Guide to Southampton Water and its Approaches.* It is a must for any visitor. Here are some of the rules of road it outlines:

Some facts you should keep in mind
1. The number of large commercial ships serving the Port of Southampton and the number of recreational craft afloat in local waters is increasing. It is essential that close quarter situations do not increase.
2. Most of the commercial vessels you meet will have a UK pilot on board regardless of the ship's flag. They will be listening to VHF R/T channel 12 or 14, the Port working frequencies.
3. Most large ships travel at a manoeuvring speed of between 10 to 15 knots whilst in the Solent and Southampton Water. The lower limit will vary from ship to ship and is "as safe navigation permits".
4. Ships often travel faster than you might expect in congested areas for various reasons.
5. Light, partially loaded or unevenly trimmed ships may require to maintain a higher "as safe navigation permits" speed in order to remain under full control.
6. It takes less than 10 minutes for a fast ship to reach you from the visible horizon in clear weather, and in hazy conditions a lot less. At 10 knots, a ship travels 1 nautical mile in 6 minutes: at 15 knots it takes only 4 minutes.
7. Large, deep draught ships cannot easily avoid small craft in narrow channels – it is up to you to stay clear. If one of these ships alters course to clear a yacht or small craft it is unlikely to regain track. The consequences can be disastrous.

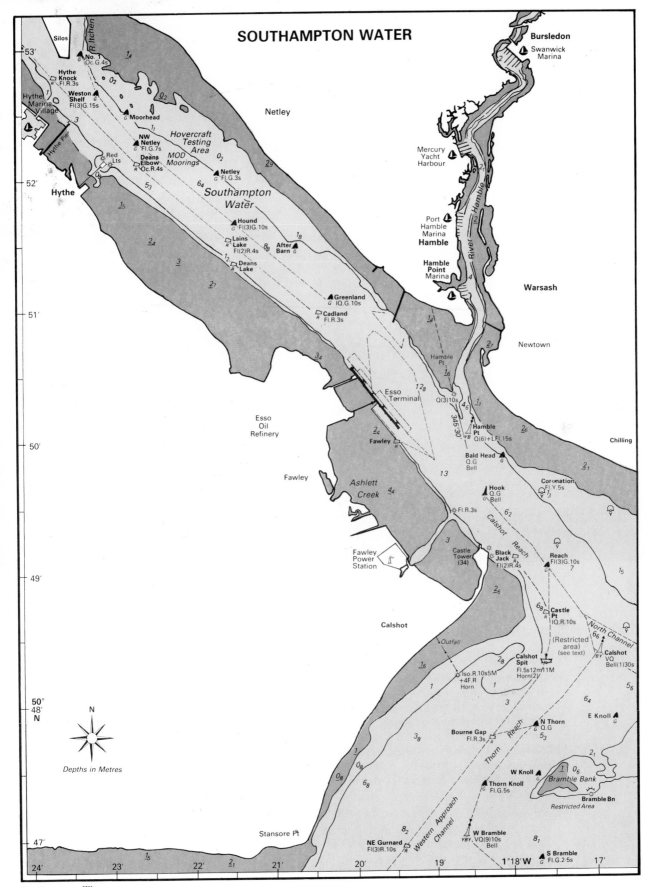

SOUTHAMPTON WATER

Silos
R. Itchen
No. 1
Oc.G.4s
G
1₄
0₂
Hythe
Knock
R FI.R.3s
Weston
Shelf
FI(3)G.15s
G Moorhead
0₂
Netley
Hythe
Marina
Village
1
Hovercraft
Testing
Area
MOD
Moorings
NW
Netley
G FI.G.7s
Deans
Elbow
R Oc.R.4s
Red
Lts
1₁
0₂
Netley
G FI.G.3s
Hythe
Hythe Pier
3
5₃
6₄
2₉
Southampton
Water
1₅
Hound
G FI(3)G.10s
2₄
Lains
Lake
R FI(2)R.4s
8₈
After
Barn
G
1₈
3
1₂
Deans
Lake
R
2₇
Greenland
G IQ.G.10s
Cadland
R FI.R.3s
3₄
Esso
Terminal
12₈
Esso
Oil
Refinery
2₄
Fawley
R
13
Fawley
Ashlett
Creek
4₄
Hamble
Pt
1₄
2₇
Hamble
Pt
1₆
Q(3)10s
345°
30'
4₆
1₁
Hamble
Pt
R Q(6)+LFI.15s
2₆
Bald Head
Q.G
G Bell
Hook
Q.G
G Bell
Coronation
Y FI.Y.5s
1₃
2₁
FI.R.3s
6₂
Fawley
Power
Station
3
Castle Tower
(34)
Black
Jack
R FI(2)R.4s
G
Reach
G FI(3)G.10s
7
1₅
2₆
Calshot
6₈
Castle
Pt
R IQ.R.10s
6₆
Calshot
VQ
YBY Bell(1)30s
Outfall
1₆
2₈
Calshot
Spit
FI.5s12m11M
Horn(2)
Iso.R.10s5M
+4F.R
Horn
1
1
3
5₆
6₄
E Knoll
G
3₈
Bourne Gap
FI.R.3s
N Thorn
G Q.G
5₃
2₁
1
0₆
Bramble Bank
W Knoll
G
Thorn Knoll
G FI.G.5s
Bramble Bn
Restricted Area
0₈
6₈
8₂
NE Gurnard
FI(3)R.10s
W Bramble
YBY VQ(9)10s
Bell
8₁
S Bramble
G FI.G.2·5s
Stansore Pt
Western Approach Channel

Bursledon
Swanwick
Marina
2
Mercury
Yacht
Harbour
2₁
River Hamble
Port
Hamble
Marina
Hamble
Hamble
Point
Marina
4
Warsash
Newtown
2₇
Chilling
Netley

Calshot Reach
North Channel
Thorn Reach

Southampton
Water

Depths in Metres

N

50°
48'
N

Calshot

24'   23'   22'   21'   20'   19'   1°18'W   17'

53'
52'
51'
50'
49'
47'

Every type of craft, from *QE* to surfboards, sooner or later pass by or through the portals of Hythe Marina.

8. A ship that is slowing down does not steer very well; it needs the propeller action on the rudder to respond. If the Captain feels that a turn will save the situation, he may not slow down.
9. When the ship's engines are put "full astern" a captain will lose control of the ship. Single screw ships with engines going astern will, in most cases, swing the ship's bow to starboard. Therefore, if you have a choice, try to escape on his port side. Remember that it takes 4 to 6 minutes and 2,000 to 4,000 feet for a ship to stop after its engines are put astern.
10. There are numerous other small vessels operating within the Port of Southampton. Watch out for ferries, hydrofoils, tugs towing barges, (especially at night, when unlit barges may remain invisible). Remember that a towing cable, which may be partly submerged, can cut a boat in two.

What can you do?
1. Stay out of the way. This does not mean that the Solent Waters "belong" to commercial ships and you have no rights. What it does mean is that the large ships must stay in the deep water channels and that you do not need to. Therefore, avoid sailing in the ship channels, especially in poor visibility.
2. Do not underestimate the speed of ships. If your boat is slow, you might not be able to take effective evasive action if you find yourself on collision course with a large ship in visibility of a quarter of a mile or less. In the time it took you to read this far, a ship cruising at 15 knots would have travelled one nautical mile.

3. Be visible. At night make sure your navigation lights can be seen. If you see the running lights of a vessel and you think you have not been seen, begin to get out of the way, using torches, search lights or a spotlight on sails, or fire a white flare to indicate your position. Carry a radar reflector high on your boat. Remember, from the bridge of a loaded container ship or large tanker, the captain or pilot will lose sight of you ahead of a third of a mile, although you can see the ship at all times!

4. Be alert. Look around every so often, especially astern.

5. Keep watch at night. Even on a clear night you will have difficulty seeing a big ship approach. You might see it first as a black shadow against a background of shore lights, or as a growing shadow – at that point you are not far apart. Remember that your lights will not be easily spotted from the ship.

6. Watch the ship's lights. To determine whether you are in the path of a ship, pay attention to the sidelights rather than the masthead lights. If you see only one side light, or if one is much brighter than the other, you can be fairly sure that you are not in the direct path of the ship. This also gives an indication of which way to move in order to get clear altogether. If you see both sidelights, you are dead ahead – move out fast but be prepared for the ship to alter course at West Bramble and Calshot. You may be safe or in great danger, as ships turn through 100 degrees or so. You must be sure of your position. Learn to recognise the mast-lights of a tug towing one or more barges and of a commercial fishing vessel towing a net.

7. Know whistle signals. The captain of a ship will frequently not use the "port" or "starboard" whistle signals when passing small boats because he is afraid the signals will not be understood and might lead to erratic changes in course. Five or more short blasts on the whistle is the "danger" signal. Check and see if it is for you – and if it is – make away fast! Three short blasts means the ship is going astern.

8. Know flag signals and shapes. Large ships proceeding seawards will fly International Code Pennant "E" flag over the answering pennant which indicates that the vessel will turn to port at the West Bramble buoy and make for the Nab (East). A vessel displaying the answering pennant over the International Code flag "W" will indicate that the vessel will depart the Solent via the Needles (West). A large ship which displays a cylinder on her yardarm during the day or three red lights in a vertical line at night indicates that the ship is severely restricted in her manoeuvrability. Please give her a wide berth.

9. Keep your VHF R/T tuned to channel 12, the Port working frequency, and listen for traffic information from the Harbour Master's Operations Room, Call Sign SPR (Southampton Port Radio). If you believe you have not been seen or you are unsure of a ship's intentions, call them on channel 12, then shift to a working frequency (6 or an alternative) for intership safety messages.

Collision avoidance check list
- Avoid ship channels. Cross them quickly and at right angles.
- Be alert. Watch for ship traffic.
- Be seen, especially at night.
- Know whistle signals – five or more mean DANGER.
- Listen to VHF R/T Channel 12 – if you have to transmit keep your message brief, say what you have to say, then remain listening.
- Use up-to-date navigation charts – read Local Notices to Mariners at your club or local marina.
- Keep in mind, that few survive collisions with ships.
- When in doubt, keep clear.
- Always be prepared for the unexpected: lifejackets do not help if you are not wearing them.

Navigational safety
The principal deep-water navigational channels within the statutory limits of the Port of Southampton are well marked by buoys and lights. These channels are in constant use by commercial vessels including large deep-draughted tankers (VLCCs) and container ships, ferries and other traffic. Recreational users of the harbour are advised to keep well clear of these main channels whenever possible, and use the recommended yacht/boat tracks and crossing areas. When main channels have to be crossed, this should be done as near as practicable at right angles. Avoid crossing the bows of on-coming commercial traffic. Large container ships and VLCCs, in particular, have very restricted visibility for quite a distance ahead when carrying a deck cargo of containers (you may be able to see her clearly, but can she see you?). Most recreational sailors take a justifiable pride in the responsible way they conduct themselves. Part of this is a realisation that hindering passage of large commercial vessels is not only bad manners but dangerous to themselves, their crews, and more particularly to the ship itself. Recreational users of the port area are particularly requested to remind themselves and observe the Collision Regulation, Port of Southampton Bye-Laws and Local Notice to Mariners.

Harbour Patrol

The Harbour Master operates a Harbour Patrol Launch service within the limits of the Port of Southampton throughout the year. This service is mainly used to escort large commercial vessels safely into or out of the harbour area to ensure that the main navigable channels are kept clear for the safe transit of these ships.

The Harbour Patrol launches maintain a VHF R/T listening watch on Channel 12 (call sign Southampton Patrol) and their crews will be pleased to offer advice and information on the Harbour and Approaches on request.

These vessels, having a royal blue hull with white upperworks, are easily recognisable by the broad yellow diagonal stripe on each side of the bow. At night, in addition to steaming lights, each carries an all-round blue light at the mast head.'

Note There is no legally laid down yacht track or small-boat channel (as, for example, in Portsmouth) but the notion is that leisure craft shall navigate just outside the main channel; that is, always to port of the main buoys. The charts show there are some close-in buoys that can be used as safe-water channel markers. Red can *Deans Lake*, green cones *Netley* and *Moorhead*, as well as other non-navigational and mooring buoys are appropriate examples.

Yacht racing courses

Associated British Ports, Southampton, establish each year during the season, the undermentioned buoys for yacht racing purposes. The navigational buoys marking the dredged channel in Southampton Water and its approaches should not be used as turning marks.

Buoy name	Shape	Colour	Position
Cathead	Spherical	Yellow	50°50'·57N 1°19'·30W
Sposa	Spherical	Yellow	50°49'·70N 1°17'·50W
Cutter	Spherical	Yellow	50°49'·47N 1°16'·81W
Chilling	Spherical	Yellow	50°49'·23N 1°17'·45W
Meon	Can	Yellow	50°49'·12N 1°16'·63W
Deck	Spherical	Yellow	50°48'·60N 1°27'·25W
Clipper	Spherical, X topmark	Yellow	50°48'·41N 1°15'·65W
Hendersons	Spherical, X topmark	Yellow	50°47'·23N 1°15'·82W
Spanker	Spherical, X topmark	Yellow	50°47'·08N 1°17'·99W
Quinnell	Spherical	Yellow	50°47'·03N 1°19'·78W
Mark	Spherical	Yellow	50°49'·52N 1°18'·86W
Jib	Spherical	Yellow	50°52'·94N 1°23'·72W

Bald Head, *Chilling*, *Sposa* and *Cutter* buoys are used mainly for sailing dinghy racing courses so that these courses can be arranged to avoid crossing the deep-water channel.

In the past it had been the custom to use the navigation mark in Calshot Reach of the Thorn Channel as the apex of a triangular course with the other two turning marks in the east and west Solent. This arrangement had two distinct disadvantages when considering the movements of large vessels entering or leaving the port. A concentration of yachts in the deep-water channel occurs when yachts converge or diverge on a navigation buoy marking such channel, when it is used as a turning mark. The Brambles bank and the East Knoll shoal were not critically marked by navigation buoys for shallow-draught craft consequently yachts tended to sheer away from these shallow patches and had to rely entirely on the navigation buoys marking the deep-water channel.

These difficulties were overcome by the establishment of the new apex racing turning buoy *Clipper* well clear of the deep-water channel. The *East Knoll* (on 3-metre contour) and *West Knoll* (on 4-metre contour) buoys are not intended as racing turning marks, but as navigation marks and consequently have been given geographical names as distinct from turning marks such as *Spanker* and *Clipper*.

The yacht racing courses in the vicinity of the Thorn Channel are now north of *Clipper* and south of *Spanker*; these revised courses will have the desired effect of drawing yachts away from the Thorn Channel.

The Solent Cruising and Racing Association have issued the following Racing Sailing Instructions: 'All yachts racing courses in the vicinity of the Thorn Channel in whichever direction they are racing, shall not pass to the North Westwards of Reach and Calshot Buoys nor to the Northward of North Thorn and Bourne Gap Buoys. Yachts crossing the deep water channel should do so as quickly as possible.'

Titchfield Haven – Hill Head Harbour

The first possible port of call is not quite within Southampton Water proper as it were, having the feeling of a much more untamed, incorrigible haven than anything suitable for modern mariners. It is accessible for craft with suitable draught and keels, for its entrance is shallow and it dries throughout.

It is the miniature harbour known as Titchfield Haven; very near to Lee-on-the-Solent it is situate at the mouth of the River Meon, and formed by a long curving spit. Titchfield once was a port, but the mouth of the River Meon was enclosed, nearly 400 years ago. The 3rd Earl of Southampton shut its mouth by damming the original river with shingle and controlling it with a sluice at Hill Head. He built a sea lock and the channel was called New River. Vestiges of the project can still be seen.

There seems to be some confusion about the actual naming of the place. Whenever I asked for Titchfield Haven, my respondent would refer to Hill Head Harbour; and the minute I asked for the harbour, back came the reply, 'Oh, you mean the haven.' However, whether haven or harbour, it is still more than home to a lively band of yachts and dinghies as well as the Hill Head Sailing Club. It suffers from access restrictions on account of its sand and shingle bars and general shallowness, and it dries completely.

The headquarters of the sailing club dominate the haven from the sea wall, gazing a little bleakly across Southampton Water. It is best suited to shoal craft, but a skipper with a good eye for withies and the ways of the water will not find it too difficult to wend his way in. It will not be immediately attractive to fast motor cruisers nor ocean-going yachts, but is of enormous appeal to visitors with little draught, modest aspirations, a wooden boat (classically) with a centre-board and a skipper (symbolically) with a pipe.

The breakwater at the entrance is a regular perch for a whole squadron of gulls, while geese and rare ducks commute from boat to boat and person to person. In winter, the whole area plays host to many varieties of wild fowl, including whooper swans.

It is a fascinating location, seemingly much more remote than it actually is; a circumstance no doubt created by the difficulty of access. You do not arrive by accident; although there is no one-way traffic by land or by sea, there ought to be, for there is no room for manoeuvre. Perhaps that is the secret of its charm: open, bleak, unspoiled, pastoral or just plain natural, according to choice.

Just to the north of Titchfield you will find the remains of a 13th-century abbey, built of stone from over the water on the Isle of Wight. Both Richard II and Henry V rested there, the first with his queen and the second while waiting for a fair wind for France. Henry VI also stayed here on account of Margaret of Anjou. In 1538 the abbey was dissolved. One Thomas Wriothesley, to become the 1st Earl of Southampton, named it a 'ryghte statelie House embatalid'. Finally, of course, Queen Elizabeth slept there.

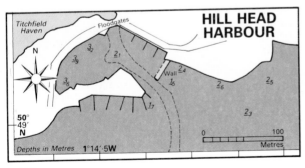

Hill Head Harbour

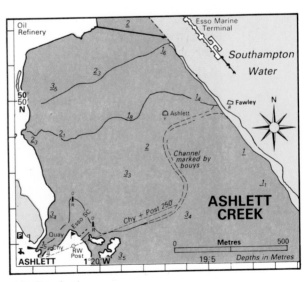

Ashlett Creek

67

Ashlett Creek

Across the water, just a little further upstream, close under the mighty works of Esso and the power station, is another almost 'lost' haven, but to be found in quite a different setting. Tucked away behind the gargantuan constructions of the Esso et al 'power-fuel' stations, protected by a maze of saltings, is to be found Ashlett Creek.

Just by the main terminal jetties is a small 'finned' red buoy named *Fawley*. From there it is easy to spot the small red and green channel markers, but I couldn't find the leading beacons that were so clearly marked on the Admiralty chart. Indeed, Captain Hall, Southampton's Assistant harbourmaster and himself a keen sailor, has gone so far as to blank them out on his personal plan of the creek.

I also found it difficult to line up the second set of leading marks, the chimney and the red and white post. In addition, there are three yellow diagonal cross beacons marking an outfall pipe; and by coincidence they have some nearby posts, and at half tide appear almost in line with a secondary channel. In fact that approach can be used, but only on the top of spring tides.

However, most of this is academic, since the buoys and the posts (a really excellent variety of top-quality withies) are so well placed and cared for, that little help is needed until the last and bitter turns; after which there is a certain amount of confusion associated with obstructions and a near-179° turn. Local knowledge is much needed.

The approach is straightforward. The channel takes four right-angle turns: one to port, two to starboard, and one to port. After that, it is tortuous enough to warrant a first trip at half flood in the dinghy. In the moonlight, or an autumn mist, it takes on something of the quality of Mystic Marshes, for there are small islets here and there, and wildlife abounds. It is shoal-draught country this, although there are some bigger boats that make it their drying home. At the top of the creek there are good drying hards and posts – and an equally good wet berth is to be found at The Jolly Sailor.

Sadly, there does seem fairly recently to be a threat of loss of water. The skipper of Southampton harbourmaster's launch reports that five years ago he was able to take in the launch that draws 1·2m when the tide gauge read 3·5m. In autumn 1988 it was necessary to wait for a reading of 4m. A loss of half a metre in five years is a serious problem. Perhaps the old tide mill could be brought back into action, as was the one at Eling where it continues to do good work keeping the channel open.

I cannot wax too eloquently about Ashlett Creek. Whether you approach it by land or water, you come upon a scene that is delightful in its simplicity: natural, rural and maritime. No one speaks of smuggling nowadays, nor of shooting duck; but in the misty mornings of late autumn their spirit rises up like a ghostly Jack-o'-the-Green. It is not quite a secret water, but it is indeed a very special place.

Ashlett Creek is no place for those with disorderly conduct in mind; for although there is the hostelry, the ambience is one of calm and sobriety.

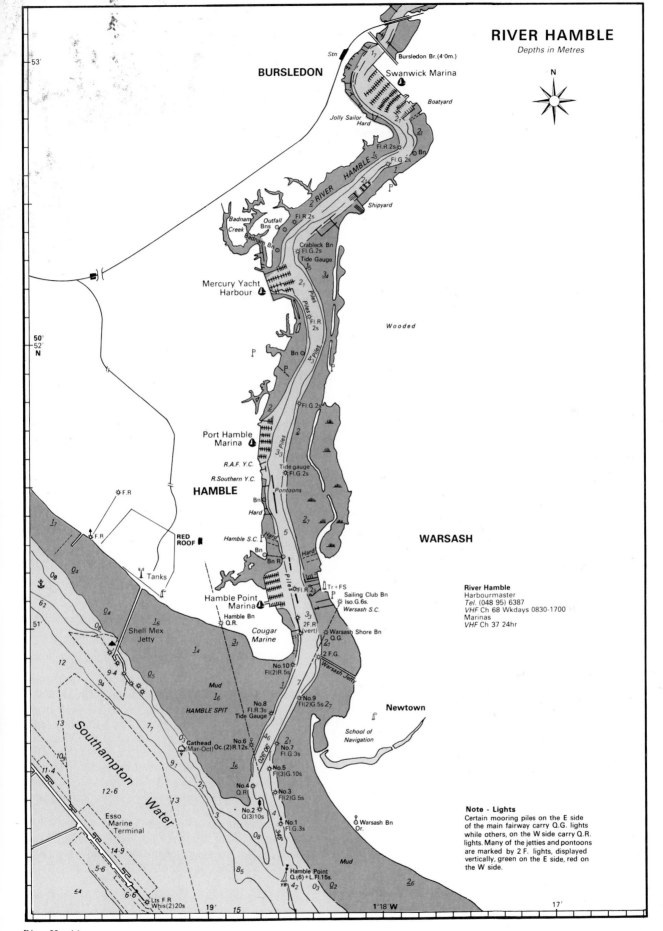

RIVER HAMBLE
Depths in Metres

N

BURSLEDON

Stn
Bursledon Br. (4·0m.)
Swanwick Marina
Boatyard
Jolly Sailor Hard
Fl.R.2s
Bn
Fl.G.2s
RIVER HAMBLE
Shipyard
P
Badnam Creek
Outfall Bns
Fl.R 2s
Badnam Bn
Crableck Bn
Fl.G.2s
Tide Gauge
Mercury Yacht Harbour
Piles
Fl.R 2s
Piles
Wooded
Bn
P
Piles
P
Fl.G.2s
Port Hamble Marina
Piles
R.A.F. Y.C.
Tide gauge
Fl.G.2s
R. Southern Y.C.
HAMBLE
Bn
Pontoons
Hard
WARSASH
Hamble S.C.
Hard
RED ROOF
Hard
Bn
Bn R
F.R
F.R
F.R
Tanks
Tr + FS
Fl.R 2s
Sailing Club Bn
P
Iso.G.6s.
Warsash S.C.
Hamble Point Marina
Hamble Bn Q.R.
Cougar Marine
2 F.R (vert)
Warsash Shore Bn
Q.G.
Shell Mex Jetty
2 F.G.
Mud
No.10 Fl(2)R.5s
Warsash Jetty
Newtown
HAMBLE SPIT
No.8 Fl.R.3s
Tide Gauge
No.9 Fl(2)G.5s
School of Navigation
Cathead (Mar-Oct)Oc.(2)R.12s.
No.6
No.7 Fl.G.3s
Southampton Water
No.5 F(3)G.10s
No.4 Q.R
No.3 Fl(2)G.5s
Esso Marine Terminal
No.2 Q(3)10s
No.1 Fl.G.3s
Warsash Bn Or.
Mud
Hamble Point Q.(6)+L.Fl.15s.
Lts F.R Whis(2)20s

River Hamble
Harbourmaster
Tel. (048 95) 6387
VHF Ch 68 Wkdays 0830-1700
Marinas
VHF Ch 37 24hr

Note - Lights
Certain mooring piles on the E side
of the main fairway carry Q.G. lights
while others, on the W side carry Q.R.
lights. Many of the jetties and pontoons
are marked by 2 F. lights, displayed
vertically, green on the E side, red on
the W side.

River Hamble

The River Hamble

The entrance

From the creek, it is no distance across the water to the entrance to the River Hamble; an entirely different experience – at least in all its lower reaches. Approaching from downstream, the entrance is straightforward and obvious, being well marked by the *Hamble Point* south cardinal marker (YB). However, it is important not to go too close to the shore after Hill Head and up to the River Hamble for the shoals reach out far into the Water. In any case, there is little to be gained by going close or trying to cut the blunt corner by the *Warsash* beacon and the *Hamble Point* south cardinal (YB).

Contrariwise, it is well established local practice for vessels to cut off the corner of Hamble Spit. From *No. 8* (the beacon with the tide gauge) onwards, even at half tide, motor cruisers, especially those that can get on the plane quickly, move straight across.

This all goes back a long time, viz Cowper: 'Having left Baldhead Buoy on the right, steer to pass SE of the Hamble Spit Buoy (conical, red), and then, steering more E., leave the first perch on the right and the next on the left. Don't go too close to the perches, and beware of crossing the spit except at high water, and then only below the last perch and the spit buoy. I have stuck here, I forget how many times, but never for very long, as I only tried this short cut on a rising tide. In fact, I never went into any of these Solent creeks for the first time except on a flood tide, choosing low water when I could. In this way I saw all the dangers and made a note of them.'

The river has been known as a haven for centuries; the Venerable Bede especially picked on the merits of its double tides, referring to it as Hamelea. The town itself is Hamble-le-Rice, and in the days of Henry VIII, Leland, the diarist, described it as an 'ood fisher town'. One of the most interesting times for boat building on the Hamble was from 1700 to 1800, when seagoing vessels were built on the river at Bursledon and Warsash. Daniel Defoe, not a writer celebrated for unbridled generosity or enthusiasm, singles it out for praise in his *Tour Through England and Wales* (1724–6). One of his fictional seamen actually sails from 'Bussledon'. It is said that the wooden door of St Andrew's church carries knife scars made by sailors. Before going to sea, they would make a vertical cut for a safe trip, and when they got back, they would add a horizontal cut, making a cross. The local records all have many entries for seamen, many of whom died unknown, and were buried 'Henry Adams'.

Cowper also said this: 'There is no place within easy reach of London that I can so cordially recommend as this delightful little pool, for really the bight below Bursledon railway bridge looks just like a pond made for toy boats.

The other day I was asked by some people going in for small yachting which I should recommend, the East Coast creeks or Southampton Water. I thought of Bursledon, and had no hesitation in deciding. But there really is very little room for more boats.'

In 1938, there were no more than 250 registered moorings; today, the figure stands in excess of 3,000.

Warsash

This small settlement used to boast the clubhouse of the oldest yacht club in Britain, the Royal Thames Yacht Club. Now they retain moorings there, but the club is now the local one with the unmistakable colours of the black lobster on a yellow ground; the Warsash Sailing Club. Warsash was the chief crab and lobster pond (pound) on the river, despatching their wares all over the country. In times gone by, HLCT (Hamble Lobster & Crab Teas) were famed for their size and succulence. One of the most interesting retreats for the cruising man must be the Warsash Nautical Bookshop, skippered by that mine of information, advice and service, Alan Obin. Do call on them, for it is perusal not to be missed; but if you can't, then phone him on ☎ (048955) 72384.

Just across the river is the base of the famous ferry that has run for over 500 years; and on the Warsash side is the small concrete shelter with the name of the Coopers', the brewers who bought the ferry rights from Winchester College at the beginning of the century.

However, there can be little doubt that the best way to travel this river has to be by dinghy, if only in order to be able to examine at close quarters the host of intriguing boats to be found there. It will take an enthusiast a long time to reach Moody's and the *Howard's Way* stuff at Swanwick; but it is well worth the time.

Cowper says: 'They are a genial, pleasant set of people up at Bursledon. The Moodys, whom I have known – father and son – for over fourteen years, are as good a type of small boat builder

Hamble
beacon
No. 8

as it is possible to come across. I was glad to see how they had flourished since last I landed at their convenient little hard. There was none of the swagger and half-concealed contempt with which a single-hander is treated in many other yacht yards of more pretentious establishments.'

The boats on the way afford real interest, and once through the Bursledon bridges, the river leads into a modest valley, idyllic in its unspoiled state. The change is one of the most dramatic on the Solent. True, the quiet of the Yar and the Beaulieu in their upper reaches makes for a contrast with the approaches, but the Hamble goes from one extreme to another. The bed is pierced by countless piles, and the river itself seems to consist of nothing but craft in serried rank and file.

It rivals the best of the East Coast rivers and the creeks of the Isle of Wight. Wildlife, nature, and natural peace go hand in hand and the further you go, the better it gets. With a dinghy on the tide, you can get to the communities of Botley and, via Curbridge Creek, to the small landing for the pub at Curbridge itself. Let me put it this way, the Hamble at its humblest is the Hamble at its best.

For those who want the services of a marina, the Hamble is well served; indeed, skippers are spoiled for choice, for in the short span between Hamble Point and the bridge at Bursledon, there are no fewer than four major operations. They are, in order of ascendancy going upstream, Hamble Point Marina, Port Hamble Marina, Mercury Marina and Swanwick Marina. There are also seventeen boatyards of varying sizes, with additional helpful bolt holes here and there, so wherever you are on the river, you are never far away from assistance.

All these facilities, and many others are shown on the extremely useful *Guide to the River Hamble* published annually by Hampshire County Council. An absolute mine of information, it is available free of charge upon request from the harbourmaster; The following has been extracted from it:

The unmistakable HQ of the harbourmaster of the Hamble.

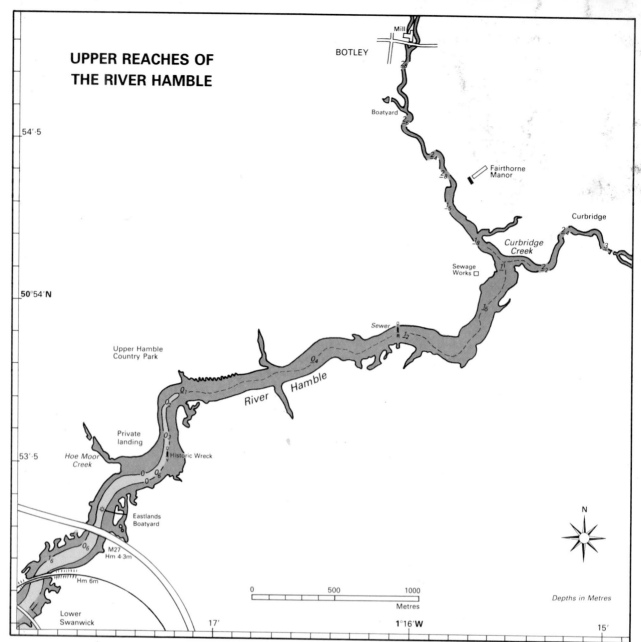

UPPER REACHES OF
THE RIVER HAMBLE

BOTLEY

Mill

Boatyard

Fairthorne
Manor

Curbridge

Curbridge
Creek

Sewage
Works

Upper Hamble
Country Park

River Hamble

Sewer

Private
landing

Hoe Moor
Creek

Historic Wreck

Eastlands
Boatyard

M27
Hm 4·3m

Hm 6m

Lower
Swanwick

N

0   500   1000
                Metres

Depths in Metres

54'·5

50°54'N

53'·5

17'   1°16'W   15'

Upper reaches of the River Hamble

The Hamble is always more or less crowded; and usually more
rather than less.

RIVER HAMBLE

Harbour Master Captain C. J. Nicholl, OBE. Harbour Master's Office, Shore Road, Warsash. ☎ Locks Heath (048 95) 6387.

Office hours Mon–Thurs 0830–1700, Fri 0830–1630, Sat (Nov–Mar) 0900–1300; Sat/Sun (Apr–Oct) (normally afloat) 0900–1830.

Residences Harbour Master ☎ Locks Heath (048 95) 82406. Assistant Harbour Master, Mr D. Walker, ☎ Fareham (0329) 283944.

VHF – information assistance
Harbour Master's office VHF Ch 68. Mon–Fri 0830–1700
Harbour Master's boats VHF Ch 16, 68, 37. Sat 0900–1300 (Nov–Mar), 0900–1830 (Apr–Oct), Sun 0900–1830 (Apr–Oct)
Marinas VHF Ch 37. 24 hour.
Solent Coastguard VHF Ch 16. 24 hour. Working Ch 67, 73, 6, 10

Dinghy racing
Dinghy races are started from Hamble River Sailing Club on Saturdays and Sundays between 1430 and 1500. Between these times other River users are asked to try to avoid the section of the River from Warsash Jetty to Port Hamble.

Visitors moorings
Visiting yachts should be moored so that other craft secured inside can cast off without difficulty. Use separate lines fore and aft not one continuous rope. For safety put out springs and plenty of fenders. If not seen by the Harbour Master on patrol call at the Harbour Office to pay dues.

Navigation
At night the outer leading line of lights (350°30′) is clearly visible. All entrance piles except No. 4 are lit. The inner transit line (026°09′) is less obvious and keeps to the starboard side of the channel. Mariners are advised to be careful not to stray to the East of the transit into shoal water. Tides are as for Southampton +8 minutes. Spring range 4·5m. There is a double high water.

Sailing in the Solent
Yachtsmen are reminded of the regulations concerning the use of the main channels in the Solent. Deep draughted vessels do not have room to manoeuvre. Small craft are required to keep clear of these channels. Avoid close quarter situations with large ships.

Scrubbing piles/Fresh water
There are scrubbing piles at Warsash, Hamble, between Port Hamble and Mercury Yacht Harbour and Lands End Hard (Bursledon). Use is on a first come first served basis. There is no charge for the first 48 hours. Water is available at the Harbour Master's Jetty at Warsash. A meter dispenses approx 25 gallons for 10p.

Above the Bursledon bridges, the Hamble becomes an entirely different experience: peaceful to the point of pastoral and sylvan to a degree.

Bursledon Bridge; head of navigation for many Hamble-based craft as well as most visitors.

Harbour notes

Speed Bye-Law 5 requires: That the master of a vessel in the River shall navigate the vessel with care and caution and in such a manner and at such a speed as shall not cause nuisance, annoyance, excessive wash, damage or injury nor danger of damage or injury to any other vessel, person, or property in the River nor to the banks of the River or any person or property thereon.

It is essential for safety and the preservation of the river bank to comply with this regulation. There is no identified top speed – some craft would need to keep below 6 knots, others might go as high as 10 knots above which speed the River is too crowded for safety regardless of wash. The speed restriction applies to the full length of the channel as far as No. 1 and No. 2 entrance piles close to Hamble Point buoy.

Navigation Vessels should keep to the starboard side of the channel. When crossing the fairway to take up a berth do so with care and avoid hampering other vessels.

Cruise vessels Relatively large cruise vessels enter the Hamble regularly. Although highly manoeuvrable in light winds, in strong wind conditions handling becomes more difficult at low speeds. Smaller craft should keep clear accordingly.

Dinghy racing Some dinghy races start and finish in the River but it is a race instruction that they keep clear of other River users.

Fishing There are some thirty fishing vessels based in the River, but net or trawl fishing within the Harbour limits is only permitted with written authority from the Harbour Master.

Sailing There is no Rule against sailing in the River but the prudent yachtsman will have his motor instantly available and lower sails when the fairway becomes overcrowded. It is unseamanlike for a larger yacht to hoist a spinnaker in the congested waters above the College of Maritime Studies jetty.

The River Itchen

Years ago, Southampton (known in the abbreviated local dialect as Soton) was the hub of Britain's water wheels. Now, after the strikers' self scuttle, the days of continuing royal progresses have gone. However, a brave new world is taking over from the good old days. Ocean Terminal, where most of the action used to be, has lent its name to Ocean Village: a massive development devoted to those with a penchant for the sea, be it from shoresides or afloat. There is little doubt that residential marinas (be they 'yachtsmen's residences', flats with boats, holiday homes with fast cruisers or mansions with yachts worth more than most houses) are one of the growth industries of the decade.

Ocean Village Marina is by the confluence of the Itchen and Soton Water, just below the new bridge (1977, height 28·9m above chart datum). One of its claims to fame is that it has deep water at all states of all tides. Indeed, one skipper was heard asking if he would be able to make entry with his draught of six feet at low water, when back came the friendly, if somewhat cheeky reply, 'Why, sir, unless your air draught is more than 20 feet, you could come in upside down if you like.'

Nevertheless, being a converted commercial dock, it can in very truth accommodate very large yachts, including tall ships. It has 450 berths with direct access into Soton Water, and has now got something of a name for itself as a venue for international sailing events. It maintains a 24-hour listening watch on Channel M, and traffic is controlled when necessary by international light signals. The staff of ex-seamen and lifeboatmen are intent on running a tight ship in a courteous manner. A very helpful touch is a notice board on the harbourmaster's boat: 'Follow Me'.

Ocean Village is an entirely appropriate name, for it is a truly amazing conglomerate of craft, starting with the spectacle of the yellow trimaran, *3026 Paragon*. There are many little ships to look out for: the Uffa Fox 'sailing-down-the-river' day boat, *Huff of Arklow*; the late Arthur Lowe's century-old *Amazon*; the training ship *Astrid*, run by a trust for young people and its attendant light ship; the sailing barge *Kitty* and the topsail schooner *Helga*, both for charter; the ex-Dutch shrimper *Isabella* run by her enigmatically mystic female skipper; the J-Class yacht *Velsheda*, sporting perhaps the tallest mast in Europe, and recently most splendidly used for her owner's wedding; the *Shemara*, once the proud gold-plated flagship of the proud gold-plated Lady Docker. In the greatest possible contrast to them all is the old cargo steamer *S.S. Shieldhall*, once a sludge and slurry vessel, now belonging to the Southampton Maritime Museum.

Shoresides, there is history for the asking. For example, the West Gate, a very significant monument for the city, and, keeping your eyes well towards the skyline, Above Bar and Below Bar (the latter is in fact merely High Street; Below Bar being a figment of the imagination of incomers). 'This important West Gate led directly to the West Quay which for many centuries was the only commercial quay which the town possessed. The grooves of the portcullis Gates and the apertures through which the defenders of the town could harass attackers may still be seen. Through this archway marched some of the army of Henry V on their way to Agincourt in 1415. The Pilgrim Fathers embarked here from the West Quay on the *Mayflower* August 15th 1620.' Southampton is rightly proud that is has more original Norman town walls surviving than York.

Southampton recalls associations with Canute: close to the Town Quay, there is an old ruin supposedly dating from the late twelfth century. While known as 'Canute's Palace', it is actually a merchant's house-on-warehouse, and the warehouse and vault are in fact 15th century. Again, near the site of the old Saxon harbour there is Canute Road, with Canute Hotel. There is also the plaque: 'NEAR THIS SPOT AD 1028 CANUTE REPROVED HIS COURTIERS'. Needless to say, there is no evidence for the tidal stream of tales about Canute demonstrating his impotence.

Now there is a bigger and better show than Canute ever dreamed of: opposite the Mayflower Monument is Mayflower Park, now famed for the International Boat Show first run in the autumn of 1969. Known as the Southampton Afloat Show, it runs for six working days each September; boasting and hosting hundreds of boats moored at the special marina built alongside Mayflower Park, just by Eastern Docks. The show spreads over three lots, with interconnecting bridges. No doubt in time, the organisers will be able to improve their layout and logistics, and then will have an aesthetic as well as a commercial success on their hands.

Overlooking the centrepiece of Ocean Village Marina itself are two contrasting edifices: Canute's Pavilion and the new Royal Southampton Yacht Club. The first is a glass monument devoted to commerce, where you reach the attractive first floor food hall via a silent view-it-all lift. The style of the boutiques, wine bars, restaurants and food hall give it a 'Covent Garden' flavour, described by one local aesthete and commentator as a 'cheap, rip-off-the-tourist-and-yachtie pit'.

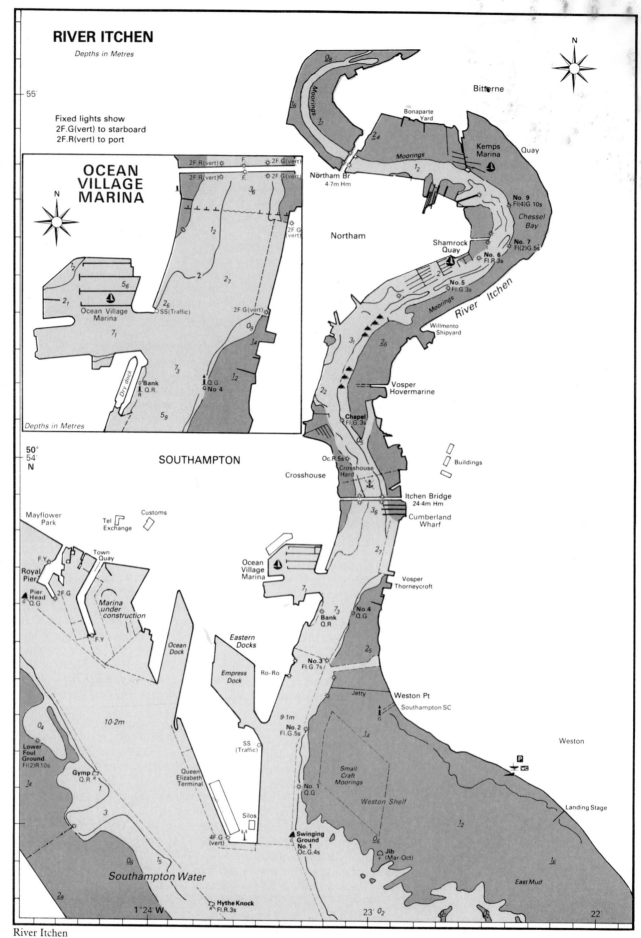

RIVER ITCHEN

Depths in Metres

N

Fixed lights show
2F.G(vert) to starboard
2F.R(vert) to port

55'

Bitterne

Moorings
0.8

Bonaparte
Yard

1.6

Moorings
1.7

Kemps
Marina

2.4

Quay

Moorings
1.2

Northam Br
4.7m Hm

No. 9
Fl(4)G.10s

Chessel
Bay

Northam

Shamrock
Quay

No. 7
Fl(2)G.5s

No. 6
Fl.R.3s

No.5
Fl.G.3s

2.6

River Itchen

Moorings

Willmento
Shipyard

3.1

2.6

3.1

OCEAN VILLAGE MARINA

N

2F.R(vert)   F.   2F.G(vert)

2F.R(vert)   F.   2F.G(vert)

3.6

2F.G
(vert)

1.2

2

2

2.7

1.7

Ocean Village
Marina

5.6

2.6

SS (Traffic)

2F.G(vert)

2.1

7.1

0.9

7.3

1.4

Bank
Q.R

Q.G
G No 4

1.2

Dry dock

Bank
Q.R

Depths in Metres

5.9

Vosper
Hovermarine

2.2

Chapel
Fl.G.3s

0.5

Buildings

SOUTHAMPTON

Oc.R.5s

Crosshouse
Hard

Crosshouse

50°
54'
N

Itchen Bridge
24.4m Hm

Cumberland
Wharf

3.6

Mayflower
Park

Tel
Exchange

Customs

Town
Quay

F.Y.

Royal
Pier

Pier
Head
Q.G

2F.G

Marina
under
construction

Ocean Village
Marina

2.7

Vosper
Thorneycroft

Ocean
Dock

F.Y

Eastern
Docks

7.1

7.3

Bank
Q.R

No.4
Q.G

2.5

Empress
Dock

Ro-Ro

No.3
Fl.G.7s

Jetty

Weston Pt

Southampton SC

Weston

10.2m

9.1m

No. 2
Fl.G.5s

1.4

Lower
Foul
Ground
Fl(2)R.10s

Gymp
Q.R

1

No. 1
Q.G

Small
Craft
Moorings

Weston Shelf

P
WC

1.4

3

Queen
Elizabeth
Terminal

SS
(Traffic)

Landing Stage

0.6

Silos

4F.G
(vert)

Swinging
Ground
No. 1
Oc.G.4s

Jib
(Mar-Oct)

1.2

1.6

0.6

0.5

1.5

Southampton Water

East Mud

2.8

1°24'W

Hythe Knock
Fl.R.3s

23' 0.2

22'

The second is a monumental p(a)lace that had its foundation stone laid, and was duly opened by its Admiral, Prince Michael of Kent. You need almost to make an appointment even to speak to anyone in these hallowed halls, which, dedicated to *fin-de-siècle* rituals and Edwardian etiquette, can echo with brandy-and-soda voices and produce raised eyebrows round each corner.

After being scrutinised by a person of the rank of something akin to a third acting undersecretary I was permitted to enter a small office where a scribbled note was hastily created before my eyes. It read:

a. RSYC new premises: bar, dining room and lounge areas.
b. Has no club berths, but many members have berths in Ocean Village Marina.
c. Club has berths adjacent to Gins Farm in Beaulieu River. Also some in the Hamble.
d. RSYC welcomes yachtsmen from reciprocal yacht clubs, and visiting yachtsmen from known clubs.
d. Marina (Dean & Dyball) has usual marina facilities which are separate from RSYC.

Having been handed the document, I was shown the door in the classic manner. It was a superior door.

Perhaps the most intriguing of the many architectural projects in the vicinity are the three yachtsmen's cabins on one floor of the RSYC complex. Each is known by the name of a famous yacht refitted by Southampton Yacht Services of Shamrock Quay, and it is this same company that is responsible for the superb woods and craftsmanship in each: *Altaire*, *Cariad* and *Jagare*. They are sold complete with all furnishings and fittings: and that means such items as CD player, TV and video recorder, all crockery, cutlery, and duvets and cover for the mini-settee that converts into a small double bed. It is said that even the proverbial toothbrush will be among those present. No doubt there will also be coffee percolating and champagne bubbling to welcome the first owners. In *Altaire*, the pseudo-skylight, with masking Mediterranean-type sun blind, displays a painting of an old-world mast complete with sails and a half crow's nest. The blinds are also in the optimistic Med-sun style. *Jagare* and *Cariad* have skylights complete with stars that twinkle, courtesy of a computer. The three cabins are, in essence, luxury bunk-sitting rooms (with full standing room, and a head and galley) and will fetch in excess of £100,000 for a 999 year lease. Each lease includes a berth of at least 40ft. The harbour itself can actually accommodate craft up to 250ft.

Leaving Ocean Village and taking a port turn into the River Itchen will bring you face to face (if you are staring well up that is) with the well known Itchen Bridge. It was opened in 1977, at long last making redundant the old chain ferry.

Of the famous and historic ferries, all that is now left of the ferrymen of old is their name, and the solitary sail ferry, the *SU 120*, in extremely nice order in Ocean Village Marina.

You may well find, lurking in the immediate environs outside the marina, fuel vessels looking for business. The Solent is the only area where I have been almost solicited with diesel, and had it brought to the door, as it were. Service indeed! In particular it is worth noting that Mr Diesel can be raised on VHF Ch 8, and by ☎ (0703) 333694. You will find he is a personable dealer who will turn out at almost any hour of the day or night if your need is urgent – and for a reasonable amount. In autumn 1988 his price was 50p a gallon, when I had been asked up to £1·25 elsewhere in the Solent.

Shamrock Quay is the oldest of Dean & Dyball's three marinas in the area. It is based on traditional boatyards, Arrow and Fay, taken over by Camper and Nicholson in 1921. The name *Shamrock* derives from one Thomas Lipton, the wealthy Scotsman. Hooked on the idea of winning the originally Cowes-based America's cup, he challenged with a number of yachts called *Shamrock*. When D & D took over in 1980, *Shamrock V*, built in 1931, was undergoing a major refit.

In no other respect is Shamrock Quay anything like Cowes: it is diamond rough and bright, and you will find you are welcomed with a personal touch by Peter Day and/or his wife (night and day) who have been there since the marina first opened nearly twenty years ago. There is no traffic signal system here, but if necessary you will be personally talked in over VHF (Channel M) by Peter or Eunice.

Indeed, most things here are organised on an informal (but not inefficient) basis. Mooring can be rather along the lines of 'Come in Number Three, your time is up!', or put another way, there is something of a family feel about the process, rather like a mother hen clucking in her chicks. Whichever interpretation you put on it, it is pleasing to be organised by people who quite clearly love their work and their clientele in the way these do.

The marina has deep-water pontoons with water, electricity and access at all states of the tides, but it must be pointed out that the ebb, for one hour after second high water, is powerful enough to demand special precautions.

Southampton Yacht Services, who describe themselves as joiners and yacht builders, specialise in 'one off' new boats, and the restoration or refitting of large yachts. In particular they are

No bittern may boom near Bitterne, on the upper reaches of the Itchen, but swans and small boats make up for any sense of deprivation.

The further reaches of the Itchen (below) are far removed from all the paraphernalia (opposite) to be found near Ocean Village and Canute's latest monument.

proud of their 15-month refit of the 1931 classic, *Altaire*. The marina has an extra wide 53-ton hoist to cope with these 90–120 footers with big beams. This new device contrasts interestingly with the heritage-old wooden worktops, complete with ancient bench marks.

Shoresides, there are extremely well kept toilets, showers and laundrette. There are all the facilities visitors could ask for: from the Yellow Welly café to the waterfront hostelry and the deluxe restaurant called Taps; from the small cabin jammed to the doors with secondhand goodies to the veritable emporium of the Shamrock chandlery; and only yards away across the road is a pub and the radio headquarters of a major speedy taxi service. There is also a water taxi that operates in season; but visitors will want to operate their own service to explore the upper reaches of the River Itchen.

It is important to be aware of the power of the ebb around an hour after second high water; it is strong enough to pin even a powerfully engined vessel against the pontoons. So, when entering or leaving, get or keep well under way when moving across the ebb (that is in and out of the pontoons across the direction of the river), or avoid that particular hour.

No one visiting Shamrock Quay should miss out on taking a dinghy right up the rest of the Itchen. It may be wide, busy, commercial and even warlike with the battleship grey of HM ships downstream, but it doesn't take long for all that to change in a most unexpected manner

If you are exploring upstream, first to catch the eye are Kemps Quay's thirty deep-water pontoon moorings in the river on the starboard hand just downstream from the yard. At the main station, there are thirty alongside berths on the outside, and, overall, some 200 berths with the majority afloat for three quarters of the tide.

There is a strong feeling of loyalty to a clientele that makes financial sacrifices to have a boat. Thus, there is no sense of threat from the nearby marina developments that provide not only all swish mod cons but also a penthouse to go with them. The yard is not to be described as run down, for it certainly is not. However, it does maintain strong links with the past, and is still redolent of an atmosphere that was all pervasive when it first opened as a rural marina nearly thirty years ago. It has a suitably personable address: Kemps Quay Industrial Park, Quayside Road, Bitterne Manor, Southampton.

Immediately upstream of Kemps, is a yard with an even more personal style. Its berths and moorings are modest, and so are its rates and its pretensions, but it is not entirely without affectation. Known somewhat idiosyncratically as Bonaparte Yard, it perhaps can best be described as the 'brainchild' of one Professor A. I. McMullen who runs it from a small office that is totally dwarfed by the premises of his other operations: Universal Marine & Civil Engineering, MM Colloid Products, and Accotec Ltd. This last is his main preoccupation: accurate pest control technology by nontoxic methods, and he is usually to be found in his laboratory, at the rear of the maritime front, working on the global destruction of mosquitoes. It is an operation of which any Hammer film would be proud.

Valcon has two sister ships. I met the first, *Old Barnacle*, in Ramsgate many years ago, so it was a pleasant surprise to come across the other, *Lindowan of Leith*, at Bonaparte's.

Upstream, the river soon begins to change its character, mainly influenced by the road and rail bridges that start at Northam and Bittern. Masts begin to disappear, boatyards become more modest, fast GRP cruisers dominate the moorings, and lived-in houseboats appear by the banks. In addition, the riverside becomes more inhabited and more cared for, yet all without losing its rural ethos. There are miniature berths and boathouses to be seen at the bottom of well mown lawns.

Trees decorate the river and, as it shallows, canoes and day boats appear from nowhere, and suddenly there are fishermen all around. There is something to catch the eye in every hundred yards.

It is difficult to imagine that Bishop Godfrey de Lucy made the river navigable to Alresford in 1200, and that Acts of 1662 and 1710 made it fully navigable to Winchester. The navigation rights have not been abandoned, but only light craft can proceed. Indeed, this stretch of the Itchen is best appreciated by rowing quietly, very close to the banks and observing the minutiae of life (wild and tame) that make up the passing show. By the time you get to Woodmill and Swaythling, there is no feel of a mighty waterway at all, and that is where most folk will stop for cream teas and ball games.

Southampton

ABP provides a short history of the Port of Southampton: 'The influence of the port runs back to 50 AD when the Romans under Vespasian founded a small fortified settlement on the banks of the River Itchen at what is now called Bitterne Manor. (North of Northam Bridge, the east bank was the river frontage of the Roman town of Clausentum; Vespasian Road is our witness!)

Successively overtaken by Angles, Saxons and Danes during the first 7 centuries, the old port rose in prosperity from around 1070 following the Norman Conquest. It continued to grow until 1338 when a French force, with Genoese and Spanish allies destroyed much of the town.

By 1450, Southampton was the third most important port in the Kingdom. However, commercial activity declined in the 16th century following Henry VIII's prohibition of the export of wool from the city.

The dawn of the New World began at Southampton in 1620 when the Pilgrim Fathers embarked for America on the Mayflower and the Speedwell.

Modern Southampton as a port began in 1803 when an Act of Parliament set up a harbour commission but it was the advent of the steam engine which led to the first steamship using Southampton docks in 1840. 1890 saw Southampton offering facilities unmatched elsewhere in the UK and by 1911 it could accommodate the great transatlantic liners like the Titanic.

Construction of the Western Docks, completed in 1934 involved the largest land reclamation ever undertaken in Britain – over 400 acres, and resulted in facilities including a dry dock capable of holding vessels up to 100,000 tonnes.

The port played a vital role in the supply to beaches of Normandy in 1944 with more than 3m troops passing through the docks, and in 1984 Southampton played a similar role in the amphibious operation to the Falklands.'

Hythe

Back in Soton Water, and across the other side, situate southeast of the reclaimed area known as Dibden Bay, Hythe Marina Village is to be found just upstream of Hythe Ferry jetty. Wherrymen, who were licensed like any water-taxi man, used to ply as hard as the winds and tides would allow them across the Water.

Access to the shoreline in these parts was never easy, and to help keep the channels open, the locals built small reservoirs with sluice gates to retain the water at the top of the tide and then to flash-flush it out at low water for a scouring effect. Although not as efficient as dredging, it was effective, always taking some top silt with it.

The marina is approached by a well marked channel, dredged to 2m below chart datum. It operates a 24-hour watch on Channel M, and the lock is opened on demand. Traffic is controlled by the usual international signals. There are free-flow periods, from about half an hour before high water. When the tide reaches 18ft, the gates automatically close, and if the tide is only 10ft, the free flow may not be initiated if there is insufficient traffic to justify it. There are also waiting pontoons if needed, but most of the time skippers expect to get in and out on demand. Inside, there is evidence of luxury, as the islands, houses, berths, canals and bridges create a waterside community. The residential side cannot be described as inexpensive, but yachtsmen are made welcome and are more than well served without being overcharged.

The place is frequently called Hythe Village Marina, especially over the VHF radio, and while this one irritates the developers, both names are actually quite appropriate for this Swiss style residential marina. Built next a site shown on a Hampshire map in 1575 as Hythferye, it consists of halfway houses; designs that lie between the strict modernity of Ocean Village and the relaxed traditionalism of Shamrock Quay. Basil Spence, from across the way at Beaulieu, might, in one of his more romantic moods, have created just such a place.

There is an actual village centre, with a social and shopping precinct. The centrepiece is topped by a classic belfry, complete with a four-faced clock in blue and gold. Its bells are muted and strike only during the hours of daylight; nevertheless, they have just the right tone to evoke the bells of ships that pass in the night. The pub is called the Lock'n'Quay, the inspired competition-winning name for which the prize was a crate of champagne. The state-of-the-art-designer decor is all of a piece except for the carpet, which contrasts somewhat unpleasantly with the rest of it.

In the village square, close by a display of fountains, is a wall with a neat mural celebrating the project: '... 225 houses, each with an adjacent berth, and a 275 berth yacht marina, together with restaurants, bars and shops. In 1985, the lock was opened by yachtsman Chay Blyth when T.S. Royalist and Virgin Atlantic Challenger led a fleet of 150 yachts through the lock.'

Hythe Marina. Berths (above), the entrance (opposite) and (below)
the head of the Test at Eling.

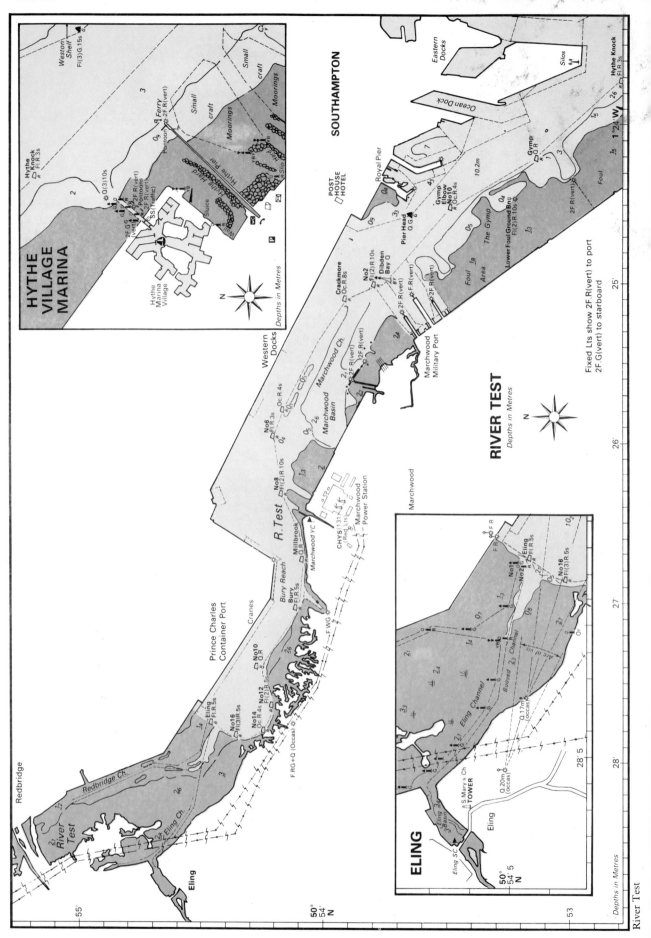

HYTHE VILLAGE MARINA

Depths in Metres

SOUTHAMPTON

RIVER TEST

Depths in Metres

Fixed Lts show 2F.R(vert) to port
2F.G(vert) to starboard

ELING

Depths in Metres

Alongside one of the private roads is a pleasing touch: the mast of the original *Shamrock V*, supported in a horizontal position to make a stout fence. Its length and girth are enough to strike disbelief and awe into the heart of any contemporary cruising man.

The asking prices for the properties range from an apparently modest £160,000 to an imaginative £750,000. This latter may seem excessive beyond the dreams of sybarites or the nightmares of misers, but having paid £1,500,000 for a yacht, and £150,000 for its electronics, such a home berth can hardly qualify as extravagant.

Hythe is an old-world kind of place. The window displays of clothes are way behind the times, however, this out-of-time ethos brings a bonus on Tuesdays, when there is an old-fashioned kind of market. It is of goodly proportions and is patronised by a busy mass of boisterous folk from both sides of the water.

But generally it is not a noisy place. There is a pedestrian precinct, but the roads themselves are quiet enough. It is easy to imagine why Lawrence of Arabia (as aircraftsman T. E. Shaw) lodged at one time at Myrtle Cottage in the village.

Quite clearly he was an unusual cove, for while he was working at Calshot, he entertained himself by translating the *Odyssey*. Here, he also worked on his last major piece, an RAF technical manual. This is an extract from a letter of that time: 'My life is as before: boats, boats, boats.... They grow more and better daily.... We work all day all week, and have no means of amusement and no leisure for it. I am glad to do the job, as the boats are of the sorts I have been pressing upon the Service for many months, personally and by reports; and they are proving what I hoped.'

There is a Waitrose supermarket (very busy – all cash tills usually have a queue) and two other shops worth searching out: the Hythe Health Food Shop where they sell some of the best yogurt in the country (made in North Devon); and a small electrics shop, where the quiet but friendly proprietor, Mr Roberts, knows more about computers and their software than does many a High Street specialist. Oddly the post office is almost out of town, near the New Forest Ironmongery, an excellent *Calor Gas* centre, where the proprietor will attend to you with garrulous Gaelic charm.

The River Test

For those who want to explore the River Test, Hythe Marina Village makes a good base. Over the VHF air waves their control is frequently nominated Hythe Village Marina, which, although apt, tends to send the management apoplectic since they have spent good money on promoting their Marina Village concept. Visitors kindly note.

Downstream, the Hythe Ferry runs its famous red boats from the jetty that feels as if it is already halfway across the water. To reach it you board the truly amazing blue and white electric train; a genuine relic that runs 'on stilts' from the mainland booking office the full length of the ancient jetty. It has toytown quality likely to appeal greatly to children and those still able to delight in simple pleasures and innocence recaptured. The ferries, two *Hotspurs* and one *New Forest*, run a 15-minute crossing to Soton's Town Quay every half hour.

Upstream, on the opposite bank, is the Cunard *QE2*'s 'ocean' terminal, from which she still comes and goes in splendour. This vast and unprepossessing jetty is followed by Ocean Dock, Town Quay, Royal Pier and the Mayflower Park, the well beloved site of the Soton Boat Show.

The other side is covered by a blanket notice, 'The shoal area along the western side of the River Test between Hythe Pier and Marchwood Jetty is foul, owing to the existence of clump sinkers with attachments.' Indeed, until you have passed the Prince Charles Container Port on the opposite side, there is little to charm here. The area is dominated by Marchwood Military Port and Marchwood Power Station. The only note of friendship or optimism is to be found at the pontoons of the Marchwood Sailing Club, where there are moorings and welcomes aplenty.

Past the Marchwood Clam Beds, Bury Creek looks inviting, but close inspection shows it to possess an associated sewage works. However, once past the Bury Swinging Ground, a much more placid stretch of water brings quite pleasing contrasts: massive container vessels and the smallest of sailing yachts; huge power stations, small havens, miniature ports and diminutive cottages; and overall, a mainly appealing mix of the old and the new.

The entrance into Eling Creek is a right-angle turn to port. Skippers with anything more than a metre draught should try for the first time only at the top of the tide. There is little room in the well protected haven, which almost completely dries out, and mooring for visitors (even with no more than a dinghy) can be problematic. Canoeing takes place above the toll bridge, where the scenery seems to be trying to improve on Constable. This is the head of navigation for most folk, who eventually retire to the Anchor pub. It is a spot not to be ignored or missed by any visitor to Southampton Water.

There is a splendid restored tide mill here, used until recently by the Eling Sailing Club as their headquarters. Now it is working and you can buy their real flour in the mill shop. The mill, with records going back to 1418, depends on a two-mile stretch of the Bartley Water for its pond and is situate by an old toll bridge that cannot possibly be as old as it looks. It was restored in 1980 and is the only working tide mill in Western Europe producing wholemeal flour (as it did centuries ago) ground with the original French Burr stones. It sells Canute wholewheat flour and bran, 'a natural product for good health'.

Inside the mill there is an explanation for the craft 'Doll Ladies' of the village that were on sale: 'A shipload of French soldiers who had been captured by us in the Napoleonic war were landed at Eling Quay. We know that the arrival of the prisoners aroused the interest of the local people who gathered on the quay to watch them being landed, for a Wiltshire clergyman wrote an account of this in his *Memoirs of a Country Parson*, which was published in the middle of the last century. These memoirs describe the French prisoners as presenting a sorry and dejected sight. The French army captain who was with them told the parson in excellent English that most of the men who had been captured with him were but country lads who had been taken from the plough and forced to fight for Napoleon. On arrival at Eling Quay they complained of hunger and exhaustion after a rough crossing from France. Their guards kept them standing on the quayside for several hours while arrangements were being made for their further transportation. Some of the Eling womenfolk took pity on the prisoners, went back to their cottages and returned with food in their outspread aprons. But a sergeant of the Dragoons who was in charge of the guards spoke roughly to the kindhearted women and ordered them away before they could distribute the food they had brought. Some of the prisoners were kept in the Eling district, others were taken to the Woolhouse, Southampton, and some went on to Portchester Castle.'

The way that tide mills work depends on a head of sea water that is filled each high tide. Here, the two miles of Bartley Water form the head (the bank) of sea water that is let through the 'great hatches' as the tide comes in. The hatches are closed at high water, and when needed the water is let out to power the mill wheels, giving about 4 hours milling time each tide. A 3ft head is enough to work them. At Eling, the wheels are nearly 12 feet in diameter.

Eling is a very quiet backwater, a beautiful spot with the strange sight of the old piles that once formed the boundary of the now disused timber pond or pound. Theirs are only small steps, while the overwhelming skeletal towers of the power pylons command the whole area with their giant strides.

Gone is the eccentric splendour of the old Calshot Light; replaced by commonplace proficiency.

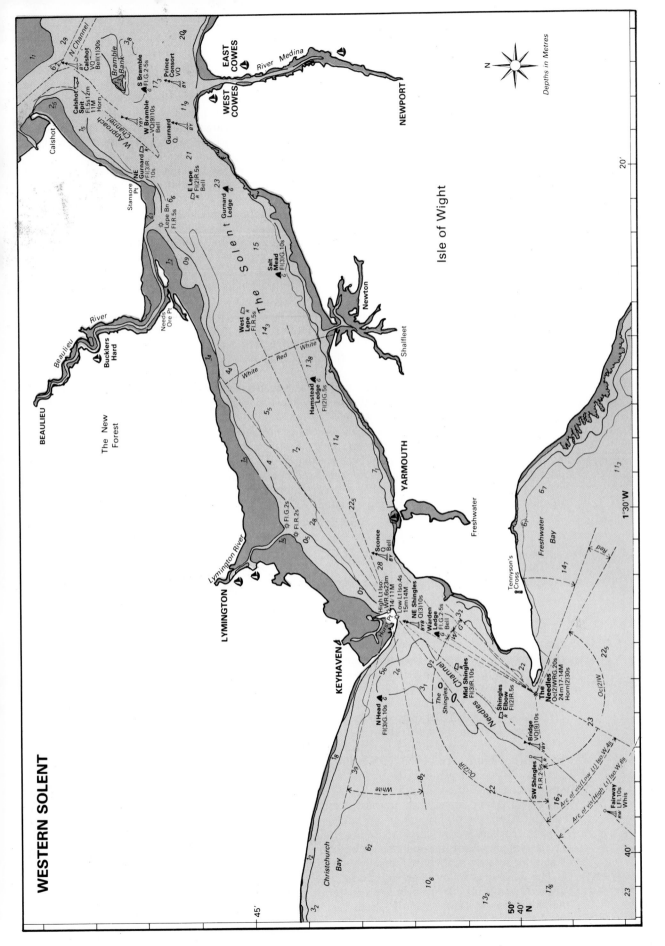

WESTERN SOLENT

BEAULIEU

The New Forest

River

Beaulieu

Bucklers Hard

Needs Ore Pt

LYMINGTON

Lymington River

Fl.G.2s
Fl.R.2s
Fl.G.2s
Fl.R.2s

KEYHAVEN

N.Head
Fl(3)G.10s

High Lt Iso.4s
High Pt WR.6s23m
14 11M
Low Lt Iso.4s
15m 14M
Sconce
Q Bell
NE Shingles
Q(3)10s
Warden
Ledge Fl.G.2s
Bell
W G 3½

The Shingles

Needles Channel

Mid Shingles
Fl(3)R.10s

**Shingles
Elbow**
Fl(2)R.5s

Oct(2)R

SW Shingles
Fl.R.2.5s

Bridge
VQ(9)10s

**The
Needles**
Oct(2)WRG.20s
24m17·14M
Horn(2)30s

Oct(2)W

Arc of vis(Low Lt) Iso.W.4s

Arc of vis(High Lt) Iso.W.6s

Fairway
LFl.10s
Whis

YARMOUTH

Freshwater

Tennyson's
Cross

Freshwater
Bay

Christchurch
Bay

Isle of Wight

NEWPORT

Newton

Shalfleet

Salt
Mead
Fl(3)G.10s

Hamstead
Ledge
Fl(2)G.5s

West
Lepe
Fl(3)R.5s

The   Solent

White
Red
White
White
Red

Gurnard
Ledge

E Lepe
Fl(2)R.5s
Bell

Lepe Bn
Fl.R.5s

NE
Gurnard
Fl(3)R
10s

W Bramble
VQ(9)10s
Bell

Gurnard
Q.

Gurnard
Fl.G.2.5s

**WEST
COWES**

**EAST
COWES**

River Medina

Prince
Consort
VQ

S Bramble
Fl.G.2.5s

Bramble
Bank

Calshot
VQ
Bell(1)30s

**Calshot
Spit**
Fl.5s12m
11M
Horn.

N Channel

W Approach Channel

Stansore
Pt

Calshot

N

Depths in Metres

1·30'W

20'

45'

40'

50°
40'
N

Beaulieu

Uniquely in England, the Beaulieu River is in private hands. The whole of the western side, from above Beaulieu to the Solent is owned by Lord Montagu of Beaulieu, as it was by his ancestors and the monks of Beaulieu Abbey before him. Lord Montagu also owns the bed of the river, a very rare type of ownership, deriving from the royal grants to the Abbey.

In the medieval days of the Cistercian monks, the river was their highway to the monastery at Beaulieu. There was a wharf on the Abbey side of the bridge. Bailey's Hard was used from about 1690 and Buckler's Hard from 1720, while another loading place, Carpenters' Dock dates from the late 18th century.

At Bailey's Hard there are the remains of a brickyard which flourished from about 1790 until early this century. In addition, there were, as in many low-lying areas in the Solent, active salterns on the river until the early 19th century.

Adlard Coles says: 'Of all the Solent creeks and harbours Beaulieu River is undoubtedly the most beautiful. From the entrance its wide channel leads west between marshes, the sanctuary of sea birds, and then takes a turn to the northward bringing the yachtsman within the "perambulations of the Forest".'

The Shell Pilot puts it this way: 'Beaulieu River is the most beautiful anchorage within the Solent. A long, straight channel leads between the mud flats to the river proper, most of which lies between deep woods on either hand.'

Cowper also found the place attractive: 'How long Beaulieu River will preserve its sylvan and retired beauty remains to be seen. Fortunately the riparian proprietors are either wealthy men or men of culture and position, so it is to be hoped they will not let the Vandal in just yet. But it is really only a matter of time, for Lepe Bar and Channel are quite as deep as the Itchen used to be before the persistent dredgers were set to work.

In fact navigating the Alde is very like navigating Beaulieu River minus the New Forest and Beaulieu Abbey, and plus the North Sea and Blackheath marshes, with Shingle Street and Orford Bar at the entrance. On the whole I prefer the Hampshire mudlark, the cosy refectory of the Cistercian monks, to the grim bleakness of the dreary keep of Robert Malet.'

The Admiralty *Pilot*, prosaic as ever, says: 'Beaulieu River is entered close around the E end of Beaulieu Spit, a drying mudflat which extends 1¼ miles E from Needs Ore Point; the east end of the spit is marked by Beaulieu Spit dolphin from which a light is exhibited.'

However, we are all agreed that it is a pre-eminent place to go, and there is no difference of opinion about the directions or ease of entry.

Directions

Once the yellow buoy (marked *Motortune* on some charts, but never discerned by me as such) has been found, the entrance into the river will be clear and plain to see. In any case, there is much on the shoreline to tell you where you are, particularly to the east where there are plenty of beacons to be marked off on the route from Calshot Spit. A particular point of interest is Luttrell's Tower: an 18th-century folly, one of many to be found overlooking the Solent. This one, however, is special: it is the place from which Marconi first tested out his radio transmissions to the Isle of Wight. It stands next the house known as Eaglehurst, from which, at one time, there was a railway line to Calshot Spit.

From the east, be it from Calshot or Cowes, you will give Stansore and Stone Points a good clearance by keeping just over a quarter of a mile off, thus leaving the red lit beacons fairly close to starboard. From the west, Hurst Point or Lymington, keep just over half a mile off, using the better water of Lepe Middle (the flats extend quite a way) until the dolphin and the leading beacons hove into view. From either direction, it is important not to be confused by the various beacons, posts and perches that are to be seen on this stretch. Stand off until you are confident you have selected the right one.

The entrance channel from seaward is marked by one main beacon, the *Beaulieu Spit*, Fl.R.5s, with 120° arc of visibility, range 3M and radar reflector; also carrying the seaward topmark. The leading markers were refurbished and repainted after the great October gale of 1987, when the trees that previously formed the background, were completely ripped away. Now the markers stand out smartly in their new bright orange array.

The dolphin is followed by substantial beacon piles. In the river, *Nos 5* and *9* (starboard), *12* and *20* (port) and *19* (starboard) are now lit, flashing red or green every 4 seconds. One of the lights shines especially brightly, fuelled by the memory of the exploding expletives when it fell on the foot of the harbourmaster while being installed in 1988.

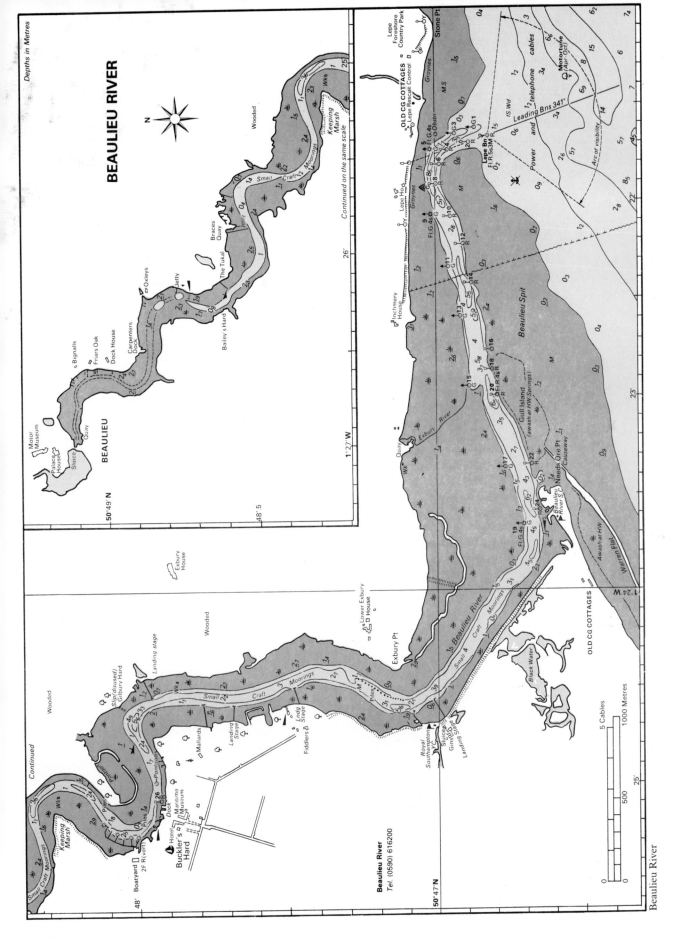

Depths in Metres

BEAULIEU RIVER

N

Continued on the same scale

1°27'W

26'

BEAULIEU

50°49'·9 N

48'·5

Motor Museum

Palace House

Sluice

Bignells

Friars Oak

Dock House

Carpenters Dock

Oxleys

Jetty

The Tukal

Bailey's Hard

Braces Quay

Jetty

Small Craft Moorings

Keeping Marsh

Wk o

Wooded

Exbury House

Continued

Wooded

Wooded

Keeping Marsh

Slip (disused)

Gilbury Hard

Landing stage

Wk o

Small Craft Moorings

Pontoon

Mallards

Landing Stage

Fiddlers

Lndg Stage

Landing Stage

Boatyard

2F R (vert)

Piles

Maritime Museum

Dock

Hotel

Buckler's Hard

48'

50°47'N

Beaulieu River
Tel. (0590) 616200

Lower Exbury House

Exbury Pt

Royal Southampton

Sluice

Gins

Landing Stage

Exbury River

Quay

Wk

Inchmery House

Beaulieu Spit

Gull Island
(awash at HW Springs)

Needs Ore Pt

Causeway

Beaulieu River S.C.

Beaulieu River

Small Craft Moorings

Black Water

Awash at HW

Warren Flat

OLD CG COTTAGES

1°24'W

25'

Stone Pt

Lepe Foreshore Country Park

Lepe Rescue Control

OLD CG COTTAGES

Groynes

M S

Lepe Ho

Groynes

Lepe Bn
Fl.R.5s3M R

Fl.G.4s

Leading Bns 341°

Power and telephone cables

Motoruhe
(Aar Oct)

Arc of visibility

IS Wd

M

Fl.G.4s

Fl.G.4s

Fl.R.4s

Fl.R.4s

Fl.G.4s

5 Cables

1000 Metres

500

0

Beaulieu River

87

HARBOURMASTER'S NOTES

Beaulieu River and Buckler's Hard Yacht Harbour

Harbourmaster W. H. J. Grindey, Buckler's Hard, Beaulieu, Brockenhurst, Hants SO4 7XB
☎ (0590) 616200.

Approach is best from *East Lepe* buoy, *Beaulieu Spit* beacon (three-pile structure painted red); light Fl.R.5s can be seen seaward and slightly west of white boathouse.

The seaward transit: dayglow orange triangular topmark on red pile beacon, should be used in conjunction with shore transit dayglow orange triangular topmark high up in fir trees, west of white boathouse. Transits in line 339°. Marginally deeper water will be found by keeping shore transit slightly open to the east.

The channel is clearly marked with red pile beacons with can topmarks to port. Green pile beacons with conical topmarks to starboard. Upstream of Needs Ore Point channel markers are withies and indicate approximate low water mark.

Beaulieu Bar

Extends approximately 600 metres to seaward of *Beaulieu Spit* beacon. A least depth of 1 metre LAT is to be found.

The Swatchway (between Gull Island and Needs Ore Point)

The Swatchway is now permanently closed to navigation. Entry or departure is through the main channel entrance to the east of Beaulieu Spit.

Caution

Vessels drawing 2 metres are advised at spring tides or heavy swell conditions to avoid crossing the bar one hour or more either side of low water.

Visitors' moorings and anchorage

Anchorage is permitted in the Lower Reach under the lee of Gull Island. An anchor trip line is advised as is an anchor light after dusk. No anchorage is permitted one mile either side of Buckler's Hard, or in a position to foul berth a vessel lying to Harbour Authority moorings.

Visitors' moorings up to 75 feet can be found at Buckler's Hard, with a capacity of up to 100 feet, by prior arrangement, on pile berths or pontoons within the yacht harbour. During the season, visiting yachts are met by launches marked 'Harbour Master' and directed to their respective mooring/berth.

Private swinging moorings

Whilst no objection is raised to the temporary usage, it is as well to be aware of the courtesies one should observe.

a. Keep within the tonnage limit on buoys.
b. Leave a competent crew on board at all times.
c. Vacate the mooring graciously upon the owner's return.
d. No rafting up. The harbourmaster's launch will be on regular patrol and will be pleased to deal with any queries.

Immediately inside the Beaulieu River, the outside world of the rush of the racing Solent is quite forgotten as an altogether other mien is called for.

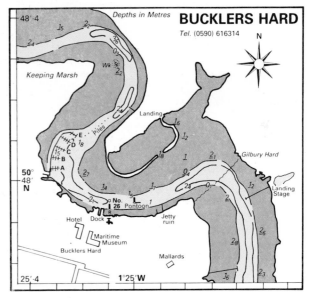

The entrance to Beaulieu river is clearly shown by the leading marks, top right.

Tradition has it that anchoring is permitted in the stretch between Needs Ore Point and Gins, but it will take a visiting skipper no more than a second's glance to see that, even if it were once an authorised anchorage, it is no longer safe or appropriate because of the profusion of moorings.

Almost opposite Gull Island, there is a landing at the small quay on the mainland. It is at the head of what is called the Exbury River. Other possible landings are on the beach and by the Beaulieu River Sailing Club's HQ at the Point.

Needs Ore Point to Buckler's Hard

Once round the starboard bend after Needs Ore Point and into the sheltered stretch, it does not take long for the odour of aristocratic affluence to impress the visitor, for it hangs over the water like any ignis fatuus the moment the major turn to starboard has been made and the river proper achieved.

The rights of the river bed, which are owned by Lord Montagu of Beaulieu, were originally granted by King John to the Beaulieu monks. It is one of the few river beds in private ownership in the UK, and the baron can also collect landing, moorage, boomage and all other nautical charges. In addition, all flotsam, jetsam and fishing are his.

The channel up the river is plain to see from the moorings, and while the yachts do tend on occasions to lie contrariwise, there is no difficulty in determining the way ahead. The worst problem is keeping your eyes on the traffic and the channel ahead, for not only do some of the

Berthing at Buckler's Hard is a popular pleasure; a privilege too, since it not easy to fall on a vacant berth – not even for a day or two.

boats at their moorings present eye-catching pictures, the scenery all around must prove a temptation and distraction to all but the strongest minded.

One of the first places to catch the eye is the intriguingly named Gin's, sometimes called Ginnes, Gynnes and Genes. Now the territorial domain of the Royal Southampton Yacht Club, it sports a most exclusive landing place, absolutely in keeping with their new lush'n'plush headquarters in Ocean Village. On the opposing side of the river, to the east, from Otterwood to Inchmery is the Exbury Estate, the property of Mr Edmund de Rothschild. His father, Lionel, acquired the manor after the 1914–18 war, and created Exbury Gardens, renowned for its rhododendrons, azaleas and camelias. In 1955, Nevil Shute wrote of the eye-catching mansion, 'HMS Mastodon was a stone frigate. It was Exbury Hall....'

Lepe House is to the westward of the leading line, and its almost next-door coastguard cottages are to the eastward. Here also is the shingle beach where the mini-river, the Darkwater, runs out. Tradition has it that there used to be a causeway here on which one could keep dry feet all the way to Wight. In the middle was a narrow channel requiring no more than a 'leap' by man or horse; hence the name.

The entrance into the river proper is achieved by a right-angle turn to port, round the long eastward-extending finger of Beaulieu Spit. Then the clearly marked channel runs parallel to the spit, past that part of it known as Gull Island, well named since it plays host to the largest colony in the UK. Some folk have it that, just like the seals in the Wash, for their 'own good' they must be protected from overbreeding; and also to create breathing space for the rarae (and weaka) aves. Thus there is a move to take their eggs – and man being man, he finds a use for them.

At one time, there used to be a swashway here keeping apart Gull and Needs Ore Point. This is referred to by some as Need's Oar, and they could be right. There used to be a coastguard station there from 1859 until 1922. Some spirited soul named Bull forged, in the 18th century, what came to be known as Bull Run to let himself in early on the tide. Over the centuries it was used by countless locals, but it grew so swiftly that Gull Island and other parts were being seriously eroded – and, some thought, in danger of complete loss. So, after much deliberation, RYA consideration and Parliamentary approval, the gap was closed in 1986, and Gull Island was restored to the mainland if that is what the narrow isthmus can claim to be.

This is how Cowper refers to it: 'There is a short cut for shallow-draught boats through a tortuous channel at Needs Oar. I have been through in a dinghy, but never is a sailing boat. The cheery author of *The Riddle of the Sands* told me he had sailed through in a boat drawing about 4ft. 6in. At high water springs I dare say it might be done with impunity.'

Although it is now the North Solent Nature Reserve Bird Sanctuary, there are those who still maintain that the swashway is open to navigation for most vessels at the top of tides; but even if that is technically correct, it is hardly fair to the birds. They have bided their time for quite long enough. In any event, landing on Gull Island is prohibited between 1st March and 31st July.

For those who do not wish to proceed up the river, there is a most pleasing anchorage in the stretch between Inchmery House, just after *No. 8* beacon, and the most westerly point of Gull Island (*No. 22*). The harbourmaster prefers, in general and when possible, for boats to keep to the Gull Island stretch. Most skippers keep well out of the channel to the south. However, there are those who, coming late at night, do not bother to anchor clear of the fairway. They can be a real pest for anyone leaving early into a low sun and mist, since they tend not to show. Anchoring is not free in the river.

From Exbury Point, all the way up the river to Gilbury Hard, there is evidence of well kept craft and even better kept fields, woodlands and pastures. The riparian lord and master does a good job all round. Two names are redolent of aristocratic weekend parties: Fiddlers and Mallards. The short leg is a most pleasing trip, and one that most people travel for the sake of arriving at one of the best known havens in the whole of the Solent.

Buckler's Hard

A most efficient and friendly welcome awaits you from the harbourmaster (W. H. J. Grindey, Esq., known to all as Bill, God bless him) and his staff, who patrol the marina in their Dory launches. They also do the rounds of the river night and morn, rounding up the latecomers and early risers, for Buckler's Hard Marina has to be made to pay. The Hard may be older than Lord M's vintage cars, but it gets no preferential OAP-type treatment; it earns its keep with all the rest.

The marina has pontoon moorings, and occasionally a visitor can get lucky and find one free. The alternative is take to the piles in the river; and even there you will need to be early for this is one of the most popular weekend retreats on the South Coast. There is a dinghy park near the actual hard and those skippers moored on the piles in the river are asked not to use the marina pontoons for landing from dinghies.

Bill Grindey, the senior Solent harbourmaster in years of service, is to be congratulated on managing to run the place not only profitably but also efficiently, politely and with a continuing welcome for all, polloi or royal. These lines from *If* seem a most suitable citation: 'If you can keep your head when all about are losing theirs and blaming it on you. If you can meet with triumph and disaster and treat those two impostors just the same. If you can talk with crowds and keep your virtue, or walk with kings and retain the common touch.'

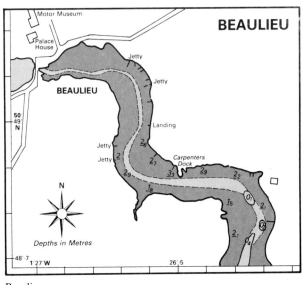

Beaulieu

BUCKLER'S HARD

How did Buckler's Hard get its name? A 'hard' is a common name in the south of England for a place where goods and passengers could be loaded or unloaded. Most of the shore of the Beaulieu River consists of soft alluvial mud, so that gravel was put down in suitable places to make a 'hard'. The first mention of Buckler's Hard in our archives is 1698, and is probably named after the Buckle family, who lived in Beaulieu at that time. There is, however, no known direct connection between that family and the Hard. But, as Bailey's Hard, one mile upstream, was named after the Baileys, who occupied Beufre Farm, it is reasonable to assume that "Buckler's" hard also derived from a family name. In the 1720's, John, 2nd Duke of Montagu renamed the settlement "Montagu Town", but after his death in 1749 the old name soon superseded the new one.

Beaulieu's museum is one of the more appealing aspects of the Boo'iful Day syndrome (although the *TS* *(Turkey Ship)* *Matthews* is just too tremendous for the entrance even).

There is a busy boatyard, the appositely named Agamemnon, but a rather poorly stocked chandlery.

In Buckler's Hard, where there is a well victualled corner shop, two long rows of houses face one another across the broad sweep of sward. It is a surprisingly wide street until you recall that it was here that all the timber was stacked when the ships were being built. Perhaps the most famous of the wooden walls to be built here was Nelson's *Agamemnon*, launched in 1781.

Alker Tripp waxes eloquently about her and her lord and master: 'Her history is well known; it is perhaps less well known nowadays that – in her prime – she bore the nickname "Old Eggs and Bacon." Captain Horatio Nelson, then aged thirty-four, was appointed to *Agamemnon* in 1793, and he commanded her in the Nelsonian manner, so that, when she went into dock at Leghorn to refit, "there was not a mast, yard, sail, or any part of her rigging, but what stood in need of repair, having been cut to pieces with shot. The hull was so damaged that it had for some time been secured by cables, which were served or thrapped round it." "Poor Agamemnon", Nelson had said, "was as nearly worn out as her captain; and both must soon be laid up for repair."'

It is all very well for us with our Johnny-come-lately green conservationism to condemn those in South America for living off their rain forests, but in fact more than 2,000 oak trees were required for a ship of just over 1,000 tons. Such a ship would also need 100 tons of wrought iron and 30 tons of copper. Buckler's Hard ships were usually coppered at Portsmouth.

The chapel on the Hard owns something of a chequered history. In the 18th century, this was the cobbler's shop of the boatyard and became the village school about 1890. Early in this century it was used as Sunday school and chapel. In 1935, it was restored as a memorial. It contains many beautiful things, including 17th-century wood panelling from Lady Cross Lodge in the New Forest, a 17th-century Spanish altar front and an old French woodcarving of the Virgin on a chopping block of the monks of Beaulieu Abbey, possibly 700 years old.

A plaque recalls the famous *Gipsy Moth* hero: 'Sir Francis Chichester K. B. E. Navigator of the skies and seas – Inspirer of the hearts of men 1901–1972. Buckler's Hard 1952–1972 Home Port of *Gipsy Moth II, III, IV, V.* They that go down to the sea in ships and occupy their business in great waters ... these men see the works of the Lord and his wonders in the deep.'

There is also the excellent maritime museum, once the New Inn, opened by Earl Mountbatten in 1963. Appropriately enough, in the entrance, is a splendid ship's figurehead, taken from a drawing for HMS *Gladiator* by Henry Adams. Part of it is based on ancient life in that very pub, and recalls with a sound and light show that brings to near life well known local characters, two of whom are Charles Pocock, the ironmaster, and Nicholas Cory, the taxing salt officer for the river.

You seldom find Beaulieu mentioned in history books, but when it is, it is usually the notorious incident involving its distant empire in Cornwall. In about 1500 AD, a blacksmith led a pathetic army to march on London. He failed and was hanged, but Perkin Warbeck exploited the cause. When he too came to grief, he fled to Beaulieu for sanctuary. It did him little good for he too was hanged.

John, second Duke of Montagu, inherited the Beaulieu estate in 1709. He wanted to build a new town at Buckler's Hard. The idea was to link commerce with the West Indies. Sugar was to be grown on the islands and refined at Buckler's Hard. The sugar project failed, when the settlers found the French there before them. However, the Buckler's Hard part got under way. It was laid out symmetrically with wide drives and a shipyard. It turned out to be a much smaller place than had been intended, a village rather than a town, with two rows of houses separated by a wide main street. It was originally going to be known as Montagu Town.

The shipyard soon prospered, and by 1800 was employing 4,000 men. Some of the famous ships of the line built there were: *Illustrious*, 74 guns; *Agamemnon*, 64; *Vigilant*, 54; *Indefatigable*, 54; *Swiftsure*, 74; *Euralus*, 36; *Greenwich*, 44; *Sheerness*, 44. Between 1745 and 1822 fifty-five men-of-war, two fire ships and fifteen merchantmen were launched from Buckler's Hard.

There is much to detain at Buckler's Hard. Just one example of how popular the place is will show: spaces and places are so much in demand that present owners will buy their new boats the correct length to fit their berths – to ensure they can stay in the marina.

There is a pleasing walk from Buckler's Hard into the village of Beaulieu. It follows the river bank most of the way, and Keeping Marsh, Bailey's Hard and Carpenters' Dock can be visited en route. Indeed, the whole area seems to have its justification in satisfying the urges of those who want to walk in attractive rural surroundings. This is not a view shared by Cobbett of *Rural Rides* fame, however, for he found the area to be one 'intolerable heath.... Never was a more barren tract of land than these seven or eight miles.'

The village itself is a classic example of a tourist trap: too many shops selling the same sort of gifts and not enough concentrating on the necessities of life. Admittedly, my judgment was clouded somewhat by finding neither butcher nor greengrocer; and only one bank, open, not all hours, but very few indeed. I was not therefore best amused by the 'Have a Beaulieuful Day' logo, when all I wanted was a (non-boo'i'ful Norfolk Matthews) decent joint of beef.

In the centre of Beaulieu, there is also an expensive hotel. It is likely that there has been some kind of an establishment here since the 1500s; and up to recent times, just like the New Inn at Buckler's Hard, it was not merely a hostelry but also the main centre for commerce. Since 1742 it has been known as the Montagu Arms. I am informed that it is the only freehold property in the village. Happily, it is of a more than acceptable standard, providing the only saving grace in this sightseer-snare of a place; other than of his grace in person, that is.

Back on the water, it is equally pleasing to take a dinghy up the river, where there are rustic panoramas to be enjoyed on each side. In addition, on the east bank there are houses to intrigue and impress. An absolute must for those with a penchant for design is the marble monument opposite Bailey's Hard, known as Spearbed House, and built by one Seymour Harris, who, I am informed, had design connections with Brazilia. In strict architectural terms it resembles the kind of edifice that Frank Lloyd Wright might have undertaken as an apprentice – if he ever was one. Nearby, is the edifice built by Sir Basil Spence that must stand as a sort of shrine to the man himself.

The peace and quiet and the friendly wildlife will appeal to all nature lovers. So tranquil is it that it comes as quite a shock to find a road bridge at the head of the navigation carrying busy vehicular traffic to and fro.

I am content to let the last words go to Alker Tripp. Having waxed lyrical about the pleasures of taking a tender up the river on a Sunday afternoon, he recalls the alternative in these words: 'But there is also a path through the covers, skirting the riverside, which in season is nothing less than a delight. It is most perfect perhaps in April, when the ground is a mass of bluebells and primroses and the covers have not yet become dense with their curtain of summer green. Spidery stems, and foliage budding like a green haze, give mystery to the distance, and the gleam of the river shines through. The cuckoo will no doubt be calling somewhere in the woodland.'

Lymington

The men of Lymington have had a reputation not only for fetching and carrying speculative goods and equally suspect chattels, but also for naughty deeds and nefarious exploits that goes far back into the murk of time. For example, about 1426 two local comrades were marked as conspirators in piracy; and in the following decades the practice of privateering (including rapine, pillage and murder) grew until it was a mainstay of employment and became supported, actively, passively or by default, by most of the populace. Eventually, piracy was superseded by that easier option, smuggling, and one of the most famous of the Lymington Lots was quite appropriately called (Captains) Morgan.

There were honorable men in Lymington's history, as there are in its present, and the arts and crafts of boatbuilding, fishing and saltering have been practised over the centuries. Today, the neighbourhood is still redolent of its past. The marshes are still calmly laid out as if eager to render up their reserves of salt; and they are still desolate enough to hint at the presence of ghostly traffickers, with the distantly open view of the Needles suggesting a direct escape route for anyone who should be in such need.

The marshes are well worth exploring, for it was here, many moons ago, that the local salt industry produced 6,000 tons a year. Just like Gandhi's followers, the people of Lymington used to gain their livelihood from the plentiful waters of the sea. There are still signs of the old quays and workings for those with enough diligence to search them out.

Indeed, for those with the right kind of mind and shallow craft to suit, there are expeditions to be made through Oxey Lake and on to the Salterns, Eight Acre and Normandy. There is also a jetty of sorts by the pipeline that extends from Pennington Marshes.

While the marinas and boatyards no longer specialise in the chisel and the adze, there is still enthusiasm enough for boats and all to do with them. The main connection with the past, however, must be centred on that word traffic, for it is in the doings of rail, road and seaways, the comings and goings of cars, caravans, ferry boats, cruisers and yachts that Lymington finds its *raison d'être*. The town jetty and the two marinas make a truly hospitable combination for indigens and visitors alike – but try to get in early or you won't get in at all.

Directions

Whether approaching from the east or the west, if you keep no less than a mile offshore, making for the (seasonal racing) buoy *Berthon*, you will discover no hazard. Pylewell Point and Lymington Spit, both shoal and drying, with the dividing channels of the optimistically named East and Pylewell Lakes, extend their sway a mile or so offshore, but the bottom shelves smoothly. While the yellow racing marks in the area are not always reliable, you can surely rely on the unmistakably conspicuous erection of the Royal Lymington Yacht Club's starting platform.

You may well spot the platform well before you espy the nearby *Jack-in-the-Basket*, although this latter is not at all difficult to pinpoint. It is the key for any stranger's approach to the river. It is said that the beacon derives its name from times past when fishermen's wives were in the the habit of hanging their husbands' victuals in it. I personally would not be surprised if it were not a small monument to some local seagoing Jack-o'-the-Green, actually put up by seamen themselves, for they can be the most superstitious of souls. *Jack-in-the-Basket* also marks the point from which HMS *Pandora* set sail in 1790 to search the Pacific for the mutineers of the *Bounty*.

LYMINGTON RIVER

Harbourmaster F. Woodford, Harbour Master's Office, Bath Road, Lymington. ☎ Lymington (0590) 672014.

HM Customs HM Customs Office, Bath Road, Lymington. ☎ Lymington (0590) 674584.

The following are extracts from the harbourmaster's notes:

'Entrance to River

The river is well marked with pile beacons at frequent intervals and has no hidden dangers. Starboard hand piles are painted green and port hand ones red. Recent dredging operations have restored the minimum depth in the channel (75 feet wide at its narrowest) to 8 feet at M.L.W.S. as far as the Railway Pier.

The R. Lym. Y.C. Starting Platform is a conspicuous mark which can be picked up on a clear day from many miles away. The entrance to the river lies between a red pile with a barrel top mark (Jack-in-the-Basket) on the west side and the starting platform and off-lying pile with diamond top mark to the east. The water around the platform is fairly shallow and should not be approached too closely at low water.

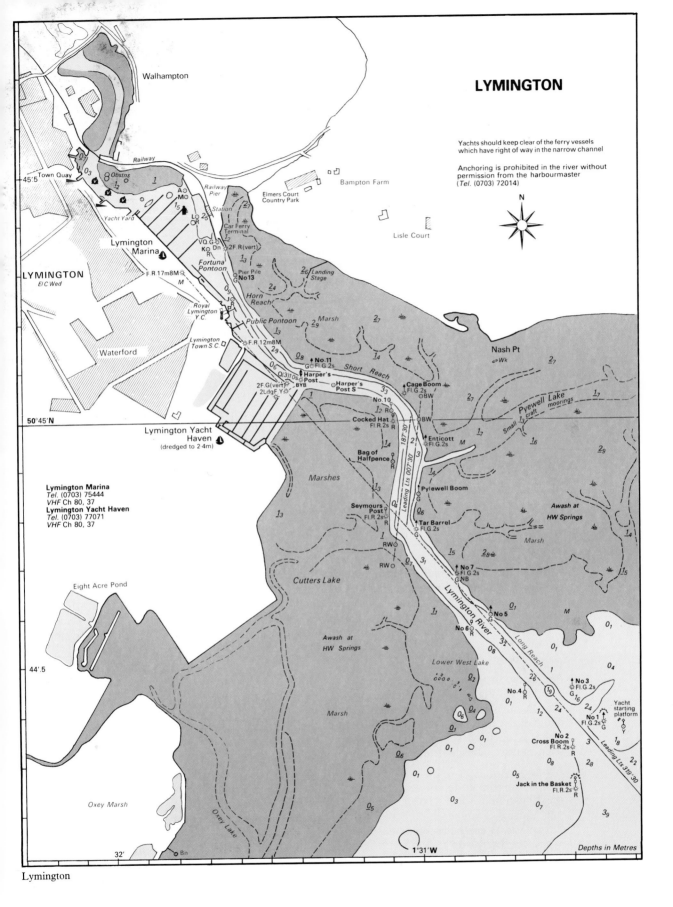

LYMINGTON

Yachts should keep clear of the ferry vessels which have right of way in the narrow channel

Anchoring is prohibited in the river without permission from the harbourmaster (Tel. (0703) 72014)

N

Walhampton

Railway

Town Quay

45'.5

Obstns

Railway Pier

Elmers Court Country Park

Bampton Farm

Lisle Court

Station

Car Ferry Terminal

2 F.R (vert)

Lymington Marina

LYMINGTON

El C Wed

F.R 17m8M

Fortuna Pontoon

Pier Pile

No13

Landing Stage

Horn Reach

Royal Lymington Y.C.

Public Pontoon

Marsh

Waterford

Lymington Town S.C.

F.R.12m8M

Nash Pt

Wk

Short Reach

No.11

Harper's Post

Harper's Post S

Cage Boom
Fl.G.2s
BW

50°45'N

Q(3)10s
2F.G(vert)
2Ldg F.Y

No.10

BW

Cocked Hat
Fl.R.2s
R

Pyewell Lake
Small craft moorings

Lymington Yacht Haven
(dredged to 2·4m)

Marshes

Enticott
Fl.G.2s
M

Bag of Halfpence

Leading Lts 007°30'

Pyewell Boom

Lymington Marina
Tel. (0703) 75444
VHF Ch 80, 37
Lymington Yacht Haven
Tel. (0703) 77071
VHF Ch 80, 37

Seymours Post
Fl.R.2s
R

Tar Barrel
Fl.G.2s
G

Marsh

Awash at HW Springs

RWO

Eight Acre Pond

Cutters Lake

RW

No 7
Fl.G.2s
GNB

44'.5

Awash at HW Springs

Lower West Lake

Lymington River
Long Reach

No 5
G

No 6
R

Marsh

No 4
R

No 3
Fl.G.2s
G

Yacht starting platform

No 1
Fl.G.2s
G

Oxey Marsh

Oxey Lake

No 2
Cross Boom
Fl.R.2s
R

Leading Lts 319°30'

Jack in the Basket
Fl.R.2s
R

32'

Bn

1'31'W

Depths in Metres

Lymington

Lymington's unmistakable *Jack-in-the-Basket* marker ...

... followed by the equally important *Cross Boom No. 2.*

The entrance to Lymington Yacht Haven is proudly announced by the *Harpers Post* cardinal marker.

Above the Railway pier the channel narrows and turns sharply to port, lying between two lines of piles forming moorings. This part of the channel up to the Berthon Boat Company is dredged to a minimum depth of 6 feet M.L.W.S. The channel then turns to starboard up to the Town Quay and in this reach depths of only 4 feet may be found.

Fixed red leading lights near the Yacht Club on magnetic bearing 320° mark the entrance to the river but care must be taken to break off from these before Seymour's Post is reached.

Warnings

Anchorage is prohibited in the river.

The Isle of Wight ferry has right of way at all times in the river.

The channel is narrow and manoeuvring space is limited.

Some of the mark posts are on drying mud.

There is no fixed speed limit but all craft should travel at such a speed as to keep their wash from causing damage or inconvenience to other river users.

Berths

Visitors' berths up to 70 feet (8 feet M.L.W.S.) are available in both the Lymington Marina and the Lymington Yacht Haven. Contact the respective marina Dock Masters on arrival. Lymington Marina, Lymington (0590) 673312; Lymington Yacht Haven, Lymington (0590) 677071. Larger yachts can be accommodated by prior arrangement.

Visitors' berths up to 40 feet (5 feet M.L.W.S.) are also available either alongside pontoons or on fore and aft moorings in the area of the Town Quay. Contact the Harbour Master on arrival.

The moorings in the rest of the river are all private but may be temporarily available; again contact the Harbour Master.

Long Reach to Lymington

Lymington River has become famously known to all as having a 'winding' channel. I suppose this was inevitable since the experts have deemed it to be so for decades. In my opinion, the river does possess what may be advisedly referred to as bends, but in no way does it qualify for winding, not when compared, for example, with the Deben or the Ore and the Alde. Indeed, once inside, the way ahead becomes quite clear and plain, and any hazard has nothing to do with a tortuous channel. There is no problem in achieving your course through the surrounding marshes since the channel is well marked all the way with regular and easy-to-see beacons. There are also two pairs of very obvious leading marks: the first, a red and white pair to port; the second a black and white pair to starboard. They mark the straight between the southerly Long Reach and the upstream Short Reach. They are in line at approximately 190° and 010° respectively.

The fact that the channel continues to be so well marked, well lit and uniformly deep (at least three metres almost all the way) must be in no small part due to the continuing service of the Isle of Wight ferries. It is these vessels that every yachtsman must watch out for. Their functional design, paying considerable tribute to fore-and-aft symmetry, makes it difficult at times to be sure whether they are coming or going – especially when two happen to be in channel together, passing near the midway *Bag of Halfpence* beacon. Ferry traffic is by no means infrequent!

Lymington Yacht Haven is the first to present itself on the port hand. Its entrance is marked by *Harper's Post*, a BYB beacon just after the red *Harper's Post S*. The immediate approach is indicated by a pair of leading marks (lit, 2 F.Y). It has a splendid location: immediately next the marshes of Waterford and hardly any distance from the open waters giving on to Hurst Point. In addition, you don't have to negotiate too many moored craft before it is reached. It has 650 berths, and there are usually spaces for visitors unless their arrival is left too late in the day (don't overlook the weekend sardine phenomenon across the way at Yarmouth). Their VHF Channel M call sign is *Lymington Yacht Haven*. This is frequently confused with *Lymington Marina* which is the prerogative of Berthons, further upstream.

The town of Lymington is easily accessible, since the yacht haven is no more than a mild walk from the many and varied services there are on offer. Lymington's facilities are comprehensive

Near the head of navigation, the river becomes increasingly popular and more and more crowded; consequently care and caution are the orders of the day – here perhaps more than anywhere else in the Solent.

in both boating and domestic spheres. At the same time it gives a genuine feeling of remoteness and release when you gaze out across the marshes to look directly onto that gateway to the west, the Needles.

Most of us have been irritated by the sound of flapping halyards, especially in the small hours of the wolf and the dog. In the telephone kiosk in the foyer of the marina office, I found the following intriguing notice that could, if sufficiently promulgated, be the saving of all of us:

'Flapping Halyards. In a modest breeze, halyards will flap against a mast at the rate of between 40 to a 150 times a minute, depending upon tightness and diameter. Taking the average to be 95 per minute this is: 5,700 times per hour; 136,800 times per 24 hours; 957,600 per week; 4,104,000 times per month. This is what it can do:

1. If your mast is aluminium, the halyards will wear through the anodising and allow corrosion to spread through the alloy until an unseen weakness occurs.
2. If your mast is wood, the varnish will be worn away, allowing water to penetrate the wood, turn it black and eventually rot it.
3. The strands of your rope halyard will fatigue especially where spliced to the wire rope.
4. Apart from keeping awake anyone trying to sleep in the immediate vicinity of your boat, the continuous Clang, Clang, Clang can give you a bad headache without you even noticing the reason. Remember if two halyards flap continuously for 6 months in one season at the average of 95 per minute this is 24,624,000 times: nearly 25 million lashes in a season.

Tying halyards back to the shrouds with shock cord is better than nothing, but it is not the complete answer. They can still hit the top. Why not tie both ends to the guard rails or pulpit or some other convenient anchorage completely away from the mast.

Please don't throw this away, it may save you money and two kinds of headache.'

That notice was only one example of the many singularities about Lymington Yacht Haven that go to make it a place that will stick in the mind. I recall my visits not only with that sigh and sense of relief that come when you have been served with friendly and quick-thinking intelligent service, but also with that rare and memorable pleasure that accompanies any meeting with people who actually listen to what you say and respond as sensitively as they are able.

They say of themselves in their extremely useful brochure, 'Lymington Yacht Haven was built in 1972 by local yachtsmen. Our aim has always been to provide a cheerful and efficient service for owners and their yachts.' I cannot but concur.

A short and pleasing river bank walk away from the marina office, is the headquarters and clubhouse of the Lymington Town Sailing Club: the old Bath House. It overlooks the open-air sea baths on the site of the King's Saltern. The official local guide has this to say about them:

'The changing-rooms at Lymington Sea Water Baths off Bath Road, are owned and run by the Lymington Town Council. There were baths in Lymington at least as far back as the 1780s, using one of the inlets from the salterns. At this time the proprietress was Mrs. Beeston, who advertised "the strengthening sea baths", and there was also Legge's baths. Terms in 1825 read "For a warm bath 3s 6d; shower ditto 2s 0d; cold water bath with guide 1s 0d; ditto without a guide 0s 6d ... every care and attention to the comforts of the invalid and the convalescent will be found strictly observed."

On March 10th, 1833, a public company was formed under the title of Lymington Bath and Improvement Company, with the intention of erecting more commodious baths with the enclosure of considerable tracts of mudland. Consequently almost £6,000 was raised by £25 shares and donations, and the main building was designed by William Bartlett of Lymington, whilst the machinery, installed under the direction of civil engineer John Silvester, afforded hot, cold, or vapour bathing, with one wing appointed for use by ladies and the other by gentlemen, with large swimming baths at the western extremity. The outside grounds were used for such sports as archery.

A few years later the company got into financial difficulties, but was rescued for a time by the liberality of Lymington's representatives in Parliament, who contributed two or three thousand pounds. Yet around 1855 the baths were sold for as many hundreds of pounds as it had cost in thousands, to Mr. G. Inman, whose limited company leased the baths to Lymington Sea Baths Company in December 1886. The Inman's property was afterwards sold and the baths became the property of Mr. A. E. Spencer. In 1902 there was an auction sale of the baths in London, and they were purchased by Mr. T. J. D. Rawlins, of Lymington. The swimming baths became noted as the largest along the South Coast, and in 1929 they were taken over by the Corporation.'

Just across the way, commanding the river, is the entirely different architectural style of the Royal Lymington Yacht Club, one of the few possessors of the Admiralty Warrant to fly a defaced red ensign. The RLYC, was started in 1922 by Major Cyril Potter, a keen member of the Royal Yacht Squadron. It began life in 1914 as the Lymington River Sailing Club, but didn't take off until 1922 when it settled in the old coastguard boathouse on its present site. There were ten members with Major Potter in 1922, and now there are more than 200 times that figure. 1925 brought the Admiralty Warrant and 1938 the Royal Warrant. Legend has it that a steward saw a stranger at the club's slip and addressed him: 'You can't land here sir, if you're not a member.' 'If I do not land here, then this club will not become Royal', replied an annoyed Duke of Gloucester. The same steward, who swept the slipway twice daily, is supposed to have said to the waters, 'Why don't you just come up and stay up!'

Of great interest by the village-square-type space in front of the clubhouse is one of the intriguing old gas lamp columns that have endured for more than 150 years. Fred Woodford, the harbourmaster told me that this one is the original beauty that stood in front of the Church of St Thomas. It lay in the council yard for a number of years after the road was widened in front of the church. It was moved to its present position in the late 1960s, as was the granite fountain berth of the RLYC which was also in the west end of St Thomas Street. Its position marks the old wooden bandstand on the green.

It was erected as a tribute to Admiral Sir Harry Neal for his munificent gift of the iron columns for the public lamps in the town in 1832; and to George Burrard, Esquire, who presented the whole of the public lamps.

Immediately opposite the RLYC building you come across a public slipway, the offices of the harbourmaster and the boathouse of the RNLI. There is a territorially sensitive pontoon at which you may tie up to unload at your own peril. (The harbourmaster comments, 'It only becomes perilous if one is selfish and stays too long!')

Further up the river, as moorings start to multiply and dominate the scene, you traverse Horn Reach and pass the Fortuna Dock Pontoon, administered by the Harbour Commissioners, on the port hand.

Almost next door on the same side of the river is Lymington Marina and boatyard of that famous name, Berthon. Their entrance is situate opposite the Lymington Pier and Ferry Station, and the river at that point is dredged regularly to a depth of approximately 8ft at MLWS. The marina covers some 10 water acres giving 300 individual yacht berths. It has five floating piers and can accommodate yachts singly at 30, 35, 45 and 55ft, with room for larger craft at the pier ends. Their VHF Channel M call sign is *Lymington Marina*.

Berthon need no special recommendation from me, for the name is known throughout the world as being synonymous with a sophisticated and cosmopolitan attitude to yachts and yachtsmen alike.

Further upstream is Lymington town quay, giving immediate access to the lower part of the town. There are mooring buoys and pontoon berths. It is an exceedingly busy spot with 36 mooring buoys. The centre row will take two vessels each, and there is room for a few more on the inside while they also build up on the outside. There is no ferry service to the quay from moored craft. The pontoon footage is not extravagant and vessels are required to follow the time-honoured custom of rafting up.

It is almost impossible to speak too extravagantly of the expensively aristocratic joys, services and benefits to be found in the town itself. You cannot fail to be impressed by all the gewgaws and goodies that fill the shops, which are to be found, hermit-crab-like, inside the original, beautiful houses with their gorgeous Georgian facades. Lymington is the kind of tourist trap that is the most successful ever; the one that convinces you are honoured to be served within its ancient walls.

Keyhaven

The unusual name of this lake is supposed to have come from the Saxon 'cy-haefenn', meaning the harbour where the cows were shipped. If true, this casts yet another question mark over the derivation of the other Cowes, some 11 nautical miles up and across the water.

From Lymington to Keyhaven is no distance at all. To the north of a line from *Jack-in-the-Basket* to Hurst Point, it is all shoal to drying; lying low in front of Oxey and Pennington marshes. For those with an urge for dinghy explorations, Oxey Lake will reveal the creek of Moses Dock, where coal, for boiling, used to come in, and salt, extracted from the nearby extensive saltings, used to go out. At one time, the local salt industry produced one tenth of the country's 60,000 tons a year.

The sea water was let into these saltpan ponds and then left to evaporate as much as it would by nature. The brine was then boiled over coal fires in suitable containers until the salt was produced. By-products were Epsom and Glauber salts: God bless *Alka Seltzer*.

It was a local tradition to throw a feast for the workers at the end of each season: for each man a leg of lamb, wrapped in dough, cooked in brine and garnished with local samphire.

Directions

There are three possible approaches to Keyhaven, and they all require the mariner to identify and then, more or less, to close Hurst Point. It is only in poor weather that there is any serious problem about the run; although due note should be taken of the strength of the tidal streams as they force their way through the gap between Hurst, the Shingles and the Isle of Wight. They will be noticeable even when coming from the east, although the leg from Lymington to Keyhaven will avoid most of their force.

Hurst Point, with its conspicuous high and low lights is the key to both haven and lake, being the major landmark in the vicinity to identify. Once you are anywhere in the area it is extremely difficult to miss its noticeable castle and lights. When making the close approach, it is wisest to keep southerly when making for the Hurst light. This will ensure that you are in good water.

From the east, Hurst castle and lights will show from miles away, and there is no intervening hazard between Southampton Water or Cowes and Keyhaven. You should make straight for the High light just to the north of Hurst Point itself, and from there you will be able to identify Hurst Road as it marches parallel to the Pebble Ridge, so reminiscent of the classic Chesil Beach and many others along this stretch of coast.

From Christchurch or Poole, in clement weather, a pleasant sightseeing trip can be achieved by cruising just under a mile off the coast. With your mind on the driving, and your hands on the wheel, you can be forgiven for letting your eyes become distracted by the sights that are to be observed on the Bournemouth strip.

This approach uses the North Channel and runs close to the shore, between North Head (the northerly shoal extension of the Shingles) and the southwest ridge beach of Hurst Point. The entrance to the channel lies between *North Head* light buoy and the Mineway Shoal. The strength of the streams here is very strong, and they seem to get up and go with a great deal of rapidity, dropping off in a similar manner; and it is from this direction, the west, that trouble can blow up if it has a mind.

I use this short-cut route as little as possible, since it takes you willy-nilly through some of what can be the worst overfalls on the South and East Coasts. In addition, there is the local eccentricity that is not known as the Trap for nothing. It is a shingle bank (steep-to on both sides hence its name) extending from the Round Fort to the south for just under a cable.

This is Cowper on the subject: 'I cannot say I recommend Keyhaven or Hurst Roads as good places, except for a mudlark or a rapid emetic. The former is a mere shallow ditch, the greater part of the way winding among miles of mud – real bottomless mud, not the spurious article they call mud at Burnham, which is a mere smear of filth on a hard substratum of clay or gravel.'

The main approach channel from the west is the one past the Needles, through the avenue between the Shingles and the Isle of Wight, and has to be a must for any first-time visitor. Ignore those few yachts and cruisers swanning along, out of the main channel, on the top of the edge of the Shingles bank as if there were all the water in the world. The truth is that there isn't all that much water, even where it may be charted; the banks can shift not only substantially but also quickly, and drying patches may materialise when they were absent only weeks before.

Many years ago, before I knew better than to move out of a main channel without enough low-water-springs direct visual evidence, I moved just outside the channel to give way to a number of Her Majesty's Navy steaming towards me at a good rate of knots. It seemed the courteous thing to do and my chart suggested there was no serious problem. However, that par-

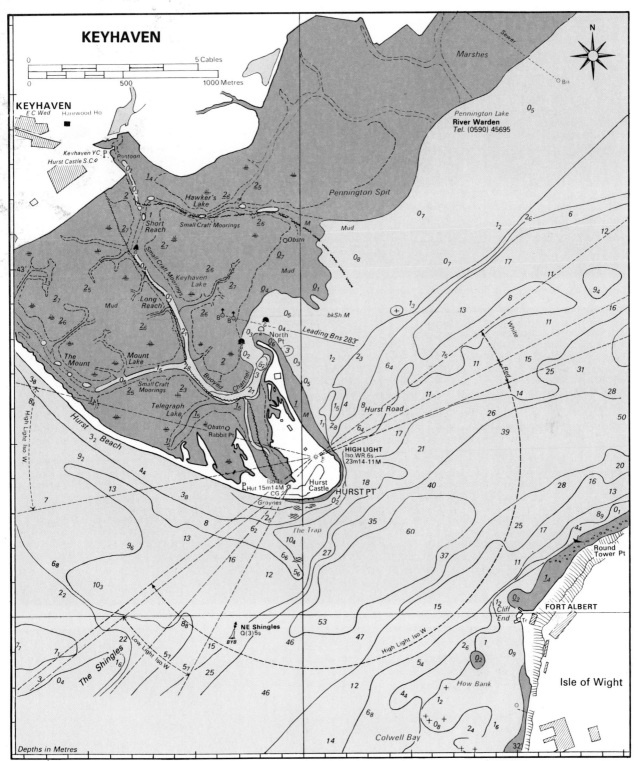

KEYHAVEN

0   5 Cables

0   500   1000 Metres

KEYHAVEN
E C Wed   Harewood Ho

Keyhaven YC P
Hurst Castle S.C.   Pontoon

Marshes

Sewer

N

Pennington Lake
River Warden
Tel. (0590) 45695

Hawker's Lake

Pennington Spit

Short Reach

Small Craft Moorings

Mud

Obstn

Small Craft Moorings

Keyhaven Lake

Mud

Long Reach

Mud

bkSh M

Leading Bns 283°

North Pt

White

Red

The Mount

Mount Lake

Buoyage

Channel

Small Craft Moorings

Telegraph Lake

Hurst Road

Hurst Beach

Obstn
Rabbit Pt

HIGH LIGHT
Iso WR.6s
23m14-11M

Iso 4s
Hut 15m14M
CG
Groynes

Hurst Castle

HURST PT

The Trap

High Light Iso W

Low Light Iso W

NE Shingles
Q(3)5s
BYB

The Shingles

High Light Iso W

How Bank

Colwell Bay

Round Tower Pt

FORT ALBERT

Cliff End
Tr

Isle of Wight

Depths in Metres

Keyhaven Lake

Hurst Castle is the usual goal of the many ferried visitors who cross Keyhaven Lake every year.

The anchorage off Keyhaven, while a generally attractive proposition, can be a bleak spot from time to time.

The leading marks off North Point when approached from the easterly anchorage.

Hurst Point. The light towers on Hurst Castle and, top right, the High Light.

ticular chart had not plotted the three drying patches that were shown when I was later able to study the Admiralty chart. Fortunately, crunching (not bouncing) *Valcon's* long, straight keel on the shingle did nothing more than shock me by its unmistakable scrunching sound. Never again!

But nevertheless, in a displacement vessel in particular, it is only sensible to time your arrival at the Needles so that the tidal stream is in your favour, otherwise you will waste fuel, time, effort and a great deal of nervous energy in covering less than half the distance you would otherwise have achieved with ease and in some comfort. The Admiralty *Pilot* gives the tidal stream hereabouts as reaching 4·5 knots at springs. It feels more!

The anchorage and run in both lie mainly parallel to the shore as it tracks from the Hurst Castle light to the point, tending northerly. About half a cable off is adequate. It is usually peopled with anchored craft and the way ahead is clear and plain. The cottages and the small landing used by fishermen and the Hurst Castle ferry at low water are all easy to spot. Quite a few folk take the tender ashore for picnics, swimming and general socialising.

On my first visit, I found myself quite unable to pick out the leading marks. The green buoys were spotted without any problem, but it was a good ten minutes before I gave up looking for the red buoy. Having timed my entry for high water on a good spring tide, I decided to go ahead without benefit of clergy (cardinal or otherwise). I later learned that the port-hand marker buoy had been dragged off station twice and was in the process of being serviced ashore.

When it comes to reading the available charts for the entrance, it is best to use the Admiralty chart 2021 (Harbours and Anchorages in the West Solent Area) or to check with the Ordnance Survey 1:25000 map of Lymington (SZ29/39). Both show water at low water at the hairpin bend, whereas previous received and printed opinion is that it actually dries. My experience is that the water is in fact there.

The approach to the hairpin port-bend entrance is extremely simple, provided the winds are not unfavourable and you are not near low water springs. Once on this course, you will come on the leading marks which you may be able to identify. I always find them difficult to spot, and some of the local pros consider them to be 'no good at all' ... 'worse than useless'.

Hurst Castle Spit, a huge bank of stones and pebbles, is the biggest of its kind on this stretch of coast. From time to time, it has been breached; and it has been reinforced by the laying down of building detritus – and some of the remains of the Royal Victoria Hospital, Netley. It is growing at a considerable rate of knots each year, and it is worthwhile noting that it now extends some distance past the black hut towards the north. The spit is fairly steep-to: twice the ship's beam (30ft) seems to be a good distance to stand off from the point, with the green buoy to starboard.

Once upon the bend, the channel is well marked with clear-to-see starboard-hand green buoys. Just inside the entrance, the channel is no more than 60 feet wide, but it does carry about 12 feet thereabouts. Local professional fishermen told me that they actually navigate around the 'wrong' side of three of the mooring buoys to find the best water. However, there still is usually enough water for a 6ft draught vessel – even at low water springs, provided the weather is settled.

The flood, the ebb and the stand are all worthy of study inside the lake. The pattern of the time and direction of the stream is changing, with the flood now entering Hawker's Lake first and coming earlier. For those whose knowledge is really local, this channel is a boon for an early get away.

Keyhaven Lake

The first 16 mooring buoys are capable of taking craft up to 35ft maximum LOA, thereafter in the main river the maximum being 30ft LOA. They may be picked up when free. They are laid to interlinked, interconnected chains, so it is vital not to anchor anywhere near them. They are inspected every winter and replaced at expensively short intervals.

Numbers 3 and 12 belong to the boatyard, but are frequently unused by them in the summer. Another is clearly marked ferry and is not to be used, since it may be required at any time of the day or night by one or other of the ferries which do various kinds of work in the harbour. It is unwise to stray too far from the channel and the moored craft for the banks shelve quite steeply. In some winds, the boats will swing with their sterns almost on the shelf, so then, and indeed in general, it is best to pass close to their bows.

One of the first of the substantial buoys belongs to the English Heritage boat that services Hurst Castle and other Heritage properties and functions in the area. The skipper and crew are approachable and friendly, and will not harangue you if you are apprehended using their buoy – provided you are prepared to move on without fuss. The river charges are extremely modest.

There is an anchorage immediately inside the run, as marked on the charts. Hooks should not be dropped after the first of the mooring buoys, since, as already mentioned, these are all laid to lengths of chain. This anchorage happens to have exceptionally good holding ground.

When there is a gale or extra-strong wind from the west to southwest, the river manager advises that you should not linger inside at anchor or on a mooring since there is little protection. Sweep and swell can soon build up, making the billet uncomfortable. The solution is to anchor outside in Hurst Road to the east of Hurst Point, where there is sound, well protected holding ground outside much used by locals and fishermen, and that is always a reassuring sign. Being able to tuck closely in and gain the protection of the spit, with luck, the wind should miss the hull, blowing directly only through the rigging.

Back inside the lake, the local ferries, fishing and work boats are frequently in evidence and will afford you a warm welcome. The ferry will pick you up and drop you off at the castle or at the quay. They operate in the holiday season and are always alert and pleased to offer their services to yachtsmen. The first trip is at 1000 and the last at 1730.

Hurst Castle is a strange affair: awesome, near ugly and almost always bleak. The naked, brutal stonework came from the ruins of Beaulieu Abbey; the oldest remaining bits dating back to 1535. The English Heritage pamphlet refers to it as being 'low and menacing on its shingle spit'. 'This castle was built by King Henry VIII for the Defence of that Channel or Passage call'd the Needles. It is a narrow neck of land shooting out beyond the mainland of Hampshire, commanding the Sea every way.'

Freedom as it might have appeared to the prisoner King Charles when immured at Hurst Castle.

Keyhaven Lake

At the castle, you cannot rely on getting refreshments, nor is there much information about the place itself – nor indeed what went on there. In particular, since King Charles I was kept there, it is frustrating not to know what happened to him and exactly where he might have been kept – perhaps in the keep? In 1854, an electric telegraph station was established at Hurst. From time to time, the place was used for herring curing, but probably its most enduring industry was brandy smuggling. To sit at anchor near it is to share something of those experiences; in the moonlight, it seems as if little has changed – a place suited to sombre thoughts and dark deeds.

Access to Keyhaven quay landing at the north head of the lake is best made by the ferry or dinghy. It is possible to take deeper-draught boats to the quay but local knowledge is required. The channel is clearly marked by green buoys right the way up, but it is a narrow twisty business and the channel does not always obey the buoyage. In any case, the landing is neither easy nor convenient, and the quay is usually crowded with working boats. The vast majority near the quay dries out.

Overlooking the quay are the fishing, boating, yachting and sailing clubs. They are all informal, but some carry the philosophy to an extreme, apparently leaving members and visitors to their own devices. 'We don't believe in organising anything. We're not keen on club cruises and rallies and events and that kind of thing. We like people to be left alone to do what they want to do by themselves without interference.' I was left mildly wondering how they managed to get together to run a clubhouse – and why?

Here also is the office of the river manager. A real charmer if ever there was one, he is as efficient and cooperative as he is friendly; a mine of information which he is prepared to divulge with generosity, and, what is more, he is round and about his patch most of the time – and does not have his office in the local pub, a habit to which many river managers or bailiffs are prone.

There is a secondary channel to the sea from the quay, now being used more and more by those with local knowledge. It is called Hawker's Lake; and to understand why, we need to know a bit about a certain *homme sportif*!

105

Hawker and his lake

From the quay it is a walk of about a cable to The Gun, the well known pub. Next door is the cottage that used to be the 'little gunning place' of one Colonel Peter Hawker. He was a great punt gunner, and in his time must have slaughtered enough species and enough birds to have a place in the *Guinness Book of Records*.

Most of his shooting was at night or early morning. He was a glutton for punishment in his punt, silently lining up a 'raft' of birds. His giant gun used to kill many birds with one shot. His diary is a long tale of this eccentric slaughter. Mary Trehearne, in her book *Keyhaven An Odd Sort of Hamlet* says this of Old Hawker:

'It is easy for the modern reader of Hawker's dairy to be shocked and horrified at the quantities of birds he shot; a bag of 758 for instance, for the winter of 1837–1838, and he let fly at anything from swans to wheatears or skylarks. Most of the game birds were sent as presents to his friends, some to the Duke of Clarence, the future William IV. But we must remember that the tables of the rich were furnished with a great variety of game which we would not consider edible. Swans and wild geese would have had to be exceedingly well-hung to be palatable, but would have fed a large household. A pie of larks or wheatears was considered a toothsome delicacy. And it was not only the rich who consumed game. Hawker describes how, when conditions were right, with an east wind and a touch of frost, the marshes would be crawling with gunners ('a beggarly army of flight-poppers'). Characteristically, he took the law into his own hands by hiring sailors with blank cartridges to drive them out of the harbour. These poor gunners would have seen the marsh as a source of food, as it had been throughout history. Many of them lived off the sea and its shores, which provided fish, game and also driftwood for fuel and carpentry.

In spite of frequent pain and broken health, Hawker was able to survive on sea or marsh under the most severe conditions. He also showed much resource and drive in the varied works he undertook in the Keyhaven River and harbour. In 1838 he supervised the digging of a new "leak", which he had cut through the mud at his own expense, to enable him to sail or row through to the Pennington leak without going round by Hurst. He marked the passage with booms given by Mrs. Whitby and cut from her estate. Since that time "Hawker's Lake" has been a boon to small boat-owners, and a refuge from rough weather outside.

This intrepid old soldier was always able to rise to an emergency and take command. It was he who got a gang working to mend the breached seawall during the great floods of 1840. Again, in January 1841, Keyhaven harbour was blocked by drifted ice. Hawker was out in the Solent with James Read and had to crash his way through the ice under full sail to get back to the quay. "I never encountered anything more formidable than this," he comments. "It was tantamount to being in a field of battle." Three days later, "Our harbour was in one pan of ice, half a foot thick, and our boats in danger every night. People defied the removal of the ice because it could not be broken. I had it cut across with pickaxe and spade. Then I put a grappling iron into it: and, having sunk the buoys by sinking them under the ice... I, by means of a long towing line and powerful lever, got the whole field of ice underway; and off it went like one large island at the first ebb of high water; making our harbour as clear as in the month of May and enabling everyone to resume his boat moorings in safety."'

And just for a little contrast, this is Cowper's view: 'Keyhaven is a small hamlet at the head of the creek which runs in round Hurst Camber. I kept Undine I in the creek for four or five years half-way up from Hurst Castle to Keyhaven, being able to see the boat from the drawing-room windows of Kivernells, my house at Milford. At high water springs all the mud is covered, but there is no sea.'

It is a mile or so to the village of Milford, where there is excellent shopping: three real butchers and four greengrocers and a first rate wine and cheese shop. Please to watch your victualling budget, for there is only one bank. Bank failure is one of the hazards of cruising; I usually manage to arrive on the one day the village bank does not open, or just after its one and only morning session, and then it is often the 'wrong' bank. In an attempt to foil the malignance of city financiers, I now have accounts with three banks and carry numerous pieces of plastic, but I am still confounded from time to time – unless I am prepared to pay the £2·00 fee demanded by some avaricious Post Office persons.

For shopping, it is wise to take a full crew with stout haversacks, for the walk, along a busy road, seems lengthy when loaded. There is a restricted bus service during school term time, and while Milford has a taxi rank, it seldom seems to house a taxi.

II. The Isle of Wight

During the Palaeolithic period, the island was part of the mainland (England, that is) and its domain spread far to the south into what is now the Channel, and was probably also connected to the mouth of the Rhine. At that time, there was a big river, named as the Solent River, that rose in far off Somerset to flow through Poole Harbour, with its channel being formed through the soft rock between what is now the Isle of Wight and Hampshire. It ran easterly for many miles until it finally reached the sea about seven miles south of Brighton.

While on things partly geological, it is fascinating to note that the seismologist John Milne (who had retired to Shide, near Newport, with his Japanese wife) carried out special measurements that showed the whole of the Isle of Wight leans one way and then the other as the tides ebb and flow around it. His research was undertaken in the cellars of the old premises of the Royal Victoria Yacht Club. I have not been able to unearth a resident who was either aware of it or who would accept it, nor have I suffered the slightest *mal de mer* when ashore.

By the time Neolithic man was leaving his remains around Bonchurch, Wight was a fully fledged island. The Beaker brethren arrived about 1900 BC and flourished near Brading. Vespasian conquered the island in 43 AD and the Romans settled, calling it Vecta or Vectis. There are those who maintain that its present name, Wight, is simply a corruption of this, thus going back to really worthy ancestors who had no linear connection with Angles or Saxons at all. Some islanders are near-paranoid in their jealously guarded separatism from (Great) Britain. But the Saxons did come, in 530 AD – fellows with sombre names like Cerdic, Cynric, Aldewach, Caedwalla and, even, Stuf. Centuries later, the Danes followed: in 896, they were repelled or pursued with much death by hanging; but in 1048 they returned with a sufficiency of forces and stayed to conquer.

The French tried again and again, and while they wrought much havoc, pillage and other unpleasantnesses, they never managed to keep their feet under any of the islanders' tables. In spite of their oft-expressed wishes to be ancestors of those Latin speaking citizens of no mean city, it is more than likely that the spelling of Wight owes nothing to Rome, and is no more than a variant of White – Ye Goode Olde Englishe. But try telling that to one of the indigens, who, while still referring to themselves as Corkheads and Englanders as Cocklers or Oveners, believe the Isle of Wight is no more a part of England than is the Isle of Man. They have a bus service called Vectis to prove it.

The Isle of Wight is shaped roughly in the form of a giant turbot, or, to be less imaginative, a trapezium or irregular rhomboid. From some parts of the English shoreline, and in particular Bournemouth, it exhibits the features of a polar bear. At its greatest length, that is from the Needles on the west to Bembridge Foreland on the east, it is 23 miles; and at its greatest width, that is from Cowes on the north to St Catherine's Point on the south, it is 13. It is 3½ miles south of Gilkicker Point and 4½ from Portsmouth Harbour. Nearest to the mainland is Sconce Point, 1 mile southeast of Hurst Point. Its total area is about 147 square miles and a circumnavigation about 60 miles.

It possesses five main rivers, three of which nearly cut right through it: the Medina, with its mouth at Cowes and its source near St Catherine's; the Western Yar, with its mouth at Yarmouth and its source at Freshwater Bay; and the Eastern Yar, with its mouth at Bembridge and its source near Niton. The other two rivers, Wootton and Newtown are really no more than creeks, but they are such superb examples that they deserve the higher ranking title of river. Other streams find their ways to the sea via bays on the eastern and western shore, and via clefts in the too, too solid rock, called locally Chines. The best known of these are Shanklin, famous for the verdant richness of its valley, and Blackgang almost infamous for its sombre grandeur and lack of ripeness. What is known as the Undercliff is so well sheltered that its plant life is often mentioned as being near tropical, gaining for Wight yet another tribute, the English Madeira.

In his book, *The Isle of Wight*, J. Redding Ware wrote in 1869, 'The Isle of Wight is the paradise of bees, flowers and invalids. Almost throughout the year there are blossoms for the buzzing bees, who are awake and careering through the air long after their English brethren have said "goodnight" to the year.'

Leslie Thomas had another point of view:

'To the garden isle came the tourist trade;
The Needles an afternoon trip,
"Five bob all round the Island"
In a snorting little ship.
But the first hard frost of winter sends
The hiker to his den,
The Islanders come, through unbolted doors,
Into their own again.
The foreigners' cars are ferried away,
The little roads are clear,
And island men in island pubs
Slowly quaff their beer.'

Sir Walter Scott wrote, 'that beautiful island which he who has once seen never forgets, through whatever part of the world his future path may lead him.' Wight has also been called the Garden Isle and the Primrose Island. I find no cause to disagree with any of these descriptions.

Approaches to the West Solent

Approaching the West Solent from St Alban's Head is just a matter of setting a course for the Needles and watching out for any set. From Poole, if following the coastline rather than making straight for the Needles, care needs to be taken to stand well off Hengistbury Head and so avoid collision with the Beerpan Rocks or too close association with Christchurch Ledge. The *Wave Research Structure* and the green *North Head* light buoy are to be identified before making a final try for Hurst Point. There is a narrowish channel, known as the North Channel by the Mineway, between the north tip of the Shingles themselves and the shingle bank on Hurst.

Finally, there is the local version of Scylla and Charybdis known as the Trap. The first part of the double bind is an eccentric excrescence extending south from the Round Fort on Hurst Point for about a cable. Its name speaks volumes: it is a shingle bank (steep-to on both sides).

The second part of the act is one of those expanses of overfalls that can throw up the most vicious of short, sharp breakers that catch you out whichever way you try to meet them. Some folk with shoal craft and different nerves from mine, go 'inside' them, risking the edge of the Trap; some go through them, apparently revelling in the 'boisterous' motion; and then there are those others, who, like me, will go out of their way to avoid them. This means picking up the *NE Shingles* and setting a course for Yarmouth; taking longer perhaps, but being infinitely less wearing.

The red marker at the gate between the Shingles and the Needles.

As I have already made plain, the North Channel and the Mineway are not to be numbered among my favourite haunts. Here, is John Glasspool's *Solent Shores* perception of the location:

'On the mainland side, the villas of Highcliffe and Milford on Sea take up most of the space. Then there's another welcome break as the gravelly shore starts its great curve to the south, ending dramatically in the white castle and twin lighthouses on Hurst Spit. Small craft favour entering the Solent by way of the North Channel, standing in for North Head buoy before steering parallel with the last mile of the Spit. There's one hazard to watch out for before turning the boat's head east into the sheltered water of the Solent. It is well named the Trap – a small but vicious patch of overfalls just southwest of Hurst Castle. Daring centreboard folk steer close to the spit and get away with passing inshore of the Trap. Strangers might find that a dummy run or two in kindly weather is helpful before trying this. Reading pilot books and their warning of tide-rips, overfalls and so on can be as daunting for the cautious sailor as reading medical books can be for the man who worries about his health. The thing to remember is that these places are perilous in breezy weather, as anywhere is on tidal water. If you are lucky with your weather and show a bit of respect, Hurst Narrows need be no more frightening than Cowes Roads. The first time I passed west of Hurst, in a 12 foot dinghy, was on a gentle summer morning, with the sun burning up the mist revealing the Purbeck Hills floating in the sky to the west. The breeze was light easterly, but I was rounded up in Hurst Roads and tied in a reef. After all, this was big stuff, going outside the Solent for the first time in one's young life. So it was a sedate exit. Far too sedate because away to the southwest the imperceptible swell was breaking on the Shingles even in the near calm. A bit of steerage way to keep clear of that was obviously a good idea. So, assuming a pose of sangfroid and listening all the while to the merry rattle and gravelly roar on the Shingles, I rounded up and shook out that reef. Once you're out, of course, in a boat of that size thoughts tend to persist of what conditions will be like for getting back, when the first of the flood tide begins to speed up and confronts a bit more breeze from the east. Both happened, but the little boat swooped gamely through the Narrows gateway leaving her young skipper time to observe the phenomenon of the tideway off Hurst, the Pinnacles. These are not rocks but small waves rising up in pyramid shapes, something like goose-pimples. A hundred and fifty feet below her keel, the old ebb was becoming the new flood. Engaging reverse gear was somehow the cause of these spiky waves.'

The Needles

Today, the Needles lighthouse is low (as is that off Beachy Head), since it was found that the ancient weak lights just could not penetrate the sea mists if they were placed, in the traditional position, at the summit.

The wreck off the Needles is that of the Greek vessel *Varvassi*. Carrying a cargo of wine and oranges, she went aground on the ledge just at the base of the light. Her wreck and the nearby Goose Rock are two very good reasons for not flirting anywhere near the area. There are those who fancy their chances by navigating (if that is what it should be called) the gaps between the rocks of the Needles. It has been referred to as 'Threading the Needles.' Just the thought fills me with anxiety and foreboding, and in spite of all the tales I have heard, I could find no one in Yarmouth who was not scornful of the idea. This is how Alker Tripp described his perceptions of this approach to the Isle of Wight:

'... perhaps the really ideal landfall is at the other end – the Needles.

To all of us who cruise hereabout, or who sail up-channel to the Wight, the approach to the Needles is familiar; and the impression never fails of its magic. Over the blue seas, the great cliffs are white and gracious; through the flying squall they loom in majesty. And, either way, they are unforgettable.

Let me recall a passage; and also I want to say a few words on the subject in general before we continue our regular exploration. We had raised the Island several hours ago, and there it now towered, its white cliffs abrupt, above the seaway. Waves were breaking to spindrift round the Needles.

The fairway buoys, that mark the regular deep-water entrance to the Needles Channel, are west of the Needles Rocks; we could see the buoys tossing in the welter of green and white. I had neglected them of set purpose, and the yacht's bowsprit was pointed at the Island. A long line of foam, a smother of white, lay between; it was right over the bows.

"Shoal!" my companion called, and he jerked his arm to point it; the gesture was eloquent.

But I held my course; I had seen this before. The waves as they broke looked ugly enough – just as if they were thrashing on a shoal with only a foot or so over it. And the wind was boisterous.

The famous white cliffs and the Needles light.

But this was only the tide-rip, as I told him, while I juggled the tiller this way and that. The tide in the Needles Channel runs at five knots or more, while in Christchurch Bay the current is comparatively slow. Along the edge, between the two tides, runs that rip of breaking sea. It looked formidable, but – beyond a little more spray about our oilskins – it would do us no manner of harm. The wind whistled, the low clouds scudded, and the yacht drove on.

Everywhere were crests of foam, not only in the tide-rip (which was a regular welter), but in the fairway too. And through the noise and tumult we steered for the Solent – itself a busy seaway today. This was a squall-wind, and was getting ragged already. Up the Solent Growler scudded. At Jack-in-the-Basket her course was changed abruptly, and she was immediately between the long, tidal flats of Lymington River, in complete shelter. We reached up river, with that singular sense of comfort and smoothness which is felt at its best only after a rough passage. A mooring was found; we furled the sails. One more day's work done.'

The Bridge and the Shingles

For pleasure craft, there is no major hazard when making for the Solent from the westerly side of the Channel. To the NW side of the approach to the Needles, are the attractively named Dolphin Sand and Dolphin Bank; while the less appealing Pot ('Belly') Bank is on the SE boundary of that approach. With least depths of 15m, it is often a site for commercial vessels dredging for ballast.

The Bridge itself is a reef just over 10 cables to the west of Needles Point, with depths varying from 2m to 10m over a very uneven bottom, seemingly made up of peaks and huge stones of chalk. It is marked by the eponymous light buoy which also stands guard by the easterly side of the entrance to the Needles Channel. Predictably, the reef is well known for its surface variations; from barely discernible ripples in calm settled weather to severe overfalls in the rough. When there are gales from the south, its delineation can be easily perceived from the marked broken water. There is substantial ground swell as well as heavily breaking seas well out from the Needles light.

The Shingles is one of the best known features of the whole of the Solent, as well as being the chief characteristic of this locale. It consists of a bank of sand, shingle and gravel, with a number of areas less than 2m and parts that dry to 1·5m. It makes up the northwest side of the Needles Channel. The southeast side of the bank is very steep, while its northwest side shelves only gradually. However, there is no threat at either side since the area is extremely well marked by standard buoyage. The SW Shingles buoy marks the southwest end of the bank and also the westerly entrance to the Channel. The northerly part of the Shingles is marked to the northwest by the *North Head* buoy, that stands by its gravel bank which carries no more than 1·5m (see also page 109).

Local tidal streams in the vicinity of the Shingles are not to be underestimated: at best there is peril of delay and loss of tide; at worst, with swell and a breaking sea, there is threat of loss of vessel. To the southeast side of the Shingles, there are overfalls to be encountered on flood tides. Less noticeable perturbations can be seen to the north on good ebbs.

With such powerful forces, it is not unexpected that the Shingles bank changes its aspect considerably as a result of the weather. After periods of settled conditions, banks can tend to show themselves even at high water, where there was none before; while tending equally to disappear after southwest gales.

Tidal streams
'The NE-going stream, which runs across the entrance to Poole Bay, divides as it approaches Needles Channel and runs ENE across Shingles, NE into Needles Channel, and E along the SW coast of Isle of Wight. The streams from the opposite direction meet off Needles Channel and run SW towards Durlston Head (50°36′N 1°57′W).

The streams in both directions run strongly across Shingles. At the entrance to Needles Channel the stream is nearly rectilinear; it runs mainly in the direction of the channel, attaining its greatest rate of up to 4·5 knots at Springs off Hurst Point; for details see tables on the charts.

On the W side of Needles Channel a set may be experienced away from, or towards, Shingles according to the direction of the stream. On the SE side of the channel the NE-going stream runs strongly. At the S end of the channel the stream runs strongly across The Bridge.'

Admiralty *Pilot*

The YBY cardinal marking the Bridge overfalls by the end of the Needles outcrop.

Yarmouth

The Needles to Yarmouth

After the Needles, the first place of interest is Alum Bay. It is formed by a deep indentation that lies between the Needles and Hatherwood Points. Its south face consists of high cliffs in that special white that is always identified with Dover, but it is the east face that is the legend here. It is a most pleasing place to anchor in clement weather, but there are shoals and drying rocks to be avoided, the best known of which are Five Fingers and the Long Rock. As the Admiralty *Pilot* says, 'There is much foul ground within the Bay.' Peter Bruce's book, *Solent Hazards* provides a useful photograph of some of the dangers, including the old pier posts. Admiralty Chart *2021* should be consulted.

The mysterious coloured layers that go to form the eye-catching feature of this bay were created on what was dry land before that strange other sea, known as the Anglo-French-Belgian Basin, part of which is, of course, the Channel, was formed. The Alum layers were put down in many different physical conditions, thus creating the Neapolitan effect. It is reckoned that there are as many as 29 separate strata. Some are vertical and some are horizontal. They were all created, as was most of Wight island, by the great eruption that brought about the Alps some 15 million years ago, a phenomenon now known as the Alpine Storm. The famous sands, which are bottled in weird containers for export to Lymington and other such foreign parts, come from ranges known as the Bagshot Sands and the Bracklesham Beds.

Nearby, there is a monument to Guglielmo Marconi, recording his famous wireless station of 1897. It was endearing to hear his widow talk of it and him with pride at the Radio Show of 1988.

Next comes Totland Bay, once a pilot boat station, but now that service has been moved to Lepe. It is a shallow-shelving bay with a pier below the hotel and towards Warden Point. It is not as popular as is Colwell Bay, a spot well worth a dinghy trip on a calm settled day. You should anchor well off since the ground is 'encumbered' with shoal and rocky ground. It is a pretty bay with good bathing, and for those who don't want to get their feet wet, there are treasures of fossils and shells galore ashore. It is a fashionable pastime for those with an eye for their individual beauty.

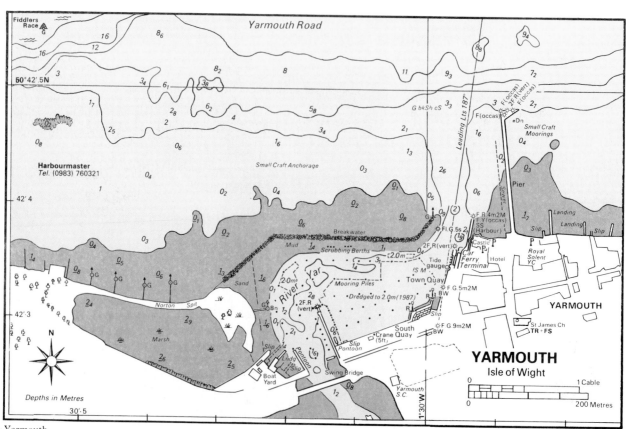

Yarmouth

Much closer to Yarmouth, I found the Admiralty chart not the only one to show two green buoys clearly marked present near the entrance. Checking up, in my usual obsessive manner, I was unable to find the second, the sewer outfall marker. I was later to discover that it had been removed over two years ago, but, nevertheless, it was still marked. The existing green buoy marks the infamous drying Black Rock, about 4 cables to the west of Yarmouth pier. The *Black Rock* buoy lies approximately 150 metres north of the shoal patch with its notorious hazard, and attendant circle of underwater, foul nasties,

This is how Frank Cowper described the approach area: 'West of Yarmouth about one-third of a mile is Black Rock. The reef nearly dries. A red conical buoy lies at the N. edge of th. dangerous shoal. It is not advisable to pass inside of the buoy. Just beyond Black Rock is a nasty bit of broken water, known locally as Fiddler's Race. There is a deep hole, and, with head winds, the sea breaks on ebb and flood violently over this spot. By keeping well out, it is easily avoided, however.'

The entrance

The actual entrance to Yarmouth is easy to spot and the leading marks are clearly visible in the harbour mouth. There are other marks (related to racing and all that) near the entrance, to seduce the careless, but considered inspection will show their true colours. The leading lights lead 188° through the harbour entrance clear of the ferry terminal. There are no racing marks on the west side of the pier; the only marks for racing purposes lying outside the Royal Solent Yacht Club to the east of the pier.

All that is needed is to open up the entrance between the jetty (to port) and the breakwater; that is, provided the red illuminated 'Harbour Full' notices (together with flags and lights) are not in operation. There are now two, since so many visitors in the past disregarded the previous single one. Yarmouth is even busier than it was, and on some of the more popular weekends of the year, it may be difficult to secure a choice berth if you arrive later than mid-afternoon on

Yarmouth Harbour delivers up most of its secrets when viewed from the ramparts of the old castle.

the Friday; although the harbour is usually only actually full on Saturday evenings. The Admiralty, in its usual cool manner states, 'The harbour is well protected and much used by yachts and pleasure craft; it has depths of 1·3m to 2·9m, and contains several rows of mooring piles. Berths are available for yachts up to 21m long.'

The chances are that one of the harbour staff will be jilling around just outside or inside to instruct on berthing. The harbourmaster and his staff are known (perhaps worldwide) for their quite amazing and energetic dedication: efficient, warm, welcoming, and apparently omnipresent. They can be outside to meet and greet (and also to ward off those who appear not to be able to read the 'full' notice) and inside to organise, instruct and help. They don't actually take your lines to the piles, but they do almost everything else – even suffering fools tolerantly if not gladly. During the season, they are tireless and peerless; no wonder they feel it necessary to do a Speedy Gonzales away from the harbour and its boats the minute their summer tour of duty is finished.

Perhaps the only serious risk in the harbour is in the vicinity of the busy ferry piers, where the wash from the powerful ferry props makes its presence felt for a good distance. In addition, Captain Nigel Hunt makes the following observation: 'I think it prudent to warn your readers of the strong ebb tide that flows out of the harbour entrance on big springs. Once clear of the harbour entrance they will of course encounter the main east/west tidal streams.'

YARMOUTH HARBOUR

Harbourmaster: Captain N. W. Hunt, The Quay, Yarmouth, Isle of Wight, PO41 0NT
☎ (0983) 760321

Berthing master's office at fuel berth alongside crane on the new quay.
☎ (0983) 760300

Mooring alongside South Quay
These berths will be exclusively for those boats taking fuel – using the crane or taking on fresh water and also at the harbourmaster's discretion for short periods by those boats wishing to embark heavy gear, stores and passengers, especially the angling boats embarking and disembarking their passengers daily. The quay to the west of the fuelling berth is reserved for loading and unloading only. The only exception being on busy Saturday evenings when it is necessary for the harbourmaster to use all available berths.

Dinghy park for use of boats moored in the harbour or quay and 3 concrete slipways in the harbour which may be used by the public (no charge).

Most visitors are arrayed and arranged by welcoming harbour staff in speedy launches – inside or outside the harbour, according to demand.

Speed limit

There is a speed limit of 4 knots over the ground in operation overall. This refers to the entrance, the pier approach, all the harbour and the River Yar.

Restrictions on mooring space

Every Saturday night from Easter to October the harbour is filled to capacity and on many occasions the harbourmaster has to turn away yachts from midday onwards. The enormous growth in yachting in the past few years has created a situation where Yarmouth harbour can no longer accommodate all those wishing to berth for Saturday nights. Entry to the harbour may be temporarily suspended on these and other occasions, when (a) by day a red flag is flown from the flagpole and (b) by night when a sign with the words 'Harbour Full' will be illuminated.

General

The original harbour was merely the estuary of the River Yar, described in an old document as 'the Eremue or Freshwater'. The present harbour is but 100 years old.

I met Captain Rose on the day his successor was being appointed, so was more than fortunate to get a full (if fast) run down on what had happened over the seven years since I had last been there, and an interpretation of future possibilities. The main change has been the building of the new jetty for the ferry – and the associated improvements along that quay wall. But as a neat reminder for those with short memories, the model for all the changes still lurks in the corridors of power.

The first piles you see after entering are now suitably red and green according to IALA standards. For many years, the 'direction of buoyage' was the wrong way in the harbour – a source of confusion to sophisticate and novice alike. Now, all the channels, avenues and lines of piles for mooring are all in a logical order and clear to understand. Mooring, fore and aft, on these piles can require very long warps, and you may be rafted with others up to six deep, so it is wise to be prepared.

Plans for the near future incorporate more water points, toilets, showers, and general quayside improvements. Longer term projects include the possibility of a brand new, extensive breakwater and a large marina-style development, all to seaward of the present harbour. Much of this is indeed to be welcomed, and it must be hoped that the new style will all be in addition to the old; for it would be sad if this last bulwark of old harbour times in the Solent were to go the way of all flesh, and entirely lose its character.

Many folk use their own dinghies to get ashore, but for those without dinghy or energy, there is the Sandhard Ferry, a service that operates only during the main summer season. It is regular and frequent, with its last return trip being suitably late for those with near midnight carousing habits. Dinghies can be left at the floating pontoon park or at the slipway. In 1988, tidying up was still going on after the building of the new bridge and the demolition of the old one.

Dinghies can also be left by the west landing which is fittingly known as Sandhard Jetty. It gives access to a pleasing shoreline walk along Norton Beach. Here, you will find small parties of fishermen with their all-night fires and their small paraffin lamps. There is also an area specially buoyed for swimming: no boating, fishing or windsurfing is permitted within the red-marked semicircle. An excellent idea upon which the board is to be congratulated – and which others will, all being well, take up enthusiastically. It is so much more life-enhancing to find an area specifically set aside for swimming than to be faced with red flags for danger, or large notices proclaiming their territorially inclined legends: 'Private Property, Keep Out, No Mooring, No Swimming'.

Yarmouth has all the facilities visiting yachtsmen need. There is the well known boatyard of Harold Hayes, manufacturers of that excellent gadget, Spurs, the antifouling line, net and weed cutter, for attaching to the propeller shaft. Their boatyard building by the Yar bridge was originally known as the Sand House, because of the flourishing trade that was conducted there: sand from Alum Bay for the glass works of Cheshire.

Yarmouth pilot cutters were well known. The last working survivor was the *Agenoria*, still on the go in 1905; but the best-known was the *Pallas*. She was the toast of Yarmouth in 1822 when she won a race against a Cowes crew. She became celebrated:

'Ye Cowes men, don't brag of your sailing,
Nor talk of the matches you've won.
Give up now your jeering and railing,
For your hour-glass of boasting is run.
Little Yarmouth has beat the big cow,
Her Pallas has shown the long trot;
While your lads were breeding a row
Hers flew away with the pot.'

Yarmouth tends always to be busy; seldom peaceful and hardly ever quiet.

The town

Yarmouth was known in Domesday as Eremud, the mouth of the River Ere, and this was later changed to Eremue. Whatever you think of the derivation, the name really sounds right and proper once you get to know the place. The town got its first charter from Baldwin de Redvers in 1135, and was famous as the HQ for King John for a time when he was gathering his fleet at Portsmouth, and he stayed again in 1214 on his way to Poitou. The place was a Rotten Borough (with no more than 9 and no less than 2 voters) and also the seat of the Captain (Governor) of the Island. It was twice burned by the French: in 1377 and in 1524.

Shopping is not entirely a disaster in Yarmouth, but it could be improved. Some establishments are especially worthy of one's attention and patronage. Jireh House, comprises XVII century tea rooms, and is a must for any student of human nature or lover of buns, baked potatoes, cakes and coffee breaks. The new Gossips restaurant, now occupying the Harbour Commissioners' old offices at the root of the pier, offers an excellent view of the Solent.

The traditional Corner Shop not only caters for a wide range of vulgar, common or garden needs, but also has a first-rate stock of esoteric foods; the chandlery combines the usual marine-type stores with a much wider range usually associated with ironmongers and clothiers; while the chemist and bookshop offer more than you might expect. Near the quay, there is a miniature studio. Known as the Studio on the Quay, it is run by Anne Toms and Wendy Franklin under this inspiring banner: 'To be part of the dynamic peace which is not a resting place between wars – but a life giving struggle to solve the continual crisis of human existence.'

Yarmouth's gateway to the only chance of solitude; the bridge between the harbour and the calmer waters of the river Yar.

The town hall (a modest building in quasi-baronesque) sits where the meat market used to be from 1271 until 1888. It was renovated in 1763. Upstairs is special, but on the ground floor you will frequently find stalls and raffles to tempt hoi polloi into supporting good causes.

The church of St James contains the amazing white marble statue of the one-time governor, Sir Robert Holmes. He was responsible for 'obtaining' gold from a Dutch vessel off the coast of Guinea. The first of these specially named coins were struck from this, and Dryden had this to say about the fellow: 'Holmes, the Achates of the General's fight, Who first bewitched our eyes with Guinea gold.'

The amazement attached to the statue is that it is supposed to have been originally worked for Louis XIV, but Holmes captured both sculpture and sculptor – and forced the poor artist into prostituting the commoner's head of Holmes onto the royal frame of Louis.

It must never be forgotten that while Yarmouth Isle of Wight is, on balance, a grand locale, it is not Great Yarmouth – that domain of bad experience and ill memory. While its harbour, facilities and staff put the other place in quite shameful shade, Yarmouth IOW, the town, does, however, have some features in common. If it doesn't quite share the Bloater Rota or the Rock Grock, it does have a propensity for the Kipper Tripper and the Kiss Me Quicker who appear in waves and droves to pour out of cars, buses, boats and ferries. The town is a place of great charm and some antiquity, marred by car queues and grot. It is a pity that its shopping amenities in general do not stay open for longer than they do; and it must be a minus mark that it has only one bank.

The English Heritage castle is worth a visit, and so is the close-by refurbished pier with its dedicated timbers and optimistic fishermen. The castle affords a splendid view of the harbour – especially for the comings and goings of maritime traffic. It is formed as a square with sides of nearly 100ft, with a sharply pointed bastion or flanker at the southeast corner. The north and west walls are open to the sea, while the other two were originally flanked by a 30ft-wide moat. It was continuously manned until 1875. In the 17th century, the moat was filled in. In 1667, Admiral Sir Robert Holmes, Governor of the Isle of Wight, built his home on it, which then became The George hotel in 1764. There is original oak in the staircase and some panelling, and visiting persons are permitted to see the room in which Charles II stayed as the guest of the Governor in 1671. Holmes captured New Amsterdam from the Dutch in 1644 and renamed it New York.

The River Yar

'Up the lazy river by the old mill stream ...' can certainly be sung for the Yar; but only those visitors who are prepared to go upstream by dinghy or along the banks by foot will be able to appreciate its joys of peace, quiet and wildlife.

At one time, visitors were permitted to take all craft through the bridge and upstream, but it seems they perpetrated such noise, such wash, such damage and such pollution that this is no longer permitted in what is, after all, not only an idyllic area, but also an SSSI. Captain Rose: 'It was really soul-destroying to see and hear them roaring around as if they were in some kind of fun fair; taking no notice at all of the speed limits or the requests to preserve wildlife. But the real end was the continuing pollution that would come down the river on the ebb: beer cans, crab shells, plastic bags, half-eaten pork pies – and worst of all, masses of sewage. So it was decided that enough was enough, and visitors' boats are no longer allowed through the bridge. It's sad, I know, and a great deprivation to those who would appreciate it with responsibility – but they are the ones who understand and don't kick up a fuss anyway. They are only too happy to row or walk away from it all and keep it as it should be. The others only have themselves to blame.'

So, take your tender (outboards are allowed) and head 'Up the lazy river by the old mill stream'. Certainly that could serve as a suitable theme song for the onetime Ere, now the Yar. Under the bridge and round the bend the aspect almost immediately changes and almost every prospect pleases. In spite of being so close to the road and quite a lot of building, the area already feels remote. First, the new, contemporary style building that is the headquarters of 'Y' the sailing club is to be seen on the port hand. Its modernity in miniature makes for a real contrast with the ancient buildings of the Royal Solent Yacht Club near the castle; itself even older, and styled by English Heritage as the 'latest of King Henry's castles', no mention of it being his last, but beautiful for all that.

Then come the piles, also to port, for the permanent berth holders. To starboard is the first creek, leading to the small community at Saltern Wood Quay. For the dinghy-less, it is fortunate that this place can be reached easily from the main harbour by crossing the main road at the new bridge and walking along the signposted creek. Boating services, including a sail loft, nestle side by side at the head of this almost remote creek, and alongside them is Puffin Fisheries: a fresh fish and crab dispensary, with a proprietor who is as much into wooden boats with big masts as he is into things piscine. His crabs and lobsters (live or cooked) are brill; and his brill is pretty good too! He is open nine till five Tuesday to Sunday, and runs a fish market in the town hall on Thursday mornings.

To port after that, along the bank from the harbour a few cables, or round the creek, is the old mill, now cared for by its fairly recent owner A. J. P. Taylor. Built in 1793, the mill was once the centre of a thriving business community devoted to exporting grain to the mainland. In those days, ships were able to sail right up Mill Creek and berth outside the front door. Today, it is accessible by dinghy, and is a splendid spot for the painter, photographer or lover of history.

Upstream, all signs of boating life are left behind. Soon, you are sharing the low banks and saltings with assorted wildlife. Occasionally you will catch a glimpse of human habitation; the secluded Kings Manor with its private jetty being one example. Going right to head of navigation, you get to Freshwater and almost reach the other side of the island; this river Yar nearly cuts Wight in two, in common with its namesake at Bembridge. There are some small signs of habitation by the tiny bridge, all apparently untouched for centuries. Nothing could be further from the hustle and bustle at Yarmouth. Even the cars on the road seem to have their exhausts muffled in respect.

The last word shall go to Alker Tripp: 'In the morning light the town was as primitive as ever, utterly remote from the twentieth century. The little breakwater was simple entirely, the old bridge was a bridge that men might have made when the castle walls – mossy and ancient now – were first built by the Tudor king. The whole scene basked in sunshine.

The hand of change has since been rather heavy, for the old bridge has gone already, and the harbour is to be dredged and modernised. The new bridge – though less acceptable than the old one is not unsightly. Under the bridge the tidal river leads to Freshwater, and is navigable at high water in the dinghy, with views that are everywhere a picture – the reed-bordered river, the copses, and the downs beyond. I have loitered up and down it at all hours, morning, noon, and night.'

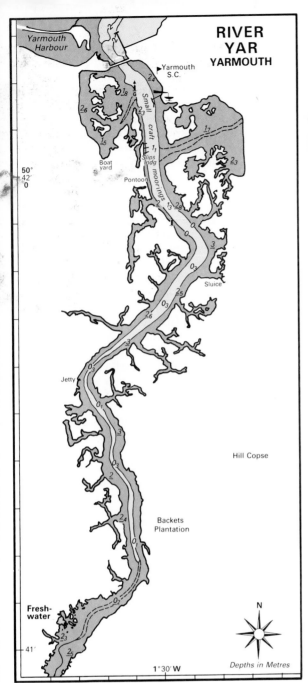

RIVER YAR
YARMOUTH

Yarmouth Harbour

Yarmouth S.C.

Small craft moorings

Slips
Ldg
Pontoon

Boat
yard

50°
42'
0

Sluice

Jetty

Hill Copse

Backets
Plantation

Fresh-
water

41'

1°30' W

N

Depths in Metres

Upriver from Yarmouth is a revelation to any visitor who knows only the town and harbour; the only rural haven for miles.

River Yar anchorage.

Newtown River

The run from Yarmouth to Newtown River is pleasant and free from hazards. You can cruise close inshore and take full advantage of the scenery, which has the modest Bouldnor Cliffs with their wooded slopes. On a first visiting approach it is best to stand off about half a mile and pick up the green buoy marking the Hamstead Ledge that extends some four cables from the shore to the west of the Point. There is also a close-in obstruction marked by an inshore dolphin.

By then, the prospect of Newtown will stand over you like an open invitation, with, rising directly above Newtown River, the high point of Hamstead. Down at sea level Hamstead Point itself heralds the entrance to the river.

Both the last leg of the approach and the whole of the entrance channel are straightforward. None of the buoys is large, but they are all in obvious positions and easy to spot when the waters are untroubled. However, they are neither substantial nor bright enough in their red and green to be easily identifiable when there is a lot of broken water about. It does no harm to remember that the whole entrance area shoals; the narrow channel running between Hamstead Point Flats to starboard and the Newtown Gravel Banks to port.

The leading marks on Fishhouse Point are a positive joy: clear, positive and unmistakable. (I have to disagree here with the Admiralty *Pilot* when it says they 'are not easily seen'.) Leading lines can sometimes be unnerving, taking you on what appears to be a disaster course. (The Deben is a good East Coast example, and the entrance to Berwick-on-Tweed, further north, is another with its dramatically off-putting doglegs.) But here, at Newtown, it is a pleasure to be able to line them up with confidence and feel, for once, reassured that not only is your course right, but it also looks and feels right.

A story is told here with affectionate relish of K. Adlard Coles (known in these creeks as 'K') who on one occasion over the years came in and proclaimed to the then harbourmaster, 'What have you been up to? You've moved the leading marks. What on earth did you want to do that for?' The immediate (apocryphal?) reply was: 'Why, Mr Coles, sir, we've put 'em where you said they were!'

The withies in the river are actually painted red and green all over, but often the weather has defeated the best efforts of men, maintenance, paint and brushes, and it is not always possible to identify the colour as such.

Strictly speaking, there is no harbourmaster as such for Newtown Harbour. The person employed by the National Trust is alluded to in their official publications as Berthing Master (BM), and the appointment is only part time. The Trust owns the 14 miles of riparian rights, and the whole area (about 300 acres) is administered and promoted as a protected area. The BM, a captivating Ken Abernethy, is himself much more bailiff-cum-naturalist and conservationist than an official administrator. In a BBC *Down Your Way* programme, he waxed eloquently, to Cliff Michelmore and Jean Metcalfe:

'You come through the second kissing gate (from the village) and the magic starts; and you can sit here for hours just looking, can't you. It's quiet. Listen, the birds; and the boats moving in and out. There's always something to see. There's always something to hear. And yet, in the winter, it can be so bleak; but yet again, beautiful.

The single file bridge through the meadow to the harbour and the boat house unnerves some of the ladies especially when they see the mud underneath, or on other occasions when they see the water lapping over the top.

The harbour is unique now on the South Coast. I can't think of any other harbour where you can just go in and drop your anchor in these sort of surroundings.

The tide can be quite speedy in the entrance. If you look at it you'll see that it is quite narrow; and this is one of the hazards of entering Newtown: knowing just which bias to give it to make the approach. We've got quite good leading marks, but if you start to meander slightly, well Hmm! It's deterred a lot of people in its time. They come up, look in and think "Oh No!" Mind you, as well, at a good bank holiday weekend, you can have 300 in; and it gets to be a bit of a game then. If you get a wind shift at two o'clock in the morning, everybody's up: Newtown Pyjama Party; and you have never seen anything quite like it. As a gentleman once remarked to me, "Don't ladies wear the strangest things to go to bed in your harbour!"

Initially I came here in the Navy. I was a diver, and we used to come down here and work on the moorings; and when I came back about 1960, I couldn't believe it. All of it used to be fields, with a herd of Frisians. In 1954, the Canvey Island floods were the big news, but this was just as big a disaster really, in its own way. But having said that, again now, it's gone back to being a marshland and we can look after it, protect it and it brings in birds like you wouldn't believe. It's magic isn't it? You can see sunsets over there, in the autumn, that beat the Caribbean.

In this harbour, you don't want someone coming in and demanding money wi' menaces, now do you? You want someone coming up, a bit cheerful, chat 'em up; then demand money wi' menaces!'

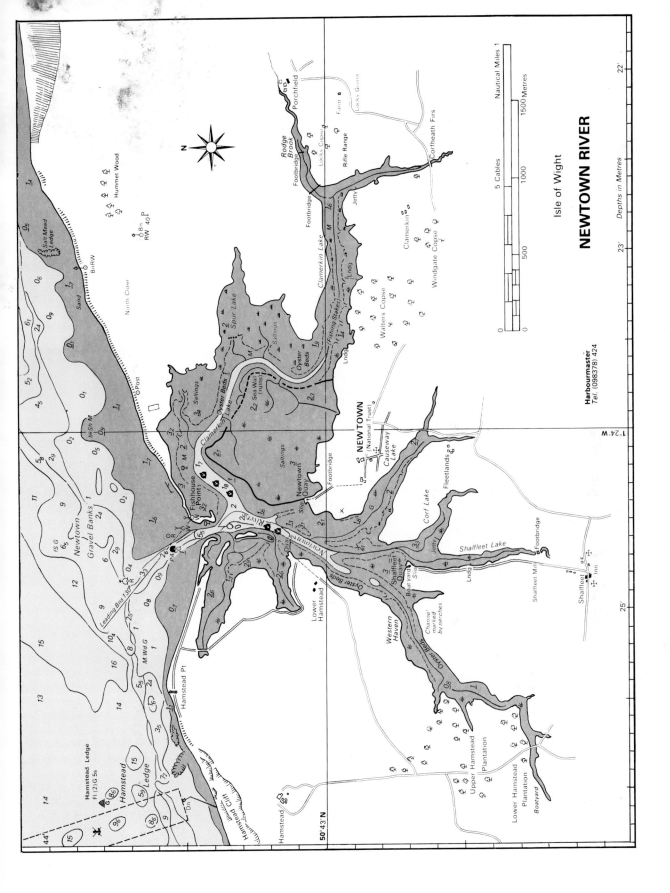

Isle of Wight

NEWTOWN RIVER

Harbourmaster
Tel (098378) 424

Some of the clearly delineated entrance markers for Newtown Creek ... where vessels come and go – or not, as the case may be.

Blandish him into telling you parts of his life story and that of Newtown and its river – and your stay will have been more than worth the Trust's modest charges. (Which, if you are a member, are substantially reduced.)

The Trust and the BM have recently been the recipients of a new dory, thanks to a local benefactor. What the BM would next like to see is the old sea wall put to rights, since, if attention is not paid to it in the near future, it will fall not only into dereliction but also into the soft mud of the river bed, thus creating channel, silting and navigation problems. In addition, there is a present danger of a breach at the entrance towards Hamstead Point, and if both should occur at the same time, it could be the end of Newtown as a navigable river – almost in one fell swoop.

The river is so attractive and comparatively unspoiled that she deserves every effort to keep her in the manner to which she was once accustomed – and now thoroughly deserves. It is difficult to imagine that during the Middle Ages this was a thriving harbour, and that only a couple of centuries ago, 500-ton vessels were using it commercially.

MOORINGS

The most important facts for a stranger to know about the moorings in the river are that (a) there are few of them and (b) those few, those happy few, are as attractive to visitors as are magnets to iron filings.

Visitors' mooring-buoy protocol in the river is as intriguing as it is unequivocal. If a buoy is vacant (meaning no boat, no dinghy and no notice proclaiming 'Back at noon') you may pick it up – even if it bears a vessel's name and is, therefore, to be deemed private. Generally, the BM will advise you if you are on a buoy whose owner is about to return soon; or, alternatively, he will arrange for a dinghy to appear on it at the psychological moment and thus fend off visitors.

On such private moorings, the rule is one vessel to one buoy. On the marked visitors' moorings (mainly nearest the entrance; that is, northerly in the Newtown River stretch itself) the rule is not only first come first served, but finders keepers. When you pick up a vacant visitors' buoy, then it is yours. Two vessels are permitted to each buoy, but the later arrival must obtain the permission of the visiting occupant. It seems that it is an etiquette that has been observed for some time, and Ken Abernethy is keen that the custom should not be observed in the breach. Here is the official stance:

THE NATIONAL TRUST,
NEWTOWN HARBOUR BYELAWS AND CODE OF PRACTICE

'The following arrangements for the management of Newtown Harbour have been arrived at after consultations with users and interested parties carried out in 1984 and 1985 and approved by the Isle of Wight Committee of the National Trust. Mooring and boomage facilities are provided subject to the byelaws of the National Trust and of South Wight Borough Council and in particular to the following code of practice.

Subject to public navigation rights access to the river is forbidden to vessels of a size and type likely (in the Trust's view) to be a source of danger or obstruction to others.

No anchoring or mooring is to take place above the mooring limits shown.

No mooring to or other interference with navigation marks is permitted.

Boat Owners are responsible for the safety and supervision of their craft at all times.

The National Trust reserves the right to move vessels or moorings at its own discretion at any time.

No rubbish or waste is to be emptied into the river.

No shooting or other interference with the wildlife of the estuary (which is a Nature Reserve) is to take place.

Fishing rights in the estuary are held by the Newtown Oyster Fishery Limited. Rod and line fishing is permitted only at the Company's discretion. Trawling or any interference with Oyster beds is not permitted.

No animals from abroad are to be brought ashore.

No access is permitted to the Eastern Spit during the breeding season for shore birds (April to September).

Camping on the shore is permitted only in the camp site at Hamstead. (Contact R. Few, Esq., Lower Hamstead Farm.)

Barbecues may be held only on the foreshore below the high tide line on the Western Spit or Hamstead Duver (outside the Harbour west of the entrance) and only if gas or charcoal braziers are used. (The reason for this is that a number of rare plants survive on the shingle above the tide lines and must not be damaged.)

The speed limit of 5 knots is to be strictly observed and no activity is to take place that may endanger or disturb other users of the Harbour, their craft or the wildlife of the Nature Reserve.

The Trust reserves the right to cancel any mooring agreement whether permanent or visitors if any of these rules or conditions are not complied with without refunding any part of the fees paid.

Moorings are only available between 1st April (or Easter if earlier) and the 15th November. At other times craft may anchor in the Harbour at their own risk but otherwise subject to the above regulations. A limited number of winter mud berths are available on request and at a charge.

Beaching, anchoring or use of moorings while re-fitting or repairing boats is permitted for emergency or running repairs only.

Moorings are available to visitors on a basis of first come first served. No bookings can be accepted.

Organised rallies should however not be contemplated without making prior arrangements with the Berthing Master to avoid clashing with other events or other problems.

Rafting of more than two vessels on a single mooring is not permitted. Rafting of two vessels is permitted only at the discretion of the Berthing Master, subject to the capacity of the mooring and prevailing or anticipated weather conditions, and not alongside craft that are subject to a seasonal mooring licence.

Riparian owners may moor a single dinghy off their property during the season with the agreement of the Trust and subject to a nominal payment.'

Anchorages

There are excellent anchorages in Newtown River. The first is one well suited to deeper draught vessels, and is found round the back of Fishhouse Point. It is an extremely popular spot, being easily accessible, close to the entrance and with good pools. The others are further 'inland', with less water, and consequently less crowded and quieter. They are further up into Clamerkin Lake from Fishhouse Point and by the junction of Western Haven and Causeway Lake, then into Shalfleet Lake and upstream towards Shalfleet Quay.

It is important not to anchor elsewhere in Newtown River for two reasons: (a) there are many delicate oyster beds that are now signposted with white on green boards; (b) in many stretches there are cables on the bottom that are seriously foul with the post-1939–45 war leavings and droppings of the RAF and Navy. After hostilities, some of the tackle was lifted with complete success; some was lifted but broke on the way up; some was only part lifted, and is now marked 'Foul Ground'; and some was completely overlooked. The upshot being that anchoring away from the permitted sites is hazardous in the extreme.

The mooring charges set by the National Trust for the river are not unreasonable: a 35ft boat uses one of the buoys for £6·00 and anchors for half that price.

Much of the murky past of some of Newtown's livelier and lovelier sons may be guessed at from the information procurable in the old town hall.

There are not many moorings available to visitors at Newtown, and any skipper lucky to obtain squatting rights is usually subjected to more than a few envious glances.

124

Newtown Quay

This is an extremely popular landing, for it is the only one that gives reasonable access to the old town. It is a small, quite unsophisticated quay that is dry for much of its life. Many people fail to get their calculations about the tide height right (or fail to make them at all) and get stranded. It is worth working out with some care, for the mud is a thick and powerful brew, and having to drag a dinghy, even an inflatable, over, through or actually in it, is not a task to be undertaken lightly.

Newtown

After landing at the quay, there is a pleasant walk through the marshes (fear not: over a singular wooden walkway) to the old settlement. First to catch the eye will be the cottages, then the church, and finally the town hall. The trim gardens and extremely well kept houses are particularly noticeable, making a stroll through the village a real delight. However, there is more: some of the cottage walls and fences carry small legends advertising fresh fruit and vegetables for sale. Not being able to resist the like, I knocked on the neatest garden door. On asking for a cabbage, I was escorted up the garden path by a true gent of the Isle of Wight school. He took me by the arm, pointed out a row of beautifully firm and plump specimens, and asked me to choose my weapon as it were. Not only was it inexpensive, but it was delicious to eat; and I had been entertained by half an hour's pleasing conversation while looking down at *Valcon* on her buoy from the high ground above. A real bonus of an experience!

In the vestibule of the church of the Holy Spirit, I came across an endearing handwritten notice pinned to the door: 'Please keep this door closed at all times lest birds fly in and die of thirst. Thank you.' No suggestion that the font might be kept filled with water – holy or otherwise. There is another more impressive notice: 'The Incorporated Church Building Society granted £50.00 AD 1970 towards repairing this church on condition that all the sittings are for the free use of the parishioners according to law.' Perhaps this refers to yet another meaning of the well known definition free house.

The National Trust is very active all around Newtown, and in particular is proud of the town hall connection. The following notes are taken from its informative leaflet.

'Newtown was the most ancient borough in the Isle of Wight. Its earlier name of Franchville (meaning a town holding its lands and tenements at a fixed rent, and free from obligation of performing any services to the Lord of the Manor except suit of court) indicates that it probably enjoyed municipal privileges before the Conquest.

Aymer de Valance, Bishop Elect of Winchester, who founded this "New Town" in 1256.

The "City Fathers" of the New Borough, which was variously known as Swainston, le Neuton or Franchville, consisted of about twenty-five burgesses whose only qualification was their ownership of borough land.

By the early fourteenth century, Newtown was a thriving community; some sixty families lived there, and in 1344 the borough was assessed at twice the value of Newport. The busy and important harbour was regarded as the safest in the Island, and as late as 1781 it could accommodate vessels of five hundred tons.

Newtown is said to have been sacked by the Danes in 1001, and certainly it suffered a number of attacks by the French at later dates, the most disastrous being in 1377 when much of the town was burnt.

By 1559 the town had lost its importance, much of its maritime trade had been taken by Newport, and a survey of that year stated that there was no longer a market, nor any good house standing.

In 1584, Queen Elizabeth gave parliamentary representation to the borough, perhaps in an attempt to revitalise it. In this she did not succeed, but nevertheless Newtown continued to elect two members of parliament during the next 250 years, among the most eminent being John Churchill, later first Duke of Marlborough (1768), and George Canning (1804), who became Foreign Secretary and Prime Minister.

In 1832, Newtown was declared a "Rotten Borough", and it was disenfranchised under the first Reform Act, bringing its political life to a close.

In 1835, a Government Commission reported that "not only does no burgess reside within the borough, but... it is not probable that there is an inhabitant capable of exercising any municipal function."

The town hall, being redundant, became a school, then a private house, and eventually an ivy-clad ruin. The annual fair, or "Newtown Randy", had ceased in 1781, and the next hundred years saw Newtown at its lowest ebb.

In 1933, a group of anonymous benefactors, calling themselves "Ferguson's Gang", came to the rescue of the derelict town hall, which they restored and presented, with an acre of land, to the National Trust. A few years later, several local residents formed the Newtown Trust, which, with limited resources but great patience, has slowly purchased much of the land of the old borough. Gradually the plots of the ancient town have been reassembled, like the pieces of a jigsaw, until now a large part of the village that had not subsequently been built upon has been acquired and handed to the National Trust.'

The town hall, which witnessed so many parliamentary elections, is now the only remaining monument to the past eminence of the borough. Built of brick with stone dressings, it stands on the foundations of an earlier building and was put up by public subscription, probably in 1699. The architect is unknown, but features such as the round-headed windows with bold keystones, the stone dressings and the interior panelling are characteristic of such a date. The stone walls and basement formed part of the previous building, while the Gothic fenestration and the four-columned Tuscan portico on the north front are additions that probably date from the late eighteenth century. One of the last acts of the old Corporation before it was dissolved was the restoration of the town hall in 1813, at a cost of £443.

After it was given to the National Trust in 1933, the town hall was used as a youth hostel until the outbreak of the Second World War, when the basement rooms made useful headquarters for the Civil Defence.

The earliest houses would have been built of wood, and thatched; there are few indications that stone was used, and there was at least one wooden house in the village late as 1880. The oldest remaining building is almost certainly the Noah's Ark (formerly the Franchville Arms) next to the town hall, so called because the ship on the inn sign over the door, reproduced from the borough seal, was thought by villagers to resemble an ark. This house is probably early eighteenth century, but may have replaced a much earlier one. Most of the present houses are shown on the map of 1768, but with one or two exceptions (notably Nobby's Cottage) were probably rebuilt during the nineteenth century. The New Vicarage, now Lamb Cottage, is known to have been built in 1847, shortly after the church itself was rebuilt.

Plans were made in 1656 to reclaim the main marsh from the sea by the construction of earth and clay banks, which are shown on the map of 1768, but it is doubtful whether the scheme was completed, and the marsh eventually reverted to the sea. The remains of the salterns (or saltings) can still be seen: great square, shallow pools, where the sea water was exposed to the sun and wind before being pumped up into large iron pans, in which it was boiled until the salt was crystallised. Although the salt industry is defunct, the ancient culture of oysters had been successfully revived, and a clam industry has also been set up. Clams thrown overboard from Atlantic liners have established themselves in Southampton Water, where the discharge from the Fawley Refinery keeps the water warm enough for them to breed; from there they are brought to Newtown Estuary, where they can grow to maturity in the clear water.

The National Trust now owns most of the estuary of Newtown River, which amounts to about fourteen miles in length throughout all its branches, and which includes Newtown and Shalfleet quays and four miles of the foreshore of the Solent. Some seventy acres of copse are also Trust property and the Isle of Wight Natural History and Archaeological Society in conjunction with the County Council has established a Nature Reserve over an area of three hundred acres, including much of the Trust's land.

'The anonymous "Ferguson's Gang" were generous and exciting benefactors to the National Trust, mainly during the 1930s. Repeated gifts, always in notes and coin, were delivered by a masked member of the Gang, whose colourful pseudonyms included Sister Agatha, the Nark, Red Biddy and the Bloody Bishop. A distinguished architect, known only as the Artichoke, restored the Town Hall before it was presented to the Trust. Other gifts were Shalford Mill, near Guildford; the remains of Steventon Priory in Oxfordshire; and Mayon & Trevescan Cliffs in Cornwall.'

The visitors' centre is a charmingly ramshackle grade one listed shack, run by local volunteers. It provides an informal and intriguing history and description of the area. I approached a congenial fork-and-spade person in the attached workshop: 'We're really closed, but if you sneak in while I'm not looking I won't know will I?' He joined me seconds later unable to resist giving me a conducted tour. In his amiable, ambling manner, he was most insistent that I should know this was the last resort of the red squirrel; and that nowhere in the vicinity were any chemicals or other additives used in the smallholdings.

His passion for things natural was not to be contained when we came to the butterfly case, 'Not one of these butterflies was caught alive or killed, they were all found dead in the area and then brought in.' At this juncture he hailed another person and insisted that she should take over: 'I'm the moth man really. She's the butterfly woman. Go on then; tell 'em about the butterflies.' And so she charmingly did.

The episode reminded me of the man I had met on the walk from the quay. I had been looking into the sun at a bird hovering. He joined me, so I said to him, 'Is it a cormorant or a heron?' His reply, in impeccable Brummigem, was 'I don't know about birds. I'm not birds. I'm flowers, me.'

However, it is a splendid spot for bird-watchers, being host to nearly 150 species of birds. In particular, the osprey can be seen in passage in spring and autumn.

Creekish Lakes

All the offshoots of the Newtown River (itself something of a euphemism, for it is no length at all) are somewhat misleadingly (but nevertheless quite prettily) called Lakes. This is in keeping with the Solent tradition that tends to designate all its small waters this way. It must immediately be asserted that they are idyllic for those who are interested in dinghy rowing, walking, and silently observing wildlife or sunsets.

According to Ken Abernethy, the sunsets over Hamstead High are the finest in the kingdom, better even than those to be found in the Caribbean; and the view from the top of the hill more than justifies a climb for it reveals all of Newtown and its river, laid out 'like a patient etherized upon a table'.

Clamerkin Lake, and the smaller associated Spur Lake (by Shepherds Hill and Lambsleaze) in spite of the sheep, the lively fish and the near immobile heron, this areas tends to be a bit on the bleak side, until you gain the head of navigation when the waters take you into a narrower creek that deserves the title 'verdant'.

Causeway Lake takes you past the soft underbelly of Newtown, giving an excellent view of some of the houses. It comes as something of a surprise to discover at the top of these mainly deserted waters that there is a road complete with bridge and vehicular traffic. Nearby is the camp of the National Boy Scout movement.

Shalfleet's name comes from two Saxon words: 'sceol' for shallow, and 'fleot' for creek; and it is just as shallow a creek now as it ever might have been back in those days. In Domesday, it is Seldeflet.

Shalfleet Lake is popular because of the nearby anchorage and the quay, where there is a boatyard with access for cars. Shoresides, there is a pleasant half-mile riverside walk (pilotage skills needed to avoid cow pats) which leads to the old mill at Shalfleet, with its old mill stream, its classic footbridges and a garden in which can be espied hugely exotic bushes and trees. The New Inn provides a meeting place for cruising regulars and is a magnet for anyone who comes into Newtown River. Although it has a reputation for good food and real ale, I suspect its main appeal is that it has become a ritualistic eating-out spot, a special treat for those who are at anchor at the entrance. However, you need to take care with the tides, or you will find to your discomfort that access can often be muddy and not always easy.

Shalfleet also advertises itself as possessing a village stores-cum-post-office (Eddy's Stores). It is an extraordinary mini-emporium, with a strangely assorted collection of goods for sale, most covered with the dust of ages: a quite hit-and-miss affair of this and that.

Years back, the village sold the church bells and gun for a wooden spire on their church, giving rise to 'Poor and simple Shalfleet people, Sold their bells to build a steeple.' The lake is navigable to the quay and just above on the top of the tide, but even at springs, it is hardly possible to get right up to the mill stream, even in an inflatable dinghy; thus confirming the validity of its Saxon name.

Western Haven must, however, be deemed to be the most pleasing of them all. Certainly it will be the most appealing for those whose hearts are imbued with the spirit of swallows and Amazons. With its many miniature creeks and diminutive near-lakes it affords the delights of unspoiled junior creeks and havens at their best. Small tenders with silent oars are what is wanted here, and there is hardly need for an anchor, since you can reach up and catch a bough from an overhanging canopy at any time. Towards the top of the lake, where there is an unexpected small bridge leading on to walled gardens and really secret waters, there is a farm with the delightful name of Pigeon Coo.

I find it extremely difficult to write about Newtown River and its creeks without appearing to exaggerate its qualities, so I will let another speak for me: 'K' himself, from his *Creeks and Harbours of the Solent*: 'There must be few yachtsmen who, after visiting Newtown for the first time, have not returned to it again year after year. The snug anchorage, the creeks winding silently through the marshes and the unspoiled countryside, combine to give the place a character of its own. Perhaps the finger prints of history linger on in some distant way to the present time.'

Cowes Harbour, the Medina and Newport

Directions

Provided you do not succumb to the temptation of cutting the corner too closely when quitting Newtown River, there is no hazard on the approach to the Medina from the west. Once clear of the entrance, there is plenty of fine scenery to contemplate on the shore. The wooded slopes and modest cliffs accompany you all the way to Gurnard Bay. There is also the measured distance from the beacons on Shepherds Hill to those in Thorness Bay, to help occupy the time.

Salt Mead and *Gurnard Ledge* green buoys are the ones to identify, although there is danger within a quarter of a mile of the shore. Soon, the *Gurnard* cardinal (BY) will show itself off Egypt Point, and this is where Cowes begins to take over the show.

From here on, the buoyage is clearly marked. The Prince Consort Shoal is no hindrance to leisure craft. The only shallow is the finger that reaches out easterly to the north off the point by Holy Trinity Church, and it is no problem. It is marked by the first (*No. 3*) green buoy. It is the traffic that is to be watched when entering, for Cowes is always busy – and from time to time it is hectic.

West Cowes

After Egypt Point, the dominating eminence of the castle begins to make its presence felt. It is the headquarters of the Royal Yacht Squadron – and all that stands for. Under royal patronage and with a privileged membership of about 400, it is a vestige, a totem and a relic all in one. It was founded in 1815 by Lord Grantham with 42 members. Members had to own a yacht of at least 10 tons, and, no doubt more importantly, to be of elevated social stature. Initially there were 25 cutters, 3 yawls, 5 schooners, 2 brigs and one full-rigged ship. The Earl of Yarborough was its first commodore. He had a yacht built in a similar style to the 20-gun corvette, *Falcon* (not *Valcon*), and started their amazing traditions of gunnery. At one time, the members had some 400 cannon privately owned between them. Rigid discipline, flag etiquette and a ritualistic approach to all things are mandatory.

Sir Thomas Lipton, the millionaire Scot, took up yachting and brought life back into the America's Cup with his yachts, all called *Shamrock*. In spite of his eminence, it was not until he was nearly 80 that he was elected a member. His grocery connections, (so disparaged by the Kaiser – of all people) had kept him out.

Members' vessels may fly the ensign of St George, and club members themselves may land at the stage in front of the castle. The notice says: 'Private landing place for members of the R.Y.S. and officers engaged on Her Majesty's Service.'

The famous clubhouse, the castle, together with its grounds and quasi conservatory, were leased from the government in 1856. The freehold, which brought with it what was left of one of Henry VII's forts, was bought in 1917. (Amazing who were thinking of property developments instead of Flanders Field. Quite clearly for some it was *Oh What A Lovely War!*). On the bastion are 21 guns from *Royal Adelaide* which are used for race signals – and, of course, for royal salutes.

In the 18th century, when Cowes was still at the height of its shipbuilding days, it was famous for fast smuggling luggers and revenue cutters, and also pilot cutters. It is ironic to note that the races started as a result of the need for speed felt by the revenue men and the even greater need felt by the smugglers. Typically, the aristocracy started laying bets on the good and bad alike as to who had the speediest craft, or the craftiest speed – for they are not the same.

Alker Tripp had some experiences with smackers of both kinds in Cowes:

'We finished our passage securely, but in complete ignominy. A Cowes smack, under motor power, came from the eastward within an hour, and her we hailed.

"Give us a pluck into the river?"

Now Cowes folk make no pretence of general altruism during Cowes week; the world is with them for a week only in every year, and they exact the uttermost – even from the most obscure hanger-on of the great occasion. The answer was obvious.

"What' you goin' to give us if we do?"

The boat slowed her engine as she circled round us; but I asked them what they wanted.

"Oh, we shan't charge you much; we'll do it very moderate. A couple of quid'll do it for you."

I had expected as much; but my reply – a brief injunction to "talk sense" – brought a reduced offer. "Say a quid, then", they shouted, and their tone was one of aggrieved generosity.

A 'must'; the first and foremost sight at Cowes has to be the prestigious castle headquarters of the Royal Yacht Squadron.

East may be east and West Cowes west, but the chain ferry ensures that the twain really do meet on a regular basis.

But I knew that the smack was going into Cowes in any case and not likely to leave the price of several drinks and some tobacco behind her. So I shrugged my shoulders and said that I was staying where I was.

"What will you give, then?" came the inquiry, now with a strong rasp and asperity about it.

Unashamed, I mentioned the sum of ten shillings, and the response was immediate. "Chuck us y'r rope over", they said. And thus, at tail of a grubby smack, we arrived among the rank and fashion of Cowes Week.'

The first recorded race was in 1788, and organised racing in members' yachts began in 1826. The word yacht was not however coined here, nor at that time; but came from Holland about the middle of the 17th century. The word was used to describe any very fast vessel, and came from 'jogt' or 'jogen' meaning 'to chase'. However, Keats would have it differently, for in a letter to Fanny Brawne, he writes, 'The Regent in his Yatch (I think they spell it) was anchored opposite ...'

In 1893, Frank Cowper had this to say about Regatta time: 'At Cowes generally it is not a difficult place to find a berth, but during regatta week obviously it is a matter requiring skill, patience, and much local knowledge.'

Upriver from East Cowes Marina is only a mite less busy than the similar reaches of the Hamble.

The Medina

The River Medina is a model reflection of its harbourmaster, Captain Henry Wrigley: it is well laid out at all times; and immaculately turned out when the occasion demands. It is efficient, proficient, sufficient and almost a law unto itself. It is also impeccably well mannered and expects you to do it the same honour.

Captain Henry (as he is affectionately known) is well aware of his responsibilities to the image of Cowes not only as the very rich man's Mecca and the aristocrat's playground, but also as the less rich man's refuge and the poor man's dream. 'The man I want to see still coming here is he with a wooden sailing cruiser, with his dinghy towed astern, ready to tuck in anywhere after a fortnight in the creeks and the bays. I hope we never lose that kind of man in Cowes, no matter how much we develop.'

He spoke in glowing terms of the marinas and boatyards on his patch, and defended their high charges, 'If indeed high is what they are. Cowes Harbour charges are probably still the cheapest in the Solent... and possibly for much farther afield than that.' He pointed out that the Crown Agents exact a costly rate of charges for the river bed, and that the local rates are deemed by some to be harsh, excessive and not at all good for business.

Ancasta Marina, which likes to refer to itself as 'The Heartbeat of Cowes' has great plans for expansion. At one time, the project was estimated at the £40 million mark; but, plans for the immediate future are more modest. They include moving the existing boatyard facilities to another site further up the Medina on the western side of the river, preferably as close to the existing site as possible. Developing the Ancasta Marina site as an hotel with associated yacht club open to all users of the marina. The hotel would incorporate conference facilities and be publicly accessible. In August 1988, the plans were to refurbish the marina and clear the boatyard site so that shoreside facilities could be brought up to the standard expected by the clientele when paying the current charges. Completions are due in time for the 1989 season.

Those are all plans. The following information is definite and is promulgated by the Harbourmaster's office:

COWES HARBOUR

Harbourmaster Captain H. N. J. Wrigley, Old Town Quay, Cowes.
☎ Isle of Wight (0983) 293952

VHF Communications
Call sign *Cowes Harbour Radio*, Channel 16, listening normal office hours and peak weekends. Usual working frequencies. Calls will be received by either office or Cowes Harbour launches, or separate call sign, *Folly Harbour Launch*.

Navigational information
All vessels enter Cowes Harbour by the main channel. Port-hand entrance fairway buoy red can marked *No. 4* Q.R.5M. *No. 8* fairway buoy is Fl(2)5s1M. Starboard-hand entrance buoy green conical marked *No. 3*. The main fairway is shown on relevant charts by pecked black lines. Visiting yachts are cautioned to remain in this channel unless proceeding direct to a particular mooring as instructed.

As from November 1988, six unlit yellow cylindrical buoys will be positioned in Cowes Roads, south of the latitude through the Trinity House mooring buoy and to the east of *No. 4* buoy. Such unlit yellow buoys are required to mark the seasonal yacht ground mooring chains on the eastern and western extremities. Mariners are advised, when entering or leaving Cowes Harbour between sunset and sunrise, to remain within the fairway approaches as shown and defined on Admiralty chart *2793*.

As from September 1988, when hydrofoils are underway within the restricted speed limit area, they will display, below the Rule 23(a) white light, an all round flashing yellow light, visible for two miles. This does not bestow any implied right of way with regard to this vessel over others.

Mariners in charge of small craft navigating the fairway approaches are advised as follows:

1. To maintain a proper lookout, which includes lookout astern.
2. To keep as near as practicable to the starboard outer limit of the fairway when proceeding along the fairway.
3. Not to impede the passage of a vessel which can only safely navigate in the fairway, which includes the present regular service of the hydrofoils.
4. Not to cross the fairway, if this impedes the passage of a vessel that can only navigate within the fairway.

The general depths vary from 9ft to 17ft. The minimum low water in the main channel is recorded at 9ft MLWS level. The port-hand side of the channel is marked with port-hand buoys *No. 6* and *No. 8*.

From *No. 8* buoy, the deep water remains mid-channel following the course to the Floating Bridge Ferry. Past the Floating Bridge Ferry moorings are found on either side of the fairway. Thence area between pile-mooring trots and the heavy commercial mooring buoys, denotes safe navigable waters. From Kingston Power Station shape course to Medham light beacon, thence main channel to Folly is close to moorings which lie on the starboard side of such channel. Yachts with draught exceeding 5ft should proceed with caution at low water from Kingston power station to Folly Reach, keeping to main channel.

General

Within the main harbour to the eastward of the main fairway, the area is used for individual swinging moorings. Mariners are advised that sailing through this area can be quite hazardous, as full appreciation of tidal sets is necessary to avoid being set on to moored yachts. The use of anchors in this area is prohibited due to the numerous ground chains required for moorings.

Visitors' moorings

Four large temporary visitors' moorings are situated off the Parade, on the starboard-hand side just past the Royal Yacht Squadron. A large notice is affixed to the Watch House Pile Beacon giving further directions to permanent visitors' moorings. These are situated on the starboard-hand side of the fairway to the south. Local marinas welcome visiting yachts.

North of Thetis Wharf (west side) there is a public pontoon landing, visitors are welcome to moor short stay or overnight.

Also there are pontoon berths opposite the Folly Inn.

To the south of the floating bridge there are pile mooring berths to suit all sizes of yachts on the port and starboard-hand sides of the main-channel; each pile berth is labelled 'For Visitors Use'. Public pile moorings are also available off Folly Reach.

Yachtsmen requiring an individual swinging mooring for a limited period should contact the harbourmaster or his assistant.

Visitors to Cowes who find it necessary to leave their yachts for an indefinite period can, on application to the harbourmaster, make arrangements for their yachts to be under surveillance of the harbourmaster and his staff during their absence. The harbourmaster invites visitors to leave small items of equipment in his yard in lock-up storage for a short period of time free of charge.

Prohibited anchorage

Attention is drawn to the prohibited anchorage areas inside the harbour, Floating Bridge and the area enclosed by the notice boards by the Power Station. It can always be assumed that where heavy moorings are present in the river, inevitably there will be large ground chains stretching across the main fairway.

Public landings and slipways
East Cowes
1. Medina slipway just north of Westland Aerospace and in front of the barracks.
2. White Hart slip, next to the Red Funnel Steamer landing.
3. Old Ferryboat slip, just south of Trinity Wharf.

West Cowes
4. Whitegates pontoon for dinghy landing, up river by T. S. Osborne (Cowes Sea Cadets) with hard for hauling out dinghies by the Cowes Youth Club.
5. Town Quay slipway between Spencers, Thetis Wharf and Shepards Wharf.
6. Old Town Quay slipway south of Fountain Pontoon.
7. Fountain Pontoon, south side only.
8. Sun slip, by the Midland Bank.
9. Market slip, by the post office.
10. Watch House slip, by the Customs Water Guard, giving access to the parade.
11. Medina steps, the next steps on the Parade.
12. Victoria steps, Parade.
13. Royal London steps, used by the Royal London Yacht Club.
14. Gloster steps, next to the Royal London steps.
15. Royal Corinthian Yacht Club slipway, used by the R.C.Y.C.
16. Gurnard Bay, slipway at end of Shore Road, near Gurnard Sailing Club.
17. Old Town Quay, scrubbing off hard, suitable for vessels 5½ft on spring tides. Free of charge.

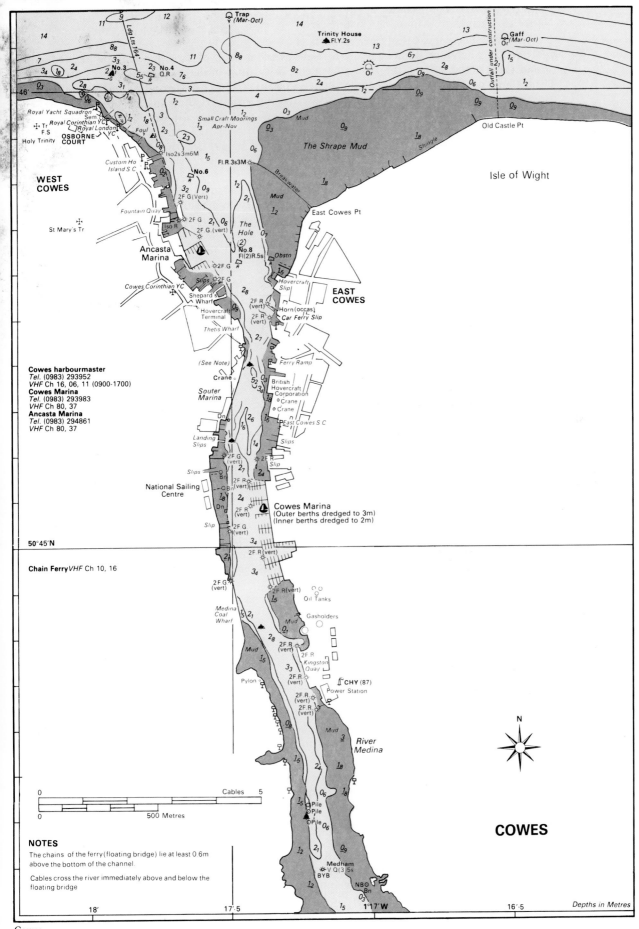

Trap
(Mar-Oct)

Trinity House
Fl.Y.2s

Gaff
(Mar-Oct)

Or

Outfall under construction

Old Castle Pt

The Shrape Mud

Shingle

Mud

Royal Yacht Squadron
Royal Corinthian YC
Royal London
YC
Holy Trinity
OSBORNE
COURT

WEST
COWES

Custom Ho
Island S.C.

Mud

East Cowes Pt

Isle of Wight

Small Craft Moorings
Apr-Nov

No.3
Q.R

No.4
Q.R

Iso2s 3m 6M

Fl.R.3s3M

No.6

St Mary's Tr

2F G(Vert)

2F G

2F G (vert)

Ancasta
Marina

Iso R

The
Hole
(2)
No.8
Fl(2)R.5s

Mud

Breakwater

Cowes Corinthian YC

Shepard's
Wharf
Hovercraft
Terminal
Thetis Wharf

2F G

2F G

Hovercraft
Slip

EAST
COWES

2F R
(vert)
Horn (occas)
2F R
(vert)
Car Ferry Slip

Cowes harbourmaster
Tel. (0983) 293952
VHF Ch 16, 06, 11 (0900-1700)
Cowes Marina
Tel. (0983) 293983
VHF Ch 80, 37
Ancasta Marina
Tel. (0983) 294861
VHF Ch 80, 37

(See Note)
Crane

Souter
Marina

Ferry Ramp

British
Hovercraft
Corporation
Crane
Crane
East Cowes S C

Dn

Slips

Landing
Slips

2F G
(vert)

Slip

National Sailing
Centre

Slips
Bn
Bn (vert)

Dn

2F R
(vert)

2F R
(vert)

Cowes Marina
(Outer berths dredged to 3m)
(Inner berths dredged to 2m)

Slip

2F G
(vert)

50°45'N

2F R (vert)

Chain Ferry VHF Ch 10, 16

2F G
(vert)

2F R(vert)

Oil Tanks

Medina
Coal
Wharf

Mud

Gasholders

2F.R.
(vert)

2F.R.
Kingston Quay
2F.R.
(vert)

Mud

Pylon

CHY (87)
Power Station

2F.R.
(vert)
2F.R.
(vert)

Mud

River
Medina

N

0   Cables   5

0   500 Metres

COWES

Pile
Pile
Pile

NOTES

The chains of the ferry (floating bridge) lie at least 0.6m
above the bottom of the channel.

Cables cross the river immediately above and below the
floating bridge

Medham
V Q(3) 5s
BYB

NBO
Bn

Depths in Metres

18'   17'·5   1°17'W   16'·5

Cowes

133

Notice to Mariners ref. Floating Chain Ferry

1. The Chain Ferry gives way to river traffic.
2. The Chain Ferry shall show at the fore end (the fore end of the ferry shall be defined as the end nearest the side of the river to which the floating bridge is proceeding) by day and by night when underway a fixed amber light so positioned to be visible all round.
3. In fog, or any other condition similarly restricting visibility, the Chain Ferry shall sound two prolonged blasts on a whistle or portable fog-horn, at intervals of one minute.

Note

(a) It is desired to stress the fact that the exhibition of signals does not grant or imply a right of way for the floating bridge. The signals are instituted solely for the benefit of vessels and craft in the vicinity.
(b) Mariners are advised to keep a sharp look-out for the small pleasure craft that are liable to cross the path of the Chain Ferry when under way, either ahead or astern of its track.
(c) Nothing in this Notice in any way diminishes the responsibility of the owner or persons in charge of all vessels to take all necessary action in order to avoid collision.
(d) VHF Radio Communications are fitted (listening and working frequency Channel 10) for benefit of commercial vessels and very large recreational craft to give warning to Chain Ferry of their time of passage.

Floating Bridge times
From Cowes
First Bridge 0530 (Mon. to Sat.), 0700 (Sun.); Last Bridge 2320, then 0010.
From East Cowes
First Bridge 0535 (Mon. to Sat.), 0705 (Sun.); Last Bridge 2315, then 2400.
Between the above times the bridge runs at frequent intervals, Tide, Weather and Navigation permitting.

I owe it to the skippers of the Floating Bridge Ferry to report that they are amongst the most co-operative professionals I have encountered: their consideration of the ways of yachts and yachtsmen is exemplary. The ferry shows a yellow light up top forward when it is under way.

However, let it not be thought that they are the only commercial skippers who show great tolerance to yachtsmen. The Red Funnel line and the visiting coasters all seem to be crewed by men who are ready to extend to leisure boaters a patience and courtesy well beyond the call of duty.

The area around the ferry is one that calls for special care because of its erratic eddies, streams and currents. In general the full sweep of a Medina ebb is a force to be reckoned with; but in particular the tide rip by the floating bridge is to be handled with intelligence and respect.

There is another aspect to the river's action: while the Edwardian Swells may have gone, the over-riding swell remains; and not only by the entrance or in the first marina – but much farther up the river than one would expect.

The town

Many are those who have disputed the derivation of the name Cowes. As far back as 1414, the Blacke Book of Southampton refers to 'Est Cowe et West Cowe', and the Earl of Southampton, in a report to Thomas Cromwell, mentions the 'ii Cowes'. In the State papers of 1512, the anchorage is called, 'ye Cowe – betwixt ye Isle of Wight and England.' In addition, the diarist Leland writes, 'There be two new castles set up and furnished at the mouth of Newport, that is the only haven in Wight to be spoken of. That that is set up at the east side of the haven is called the East Cow and that that is set up at the west side is called the West Cow and is the biggest castle of the two.' The reference is to the two blockhouses or forts built by Henry VIII in 1539.

> 'The Two great Cows that in loud thunder roar,
> This on the eastern, that on the western shore,
> Where Newport enters stately Wight.'

Whatever the derivation, nothing stands in the way of the old punning comment, 'The cream of true pleasure flows freely from Cowes.' Historically, it was sound, with ships of war being built there in the reign of Elizabeth I; a business that continued until the Second World War.

Meanwhile, back in the present century, the business of shopping leaves something to be desired with Gateways having a near monopoly in the super-grocery-market stakes. Harbour Supplies are worth the longer trip up the hill, to the north. In common with The Wine Shop (by East Cowes Marina) and many other establishments on the island, they carry a really wide range of foreign beers – a near worldwide selection. True, some of them are greatly over-rated and equally over-priced, but they are interesting and different.

Back in the main street, there is a real butcher who has supplies of authentic pork pies on Thursdays, and makes his own spiced belly pork and beef. Nearby, there is another purveyor who is worth searching out: fresh by fish and fresh by nature, he is a monger of many piscine goodies – as well as many a snapper catch answer.

In the main drag, Cowes is frenetic: if it is not being weakened by the annual week; tripped up by the hourly and daily trippers; it is in danger of being enveloped by the developers. However, up the various side roads, is to be discovered an entirely different experience. The atmosphere changes instantly, thanks to the architecture in the back streets undergoing a sea-change into a 'yuppy-to-with-it' style. House refurbishment goes on apace, and many of the older properties are being renovated in a splendid manner.

Any skipper with a love of old wooden boats (renovated or otherwise) will want to pay a visit to the diminutive office of Wallace Clark Ltd, 70 High Street. A look in the window tells most, but for all, you need to step inside. A word from Wally (I have never heard him referred to as Wallace, Mr Clark or anything in anyway formal) brings the past winging back and you can feel the spirit of Maurice Griffiths hanging in the air as the master talks of this or that classic (or just old) wooden boat. I was privileged when he took me by the elbow up and down the high street from his own premises to show off with pride the number of shops that still possess their original brass window frames. Sadly much of the brasswork is now (and probably has been for decades) painted over in some strange and often unattractive colours, but the opportunities remain for those who wish to refurbish and conserve.

Close by, is Prospect House, and the Max Aitken Museum with its fascinating collection of maritime memorabilia; the Harbour Lights hostelry; and the house in which used to live the light of Cowes himself, Uffa Fox.

Another house worth a nod is situate at the other end of the town, in Birmingham Road. It is where Dr Arnold of Rugby fame was born to a father who was the town's Collector of Customs. The house needs some upkeep other than the red plaque noting the birth. Nearby is the only laundrette.

East Cowes

Not far up the river, on the other side and across the tracks as it were, the first major berthing attraction is the marina at East Cowes, where another £40-million development scheme is in a pipeline. In August 1988, the East Cowes Marina was still what it had been for 50 years or more: an informal family affair, with a rustic flavour and views of the cemetery; a truly rural relief from the razzmatazz of fun times in West Cowes. But time marches on, and as soon as the owner finally clinches a deal that is to his taste and financial expectations, no doubt the proposed changes and developments, for which planning permission has already been granted, will be realised.

The nearly ancient monument of the marina office is due for demolition. Immensely sad this, for it is an excellent piece of Bauhaus-cum-Bexley design from the late 1930s, deserving a preservation order and ordered preservation. The equally neat and idiosyncratic floating bar is available for sustenance.

For those who want to get from here to there (usually east is east meeting up with what has gone west) there is a dory-type ferryboat based in the upstream marina bay, that whistles about from marina to marina. The skipper is to be contacted either at Pontoon 'A' or over VHF on Channel 10.

Shoresides, there is a small shop with modest supplies on the presently open and exposed landscape site. Not far away is the mini-centre of East Cowes, with the ferries, the floating bridge, and a good selection of pubs and clubs. However, there are only two banks (with Lloyds open only from 10–12 Monday to Friday), and, once again, Gateways heads the shopping scene, but with a new Spar not 25 metres away. In fact, for the yachtsman, shopping is actually better nearer to the marina. The local 'open all hours' corner shop is well above average; and The Wine Shop, up the small hill, has a splendid range of special beers as well as the usual off-licence liquids. It also has an intelligent and informed proprietor.

Nearby, and easily accessible in no time at all by grace and favour of the Southern Vectis bus services, are Osborne House, the associated vineyard and the metropolis of Newport.

Osborne is Palladian in style and was designed by Thomas Cubitt and the Prince Consort – and one is tempted to wonder how much design the former was permitted. It was completed in 1846. The Durbar (a minor miracle of teak), the Antler (a major nightmare of dead stags royally shot), the Billiard, and the Dining Rooms, together with the private apartments are open to visitors. Just as Victoria kept Albert's rooms as they were after his death (even to the macabre rituals of laying out hot water and a clean night shirt) so have all these been kept as Victoria left them in January 22, 1901.

The canny queen made her servant, Abdul, her close adviser on all things Indian; providing him with a bungalow near the house, and apparently being not entirely unamused at his harem, which he described as 'my aunts'. Swiss Cottage is nearby: an 1853 example of a glorified doll's house built for the royal offsprings' model farm where legend has it they studied the theory and practice of domestic and rural economy. Also in evidence are other equally esoteric edifices: their museum and the Victoria & Albert Almshouses for Royal Pensioners.

The church of St Mildred at neighbouring Whippingham, was 'designed' by consort Albert. One incisive appreciation of his work described it as 'both ordinary and pretentious'. Perhaps our own dear prince will do better. Also close by are the Barton Manor gardens and vineyard – also under Victoria's spell. Situate at Whippingham, they consist of 20 acres of gardens originally laid out by that lady and her consort, and later extended by Edward VII. There is the magic water garden (even more magical when it was the skating rink of the royals), the scented secret garden, Italian marble fountain and the eerie Cork and Ilex plantation. Perhaps of more sparkling interest are the English vineyard and winery – with wines for sale by the glass or bottle. Opposite the church, on the other side of the river, is the road to Albany, Camp Hill and Parkhurst prisons.

When entering or exiting the marina, it is worth noting that if you are doing so against a powerful Medina ebb, you can have your work cut out, for it is easy to get pinned against some of the outer pontoons. A little forethought and extra care in boat handling will pay dividends.

Moving upriver again, the spit on the east bank just above East Cowes Marina dries far out – almost to the centre of the river. Red can buoys have been laid by Captain Henry Wrigley for local navigational needs, but they do not appear on the charts – Admiralty or otherwise. With or without charts, navigating up river at low water will almost certainly take you aground sooner or later if your draught is much more than a metre.

Folly Reach

Most people going upstream of Cowes Marina do so for only one purpose: to visit the the Folly Inn, the classic calling station on the river. The official harbourmaster's notes are as follows:

'A most delightful quiet stretch of the Medina River is found in the Folly Reach. Many pontoon moorings are available to visiting yachtsmen on the pile trots. Vessels with a draft up to 5ft. can navigate to these moorings on ordinary low water conditions. Larger vessels with a draft up to 8ft. will find heavy moorings in Medham Bay, which is to the north of the mooring lines in the Folly Reach. There is a pontoon landing Pier for dinghies. (The Folly Pontoon, that dries at low water springs, has a small water tap.)

Visitors requiring additional mooring information and any other assistance, should contact Mr. L. A. Cundall at the Folly Harbour Office (☎ (0983) 295722 or Channel 16 VHF (Call Sign "Folly Launch" then to Channel 6), who is acting in the interests of both Cowes and Newport Harbour Authorities for the benefit of visiting yachtsmen, or contact the Cowes Harbour Master. Cradles for hauling out boats of up to 35ft. and 5ft.6in. draft are available together with a High Pressure Hose on application to the Folly Harbour Office. In addition, visitors may leave their yachts on the moorings to the direction of Mr. L. A. Cundall or the Cowes Harbour Master, who will also arrange a "caretaker" service to look after the yachts should the owner or crew be obliged to leave it for an indefinite period. Winter laying-up berths (afloat between piles) are also arranged at most reasonable terms – contact Cowes Harbour Master. Fresh water is available at the end of the pontoon landing. Three minutes walk from the landing stage is Medina Park offering a fully stocked supermarket and off-licence and a bottled gas service.'

The Folly Pontoon is much used as a landing stage for dinghies. It is also extremely popular with larger craft with larger crews in search of victuals and spirituous liquors. It is worth noting that the said pontoon dries at low water springs, even though it has a small water tap.

The Folly has a long history. In the 1700s a large wooden barge was washed up onto the beach and abandoned. There are several theories, the most popular of which is that it was the seagoing barge *Folly* which sailed between England and the East Indies. Another theory is that it was *La Follie*, a French barge. Shortly after this someone moved onto it and started selling beer and rum to the mariners travelling to Newport and to the local inhabitants. The first mention of it as a building was in 1792 and over the years it has been built upon and added to. A piece of the original timber from the hull is on display in the bar, and parts of the original deck and hatches still exist in the roof. Also well established these days is the Folly Regatta:

'The First Folly Regatta was held on Saturday, 20th September 1913, under the patronage of Rev. Canon Smith (Rector of Whippingham), Sir R. Chatfield Clarke JP., Messrs. F.

Templeman Mew JP., N. Harvey, T. Sopwith, H. R. Buster, T. Roach, N. H. Grace, R. H. Grace and the Shell Motor Spirit Co.. Croucher Ltd. of Newport generously loaned their motor barge *Tally Ho* as a committee boat. Additional events included a duck hunt, walking the greasy pole, a ladies tug-of-war – married versus single (the latter won) and a treacle bun eating competition for schoolboys.' Uffa Fox recollected: 'Our little gang thought it sensible to revive the old Folly Regatta that had ceased to function many years ago. Therefore at six in the evening, opening time, there were twenty-three of us on the doorstep. We knocked, and were welcomed in by the Landlord of The Folly Inn, Bob Savage. We had all been great friends for many years and knew each others' hearts and minds, so it was a friendly gathering.

At the outset, Lennie Mew, the brewer, proposed that I became the first President because of my knowledge of sailing, seamanship, rowing and because I owned a house with grounds stretching a quarter of a mile along the Regatta course. All were in favour. But, before accepting I said that there were things I would like them to listen to and if they were in favour of these three things, I would be President. So all was silent.

One – we formed a large committee of thirty people composed of ten small committees, with three men on each, a Chairman, Secretary and a Treasurer. Each committee dealt with one aspect of the Regatta. Each committee would have full power to act and spend money in its own province. There would be a Sailing, Rowing, Swimming, Shore Sports committees and an Entertainment and Finance Committee, and so on. I, as President, could be called on to any committee that required me for advice, but not to vote. We all agreed that this was fun and sensible.

Two – as we could not start a regatta without money, each of us would put a guinea in the funds. All agreed, and did this there and then.

Three – that we all drank a pint. This was joyfully agreed, so I ordered twenty-three pints of bitter beer and we soon wrapped ourselves round our first pint and felt better for it.

As Chairman and President, I had a simple and direct approach to every problem, and every time a man suggested something new I would say "right, you are the Chairman of this, all you have to do is collect a Secretary and Treasurer to form your committee and proceed full speed with this part of the Regatta".

As the evening proceeded all twenty-three chaps stood a round of pints. By the end of the evening we were very mellow, and felt that if we tilted our heads slightly sideways, beer would run out of our ears. This was the only occasion on which I knew how many pints I had drunk.

Very late that evening, Captain George Barton, the HM of Cowes, said "I suggest we have fireworks". "George, you are right in. You are the Chairman of the Committee, proceed with full speed, spend what money you think sensible." George thought better of it, when he realised that he had all the work to do in connection with the fireworks, so we never did have any. This system of mine of allotting the job to anyone who suggested it, eliminated a great deal of idle chatter, for all there knew that once they suggested something they should be running it for all the years to come. It was a happy and joyful evening, and all of us enjoyed every moment of it. We arranged a regatta date to suit the tide and to avoid conflict with other regattas. All the various committees were formed and the skeleton plan of the Regatta set out so well that there was no need to change any details afterwards.

We laughed until we ached. Finally we left The Folly Inn, but not all of us for home, as some of us by this time had reached the mood where we wanted to continue the fun, so we went to Leonard Mew's house in Crocker Street, Newport, a part of The Royal Brewery. We continued laughing, drinking and talking until about five o'clock in the morning, and then wended our way home to roost. As can well be imagined, none of us felt very strong the following day through having so little sleep. This meeting, the first, set the pattern of the Regatta Committee Meetings, and ever since they have been joyous occasions.

The following day, Alec Purdey, several times Mayor of Newport, telephoned me. "Uffa, soon Newport is holding its carnival and I think we should put a tableau in the carnival." "Alec, you are the Chairman of the Entertainment Committee and a tableau is entertainment so I suggest you contact Lenny Mew, the brewer. See if you can borrow a brewer's dray and horses, set up your tableau on this, and you three on the Entertainment Committee form the main piece of the tableau. If you cannot get a dray from the brewery, you of course have full power to spend money if you must hire one."

Alec had the brewer's dray and three men on the Entertainment Committee but, anxious and puzzled, asked for ideas and received many good suggestions.

Many events were just sheer fun. In one a tub of beer was tied up on a pole, the boats to row and race to this. The first to get the tub in his boat won it. The innocent thought that they only had to win the rowing part and arrive first to get the barrel, but it was well and truly lashed. Before the early swift innocent rowers could untie it, the rest had arrived. We knew that before it came down, every boat in the race would be on the spot, jostling and bustling each other about long before the beer came down.

Soon the river was full of sunken boats, swimming men, oars and paddles floating all over the place, 'till finally all in the race swam ashore with the barrel between them, and shared it out amongst themselves.'

The Folly Regatta Committee is still run in much the same way today, members still have to be very careful and think before they air any ideas, as the motto of the Folly Regatta today is the same as it was then ... 'you says it, you does it.' (Pronounced 'dues it'!)

A few hundred yards up the road (round the bend and in the caravan site) is a seven-days-a-week shop with attached telephone (obvious) and nearby post box (nearly hidden in the wall). The shop is an excellent example of a place with a place for everything and everything in its place. They have an unexpectedly wide range of goods and goodies.

The harbourmaster referred to above as Mr. L. A. Cundall is in fact best known to all Folly fans as Alan. He first started collecting dues from a sailing dinghy, and this has been his patch for 25 years. Talking to him will convince you that there is hardly a boat on the water, a ripple on the surface of the water, or a hump or hole in the river bed that he does not know intimately. There are those who have the gift of the gab; there are those who will give you the Old Barnacle Blarney; and then there are a few like Alan, who have really kissed the Blarney Stone, who really know what's what, and who will down the real thing (Uisgebeatha, the Water of Life, not the Medina) to prove it.

All the river moorings are laid to chain, and all the gear is lifted and checked annually. So, it is important not to anchor anywhere in their vicinity, since fouling is more than likely, and the chain is of such calibre that you will certainly lose your anchor.

There are three visitors' moorings to be found above the Folly piles. They are clearly marked MBC. Once past them, it is permitted to anchor out of the fairway, on either side of the river, but you will generally dry out. In the summer season, mainly during the weekends, there is a ferry service running between the visitors' moorings and the Folly Pier for the benefit of yachtsmen.

With regard to navigating the river at low water, it is possible for a 6ft draught vessel to get to Folly piles at all normal tides – and that includes low water springs; but with abnormal tides (those at the equinoxes for example) your draught will be restricted to no more than 4ft. When navigating at low water, it is best in general to tend to the starboard side of the river, where the lines of mooring piles will indicate the way ahead. There is a particular shoal patch, the Horse, that is to be avoided at low water springs. It lies between the Floating Bridge and the East Cowes Marina, about quarter to half a mile up river from the Floating Bridge.

There is also another mini-hazard (mini, that is, until it catches you) to be avoided on the port hand going up. It lies just off the church at Whippingham. It is the remains of a derelict jetty, built years ago from the stones of the old church. There is a large warning sign, but nevertheless, the hazard usually claims one or two bottoms each season, in spite of being very close in to the side of the banks, and so well away from the channel proper.

The way the tide runs in the River Medina at the Folly Reach is worth special consideration. Alan's advice is that it follows this rule: immediately after low water there is a flood for 2 hours 30 minutes; then comes a stand for 45 minutes; next there is another flood until −0045 HW Portsmouth; finally it stands again for 2 hours.

The river is well lit at night, and the major lights to watch out for are: Kingston red; *Medham* beacon white; *Folly* beacon green; Newport red leading (diamonds by day). You are advised not to be misled by the possibly doubtful siting height of the Island Harbour red navigation lights; nor by the two greens exhibited on the private jetty on the west bank, that stands on the opposite side of the river to the Folly Inn, guarding its own near-lagoon of a lacuna.

The River to Newport

Up to the red signpost at the Folly piles is administered by the Cowes Harbour Commissioners; upstream of that point is under the jurisdiction of the harbourmaster of Newport, the head of navigation. There are red and green buoys above the Folly Reach to Newport, mainly marking the mud spits on the bends – which reach out far into the centre of the river. There are also massive hulks on both sides of the river. Some of these are clearly to be seen before arriving at the next port of call, Island Harbour.

About 6 cables southward of Folly Inn Point is the lock entrance to the Medina Yacht Harbour on the eastern bank of the river with 180 pontoon berths. The lock is approximately 80ft long, 30ft wide and the harbour maintains a constant depth of 6ft or more. Access to the lock is four hours either side of high water and there is a waiting pontoon outside. The channel leading to the lock is marked by red buoys on the port side. Facilities include fuel, water, electricity, provisions, gas, slipway, restaurant, toilets and showers. ☎ (0983) 526733. The *Ryde Queen* paddle steamer is in the adjacent pond.

On my first visit, I was accosted just outside the entrance by a gaff rigged smackish sort of vessel. The skipper wanted to know what kind of place it was, because he hadn't found it in his guide. I got a similar story once inside; indeed, the plaint went up that most people were inclined to refer to it in these terms: 'We didn't know where it was. We had great difficulty in getting here. We had never ever heard of it. Why didn't you tell us it was here?'

True it is a quiet and fairly secluded spot, but not all that remote – nor difficult of access, once you know it is there. Outside on the river, the entrance channel is marked by red and green painted beer cans. This channel, and the area by the newly erected waiting pontoons, are to be dredged. These pontoons are marked by green piles, and close by the lock gates there is one red pile. On site there is a small shop, a laundry and toilets, and, in an altogether different scene, a laid-up steam packet for the edification and entertainment of one and all. There is also something of a specialty in the form of a welders' shop that offers unusually comprehensive services.

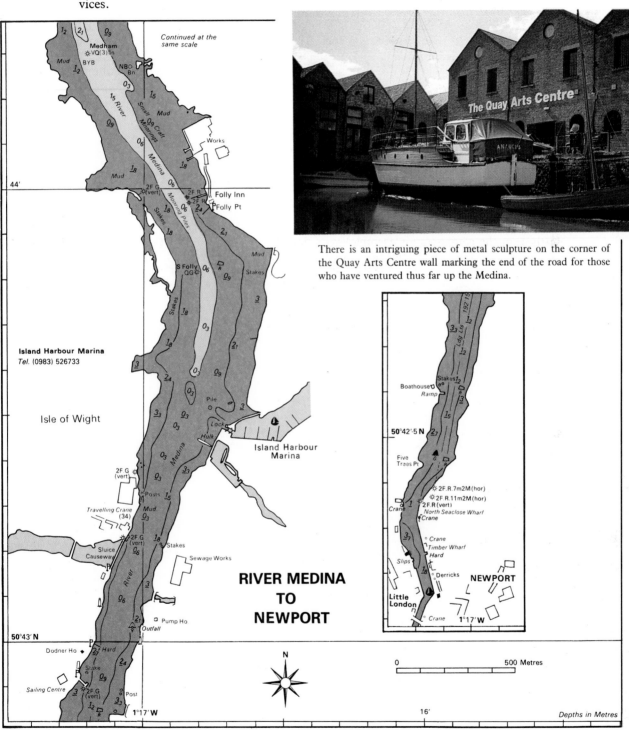

There is an intriguing piece of metal sculpture on the corner of the Quay Arts Centre wall marking the end of the road for those who have ventured thus far up the Medina.

RIVER MEDINA
TO
NEWPORT

River Medina to Newport

139

In common with many of the older marinas and boatyards, expansion and development is due to take place. Dwellings (with tied berths), be they houses, flats or mansions are to be erected to form what is advertised as a 'unique waterside lifestyle'. From the plans it does not appear likely that the presently rural and unspoiled nature of the place, with its tree-capped view of Whippingham spire, is going to be destroyed.

Nevertheless, I was accosted by some berth-holders and other locals who told me with some glee, of the sad fates of some previous proprietors who had been dealt financially fatal blows when attempting the same kind of endeavour.

Newport

River Medina – Folly Inn Point to Newport: the *Folly* beacon is a green pile, exhibiting a Q.G light, on the west side of the river about 1½ cables south of Folly Point and at the end of yacht moorings.

Further up the river to Newport, there are games and sports fields on the left bank, which is pleasantly treed, with a gentle slope to the water's edge; and there equally gentle fishermen casting off the right bank; they are an extremely pleasant bunch of fishermen, quite unlike the traditionally glum-faced hater of boats.

The Folly Inn on the River Medina.

NEWPORT HARBOUR

Controlled by Medina Borough Council

Harbourmaster Wayne G. Pritchett Town Quay, Newport.

☎ (0983) 525994 and (0983) 520000 Ext. 2144

Newport Radio VHF Channel 16

The harbour notes read as follows:

'Depths of water between Folly Inn Point and the Cement Wharf are M.H.W.S. 18ft to 16ft and M.L.W.S. 5ft. to 1ft. Southwards of this point the river dries out at Spring Tides. Half-a-mile southward there is a small jetty and pontoon on the west bank, exhibiting two green lights placed vertically, about half a cable from the centre of the river. All shallow points above this jetty are marked with red and white Port Hand marker buoys. The headquarters of the Newport Rowing Club is conspicuous on the west bank.

Leading beacons will now be seen on the north end of Newport Quay on the east bank of the river. Each has a 6ft. x 4ft. white diamond shape, and at night each shape shows two red lights placed 2ft. apart horizontally in the middle of the diamond. When in lie these bear 192°T and mark about 1½ miles of the approach channel. Depth of water in this channel are M.H.W.S. 9ft. to M.L.W.S. nil to 1ft.

Depths of water alongside quays are from 8ft to 10ft M.H.W.S. but nil at low water. There is often more water alongside the quays than in the approach channel due to the continual movement and grounding of vessels alongside.

The harbour runs out dry for about four hours each tide, but for a short stay one can lie here for up to six hours without any worry of going aground.

Pontoons provide convenient moorings and are ideal for bilge keel craft and multi-hull craft. There is almost unlimited space for mooring alongside quay walls. Toilet and shower facilities are available. Water and electricity are also available on the pontoons and litter bins are on the quays.

Newport is the capital town of the Isle of Wight, a port and a market town. Receiving its first Charter in 1180, altogether fourteen Royal Charters were granted up to the reign of Charles II in 1684. The town also holds the old town maces which date back to the 17th century. An ancient visitors' book called the old Ligger has many historic names including the present Queen Elizabeth and Duke of Edinburgh. Places of interest include Carisbrooke Castle, The Roman Villa in Cypress Road, St Mary's Church in Carisbrooke, the Newport parish church of St Thomas a Becket built in 1857 on the site of an earlier church dated 1175. There is a small photographic display in the Harbour Office depicting the harbour as it was in times gone by.

Odessa Shipyard (Mr. P. Foster) operates two patent slipways (No. 1 – boats up to 100ft and No. 2 – boats up to 30ft) on the west side of the harbour at Little London. Diesel fuel is also available there. Close by is Riverside Motors Limited with a slipway capable of hauling craft up to 35ft and facilities for engine repairs. There are also two public slipways.

Mobile cranes are operated by Vectis Transport, Town Quay, for lifting out vessels on the quay and a self-operated hand crane is also available for up to 10 tons at £7·00 per lift.

Further south on the west bank is the Cement Storage Depot and Pioneer Concrete Marine Gravel Ready Mix Plant Wharf. Two pairs of green lights, placed vertically, are exhibited one on the Pioneer Wharf (north end) and one on the Cement Wharf (south end).'

Newport Harbour itself is filled with a conglomeration of strange vessels, many on their way to being hulks; and many possessed or even lived in by hostile persons whose 'welcome' may be one of abuse and threats. Their territory is definitely insalubrious. However, a recent revision order has been implemented to control the numbers of houseboats and I am reliably informed that some of the least desirables have now left the harbour. A particular specialised houseboat site for a limited number of craft is being established.

In contrast to any disappointment in this area, the pontoons for visitors are in very good order. Because the river dries out, there is a legend stating, 'Bilge Keels Only – No Fin Keels'. There is water at these pontoons. Vessels with fins or long straight keels and all others go to the wall above the 'new' road bridge. Here is to be found another notice: 'Nurosis Berth'. This part of the quay could do with some repair, replacement and refurbishment. Much of the head of the navigation has been improved, and there is an arts and crafts centre with sculpture hanging over the water to prove it, but the wall and its appurtenances need help. Wayne Pritchett (the harbourmaster) and I are not in entire agreement about this matter, for his opinion is:

'I must disagree that the quayside around the area of the old yacht *Nurosis* berth is in need of repair, but I admit that the western quayside opposite by the Newport Squash Club is in a poor state and not recommended for yachts wishing to take the ground at low water.

I would like you to add that there is still a little movement of commercial craft from time to time, and that ships of up to 500 tons have been discharged here recently. Also: charts of the river from Folly to Newport are on sale at the harbour office.'

The harbourmaster's office is close by the pontoons, a little way ashore. There are special toilet houses with labels for 'Yachtsmen' and 'Yachtswomen'; no common Gents or Ladies here! In common with many harbourmasters, river managers and bailiffs of water patches that are a little remote, the Newport harbourmaster does not always readily show himself. His office door has one of those 'IN-OUT' sliding notices that can be changed. Not that it is to be relied on, for I personally changed his 'IN' to an 'OUT' more than once.

But do try to search him out, if for no more than a splendid dose of crack. He has been dedicated to the river/quayside at Newport for the past 27 years, and has now been harbourmaster for more than five. However, in addition, the family claim to local fame goes well beyond such mini figures, for he is the seventh generation of the clan to have worked on the River Medina at Newport since 1748. His son is the eighth generation, and is also on the harbour staff.

It would also be an improvement not to have to gaze upon the pseudo *Pirate Ship*. Its brash presence and poorly made up 'crew' show what the love of lucre can do. This eccentric vessel is to be moved to another site further north in the harbour.

The town shoresides

Keen food fanatics are in for a treat here. I was told that the Gateways' monopoly is to be broken at last by Safeways. Really well stocked greengrocers abound, but there is a dearth of butchers of excellence. I was also informed that there are two very good fishmongers in the town, but I was unable to search either of them out. It is difficult to understand why there should be such a dearth of such fish-purveyors-mongers. (This is so almost all over the island. East Cowes, for example, has to be content with a purveyor who trades occasionally from the back of a van. There is one shop of excellence in West Cowes, but on the whole, it is possible to do better in Leeds where you can hardly be further from the sea.) So, where is the treat? The cave of goodies worth a special trip is the delicatessen and wine shop known as Benedicts. Large haversacks and well furnished wallets should be at the ready, for the choice of food is mouth-wateringly alluring, and the selection of booze is tempting to say the least. They stock a first-rate sparkling burgundy; an effervescent delight indeed.

Newport is old: it received its first charter just before 1200 from one of the omni-present all-powerful de Redvers. In those days it was literally the New Port, with Carisbrooke the seat of government for the whole island. In the best traditions of 'Rottens' it had two MPs for centuries; among them, the Duke of Wellington, Lord Palmerston and George Canning.

In the 16th century, according to Sir John Oglander, '... the stretes weare not paved, but lay most wet and beastlye with great stoppels to stepp over ye Kennell from ye one syde to ye other.'

There is a monument in the church raised by Victoria to Princess Elizabeth, second daughter of Charles I, who died Sunday September 8th, 1650, a prisoner in Carisbrooke aged fifteen. She is supposed to have caught a chill while playing bowls with her young brother Henry; but there are those who point the finger of regicide.

Keats, who once lived at Newport, wrote, 'I have not seen many specimens of Ruins – I don't think I shall ever see one to surpass Carisbrooke Castle. The trench is overgrown with the smoothest turf and the Walls with ivy. The keep within side is one Bower of ivy – a colony of jackdaws have been there for years.'

Part Roman, part Norman and part Elizabethan, it is now famed as the last resort of Charles I to which he turned after hiding at Titchfield Haven. It proved to be a poor choice and he was made prisoner, trying to escape twice; once through a narrow window on the assumption that where his head could go, his body could follow ... a rash policy that cost him both. After Carisbrooke he was imprisoned in the local grammar school and later forced to cross the water to Hurst Castle.

A bowling green was created for his pleasure, and you can still walk round it and let your imagination run riot. If of a mind, you can actually see the window from which he tried to escape. You can also watch the donkeys, who have just about as good a chance of escaping, treading the wheel to draw the water bucket up from the 161ft deep well.

All in all, it must be granted that Newport, Isle of Wight, at the head of the River Medina, offers a more than fitting variety of entertainments for those who have navigated so far.

Wootton

Directions

Leaving Cowes for Wootton, the Medina estuary (if estuary indeed it be), is so well marked by stationary buoys and fast moving traffic, that the Shrape Mud offers no hazard; and once the flashing red off East Cowes Point has been passed, those with the right draught at the right state of tide can steam quite close in. It is worth trying for a close inspection for the scenery from here to Wootton (as befits a royally patronised patch) is memorable.

Old Castle Point, is one of the two most northerly tips of Wight; the other being Egypt Point to the west. It is here that the first of the views is to be seen: cared-for copses on modest headlands, allowing, here and there, glimpses of mansion-like homes erected in splendid isolation. Shortly after this impressive and attractive outlook comes the impressive but gloomy facade of Norris Castle. Built nearly 200 years ago, it is another of the fanciful creations that were erected all over Wight and euphemistically described as examples of architectural expertise. However, they kept local builders in good work; and it is well known that Albert was no Charles, so they were never in danger of improvement or demolition.

Next comes quite a different experience, the majesty of Osborne Bay and its attractive scenery. A break in the trees offers a splendid view of a castle on a hill, with its associated small stone building on the waterline. This miniature curiosity was described to me as Queen Victoria's Tea Rooms; the retreat she and Albert used when in their Garbo moods.

It is easy on this part of the approach to find yourself spellbound by the compelling facets of Osborne House as its aspects and prospects tantalisingly appear and disappear. So, care needs to be taken not to risk either the East or the West Patch Rocks by Barton Point if you are tempted really close. Standing off north of Peel Bank will offer a good view of Osborne itself deeply set in the trees of Barton Wood.

Between Barton Hard and Peel Wreck, is the diminutive inlet leading to King's Quay and its associated creek, deriving their names, it is said, from King John. Needless to say, Charles I also passed this way, failing to get his own way once again. Now it is all privately owned or in the hands of the Nature Conservancy Council; but an exploration in a clinker dinghy rowed with muffled oars will bring forth no protest and the explorer will find a quietly proud contender to all H. de Vere Stacpoole's locations, real and imaginary.

At sea level is the long line of a sea wall in various states of repair, disrepair and apparent abandon. Shortly after, Ryde Pier reveals itself like a long enquiring probe out into the eponymous Roads. A straight course that clears all dangers off Wootton is made by standing off to line up Norris with Ryde's famous All Saints' church spire, which really is conspicuous in spite of the many other competing churches. Such a course clears Peel Bank and leads closely towards the approach beacon.

The entrance

Wootton Beacon is not easy to spot against the background of trees and the cluttered shoreline, but in its vicinity are half a dozen small marker buoys. Some are esoterically shaped, but all are the work of the Royal Victoria Yacht Club's racing brethren, and can easily be identified as such. There is, of course, the official red buoy marking Wootton Rocks, but there is also a withy with a white topmark, close in, marking the inner limit of the rocky spit. A new sandbank has appeared recently to port on entering the creek.

Once any of the marks has been identified, the beacon and the entrance will not be difficult to spot. The ferries move in and out frequently, and it is quite amusing to watch them as they perform their disappearing tricks behind the trees of the entrance.

The entrance is not a wide channel by any means, but since the ferries manage quite well, there is little problem for yachts. In any case, the occulting red, white and green sector lights make it quite straightforward. If you get 'caught out' by a ferry, you can, if necessary, creep just to starboard of the starboard pile markers; but there is little leeway in the channel itself let alone outside it.

Wootton Creek is formed by yet another small bite that the sea has taken out of the Oligocene clays and marls. The most demanding landmark is the 'new' Quarr Abbey, built for French Benedictine monks in pink Belgian brick and completed in 1914. Claiming to be the largest brick building for many miles, it sits near the site of the original Quarr Abbey that took its name from the quarries that were once busily worked; sending stone to Chichester cathedral and Winchester school and cathedral, as well as to the old neighbouring abbey.

The Royal Victoria Yacht Club has a splendid view of the lower allotment of Wootton Creek.

Some ruins still exist of the old buildings, built in 1132 by Baldwin de Redvers, Earl of Devon and Lord of the Island. Of considerable interest to yachtsmen, must be the knowledge that, in the fifteenth century, the then Abbot ran his own fleet to import wine.

The close approach shows an entrance shore with pretty white houses, with the new and the old ferry slips mainly dominating the scene, but permitting the clubhouse of the Royal Victoria Yacht Club neatly to appear. In contrast to the *ancien régime* of the Quarr days are the high-rise lights that stand ready for Quatermass or Tomorrow's World.

Wootton Creek

Immediately next the ferry station, just inside the creek there are some visitors' buoys, and also some piles. The buoys are laid by the RVYC in what is still known as the Pool, although it is no longer what it used to be. Most of the moorings carry 1–2ft at low water neaps, but piles and visitors' buoys dry out at low water springs. The mud under the buoys is fairly soft, but not so under the piles. Due to silting caused by the movements of the ferry it now has banks and ridges.

The Commodore anchors in the Pool; and some unwary or unthinking visitors have been known to misinterpret this, taking it as carte blanche to follow suit. Even craft with less than a metre draught will get well and truly stuck at half tide should they drop their hooks just to the seaward side of the leading marks. Anchoring is prohibited in the Pool itself.

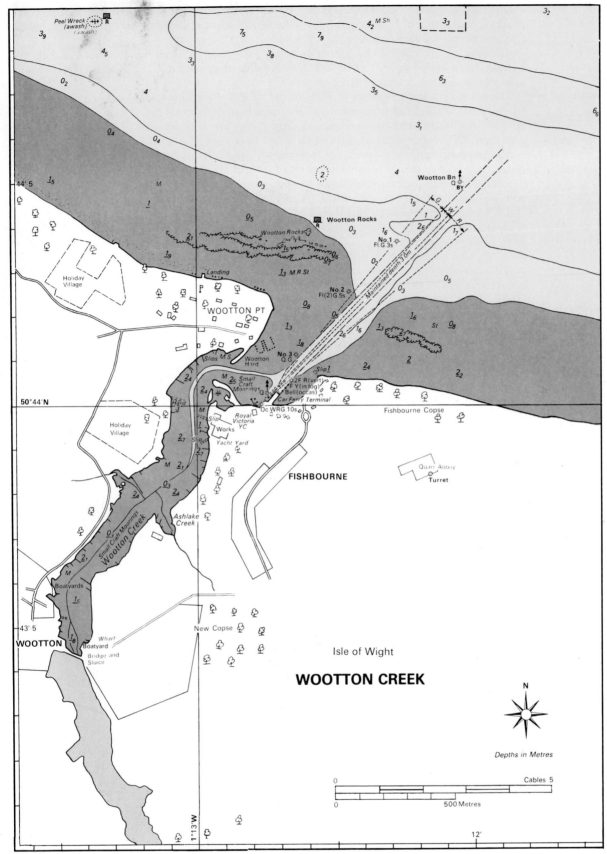

Isle of Wight

WOOTTON CREEK

Depths in Metres

N

| 0 | | | | | Cables 5 |
| 0 | | 500 Metres | | | |

Wootton Creek

However, it cannot be forgotten that it is Sealink 'ferritory' and the commerce of the big ships makes it something of busy, noisy spot. The ferries leave every hour on the hour, or, when traffic demands, a shuttle service.

Anchoring is permitted, but must be well away from the buoys and clear of the fairway. Visitors have been known to overlook this sensible requirement. The Royal Victoria's generous attitudes to visitors deserves better respect.

There are very few moorings at Fishbourne with 3–4ft at low water, and they are to be found to the north of the Pool, alongside the ferry terminal. It is to be noted that Sealink have ordered an additional ferry; and two linkspan landing ramps are now planned. This additional ramp will cost the RVYC some of the already small area where there is a good depth of water.

All the moorings in the creek are fore-and-aft; and visitors anchoring in the upper reaches or picking up buoys, should secure themselves fore and aft.

Some authorities refer categorically to the presence of the Wootton harbourmaster. I was not able to unearth (or should the word be unwater?) any trace of such office or officer; but river bailiffs, creek commandants and their like are rarae aves (or should that be rarae pisces?)

In fact, the harbour is under the jurisdiction of the Queen's Harbourmaster at Portsmouth, with all day-to-day running of the creek and the allocation of moorings being in the hands of the Wootton Creek Fairways Association. The Royal Victoria Yacht Club is the fount of wisdom to which all visiting yachtsmen are first recommended to refer. It is one of the most friendly and non-poncey royals that I have ever set oilies in, in spite of the fact that it has such an impressive lineage. The view from its bar must be one of the most pleasing on the island; an extremely pretty combination of marine and rural shoreside life. A good example of riparian efforts at their best.

Inside the bar, there are many papers of historic interest, from their own recent newsletters to the instigators of the America's Cup. In addition, there is this relic: 'To their Royal Highnesses The Prince and Princess of Wales. May it please your Royal Highnesses on behalf of the flag officers, committee and members of the Royal Victoria Yacht Club, I am directed to approach your Royal Highnesses on the joyous occasion of the twenty-fifth anniversary of your Royal

The clubhouse and steps of the Royal Victoria seen from the vicinity of the famous Pool.

Highnesses happy marriage on the 10th March 1863. We venture to offer our heart-felt congratulations on this auspicious occasion and unite in expressing the fervent hope that Your Royal Highnesses may be spared for many years to enjoy the love and esteem of a loyal and devoted people. Commodore, Royal Victoria Yacht Club, March 10th 1888.'

Had I too been royalty (a disturbing if unlikely thought, I confess) I could not have been afforded a more royal welcome. In the holiday absence of the manageress, the temporary club steward, Digby (a gradely chap he, Dickensian in stature and in character) saw to my every need with patience and twinkle. There is little in the club that a visitor is likely to want for. The following extracts from recent newsletters furnish a good idea of the spirit of the club:

Newsletter of the Royal Victoria Yacht Club, Fishbourne. September 1988. Comment:
'What a boring old summer it looked like being. Especially for the frustrated staff of your favourite Newsletter. No boring reports of how our Club boats fared in the ROUND THE IS-LAND RACE, in spite of placing the whole of our reporting staff on St Catherine's Point to observe and report. No tired old articles on Club members' performances, if any, during COWES WEEK. No Club members went anywhere and the very bored CRUISING section were bored stiff with our monotonously gale swept Saturdays. Just the same old boring news of dog mess and Cola cans, in ours, as in every other dinghy park. Just the same old sight of boyish and girlish bums as adolescents giggle and grunt on the Club's lawn, to the bored amusement of the veranda audience – Club members supping BURT'S ALE and visitors old-fashioned enough to have paid their mooring fees, yawning over their PIMM'S. So boring in fact, that our worthy Editor wandered his tired way, with our weary Production department, off to the wet and boring West Country, just when it all changed.'

My personal contact at the Royal Victoria was one John Triggs, who gave up his own mooring, moving his own boat, so that I should be able to stay afloat at all states of the tide. 'It's good that you are actually coming in here, since a lot of what has been written about us is either so old that it isn't relevant or is just plain wrong.'

Leaving both club and pool behind to make for the creek proper, you will immediately see that the channel turns noticeably to starboard. Shortly after, it turns noticeably to port before it turns to starboard again; finally settling on a straight course. The turns in the channel are tighter than they appear on the Admiralty chart, since they are governed by moored craft. As usual, the lines of the larger vessels give a good indication of the best water. Look out for the many isolated small buoys that are used for fore-and-aft mooring. However, the channel is also marked by small red and green buoys that are not shown on the Admiralty chart. They are rather strange devices, looking like mini-Michelin watermen. Each wears a kind of tyre corset and is entirely in keeping with the idiosyncratic designs of some of the private markers in the bay.

At half tide, the near 180ft turn round the spit is very clearly defined by its steep-to shingle banks. There is evidence of these banks shifting and encroaching, as the traffic of the ferries to and from the terminal increases; with the spit growing at a rate of about one foot each year. Still, those same craft do keep the channel well dredged. The shingle spits and banks are not as yet closing the gap into the inner sanctum, and at half tide and more they afford really excellent protection against any inclement blow.

When the wind is in the north to east, there can be a quite unpleasant swell in the main entrance; and it is on these occasions that the spit comes into its protective own, providing a first-rate refuge. Further up the creek, that is to the south, you are fully protected, and since the creek itself is in the main unexposed, there is hardly any discomfort to be experienced. Indeed, Wootton Creek was one of the few places where I saw little evidence of the work of the October hurricane of 1987.

Ranalagh, the boatyard just round the bend, has mooring piles that dry out, and no objection is taken to a stranger using one for a tide or two. There is no visitors' mooring in this part of the creek, and anchoring is permitted only absolutely clear of the fairway. However, many rogue skippers do precisely that, much to the inconvenience of local traffic.

By Ashlake Creek, you are poised between the almost hidden Fishbourne and the slightly less hidden holiday village of Little Canada. This latter could hardly have been more discreetly placed and executed; and there is no feeling of a glazed gaze coming across the water at you such as is frequently experienced near East Coast holiday resorts. The shores of the creek are fringed with bushes, trees and copsewood and the whole is a quiet idyll of riverside life. Private houses and mansions, themselves tucked away and hardly to be seen, all have private pontoons at the bottom of their gardens. Particularly charming are the examples of old and new boathouses. The whole of the Fishbourne side of the creek is privately owned; the riparian owners took the Crown to court in times bygone, winning the day and their case.

This is an extremely beautiful part of the creek, hardly busy at all, and with a ground rent for permanent residents so inexpensive as to defy the imagination; and since the ones that dry are only half that it must be a veritable yachtsman's paradise.

Up towards the Old Mill Pond and the village of Wootton Bridge, there is hardly a hulk to be seen, and while most of the head of the creek is taken up with private houses with private jetties, the folk who live there are not so territorially minded that they are unapproachable by a stranger who goes to them in the right frame of mind.

Once there was a lock into the Old Mill Pond above the bridge, but as a result of local feuding and infighting, it was destroyed by various midnight raiders and now the water sluices out. There have been, and still are, plans to refurbish and/or to promote lakeside developments, but little progress seems to have been made. But in 1989, the new owners of Lakeside constructed a footpath and replaced the sluice gates adjacent the bridge.

Wootton Bridge is clearly the favourite village, rather than the nearby just plain Wootton. It may be a small community, but it has an excellent range of shops, and they cover most visitors' needs. In particular, there is a garage, a laundrette, a real ironmonger and a real butcher.

There is still peripheral boatwork going on in the creek, but naught to compare with the days when the Earl of Yarborough (he of the Royal Yacht Squadron) had his *Falcon* built here. For a time, Wootton also played host to Erskine Childers' converted lifeboat the *Vixen/Dulcibella*; the one used on the Frisian and Baltic cruises for his inimitable tale, *The Riddle of the Sands*.

Quite clearly, Wootton was a favourite spot for eccentrics. This is Cowper on the place:

'From Ryde to Wootton Creek is about three miles. This creek has very little water in it. The bar nearly dries out, but just inside the mud flat, off Chapel Corner, opposite Fishbourne Coastguard boathouse, there is a depth of about 4ft nearly as far as the hard, N. of a long red brick half-timbered house in woods, called Lisle Court. There is a private hard to this place, and off it I used to keep my Undine I. She remained always water-borne, and I never wish to find a better place for a small boat. At high water the scene is lovely and the sailing excellent. The entrance to the creek lies some way out, but is well marked by large booms. I was instrumental in getting the Portsmouth authorities to renew these in 1889, and they were placed more in accordance with the channel. It is a lovely place, and delightful at high water, but very tricky for a stranger.'

To conclude, he also has a nice story to tell that emanates from Wootton:

'But there is the band on the St Vincent playing "Rule, Britannia; Britannia rules the waves", which reminds me of a quaint and touching incident that happened to me as I was taking across from my house, Lisle Court, in Wootton Creek, to Portsmouth, an Indian gentleman high in office at the Court of the Rajah of Pattiala, and one of the invited guests of the Empire on board the Serapis. He was in full Indian dress, flowing robes, turban, yataghans, and tulwars galore. As it was calm and we were late, I took to the oars. My guest insisted on rowing too, and he did it with a will. As we crossed the lines of magnificent ships – for it was the great Jubilee Review of 1887 – suddenly "Rule, Britannia" struck up close by. A liner chartered to bring visitors round from London was passing down the lines and rousing the patriotism of its passengers by these historic strains. The effect was electrical on my swarthy guest. He threw down his oar, raised his arms in emphatic gesture, declaring, with deepest conviction, "And she always will!" "Amen!" say I as fervently.'

Bembridge and the back of Wight

Quitting Wootton Creek, the huge brick building of Quarr Abbey, in its pink Belgian brick dominates the wooded shoreline. Once away from its influence, there are numerous signs of boathouses, small habitations and moorings by Binstead, its hard and its rocks. But soon your attention is taken by the pier, town hall and church of Ryde; as well as the many and varied blocks of contrasting architecture that go to make up the patchwork pattern that is the essence of the town's style.

Ryde (or Rye or La Riche as it was in the 14th century) is best seen from seaward; and, not so long ago, all ferry passengers had ample time to do just that since they had to be shifted bodily from their boats into carts that were then pulled by horses through the mud and water to the shore. This sorry state was the target of the novelist Henry Fielding, in 1754: 'There is an impassable gulf of mud and sand which can neither be traversed by walking or swimming so that for nearly one half of the twenty-four hours Ryde is inaccessible by friend or foe.' He waited at Ryde for another boat to take him to the continent, and died shortly afterwards in Lisbon. It is not recorded whether being carried by cart contributed to his early demise. Four years later the Lord of the Manor, rebuilt the quay in Gurnard stone at the cost of £238.6s.9d.

The pier, which, with its pierhead at 636ft is unmistakable, was built in 1813, and radically altered the life of the town, which previously had a population of no more than 1,000. It reaches half a mile out to sea and is made up of the old pier for pedestrians and cars, the railway and the (disused) tramway. Trains run in connection with the ferries, and in contrast with the rest of the island, which has been nearly denuded of its trains and stations, Ryde Pier has a station at both ends. Although not particularly accessible to visiting yachtsmen, Ryde can be easily reached from Bembridge. It is worth noting one or two intriguing remarks that have been passed about the place in the past. For example, 'The chief trade seems to be in tourists, who are taxed, tolled and touted for by purveyors of entertainment for man and beast, the managers of excursions, and the enclosers of natural curiosities.' Its architecture has been defined as, 'classic, rustic, Gothic, Swiss and nondescript'. Its general slogan was one up on Skegness: 'Bright, Bracing and Beautiful'.

Ryde has also had its share of the good and great. In 1870, after Napoleon III's Second Empire collapsed, the Empress Eugenie, a friend of Queen Victoria, fled to Ryde in Sir John Burgoyne's yacht. However, no accommodation suited her delectation, and she did not stay.

Ryde Regatta was an amazingly grand affair, to be compared with Cowes. This is an extract from a contemporary account: 'Fashion, beauty, flirtation, gossip, scandal, costumes of myriad orders, yachtsmen and women of every conceivable graduation, nautical attire of all degrees of eccentricity, curious persons, people you meet everywhere, and people you have never met before, the belles of last season, and those who were belles once but many season ago; damsels fresh and faded; widows whose garb betokens every grade of not irremediable grief; the inevitable Russian count, whose wealth is fabulous; the hero of the last divorce case, and the heroine of the last elopement – que voulez vous? Go to the pier at Ryde and you have them all.'

From the east, Ryde rises dramatically out of the mound of trees that appears after Nettlestone Point. Indeed, so do other heaven-searching edifices: for some time, the major features will have been the 180ft tower and spire of All Saints' church in Ryde, and the No Man's Land Fort off the Point.

Neither Mother Bank nor its spit is of any threat to yachts. A course just to seaward of the red can *SW Mining Ground* clears Ryde Sand, and will also keep you well away from the Sturbridge Shoal, taking you on to No Man's Land Fort. There are red beacons in the vicinity and they do not appear to agree with what is shown on the Admiralty chart.

The same applies to the presence of the underwater barrier. I never actually saw physical signs of danger, but since the appropriate legends appear on the charts and that pearl above all others 'local knowledge', usually so reliable, consistently brought forth merely conflicting opinions, it seemed prudent not to court any potential protuberances too closely. In any case, under such circumstances, my policy is to shy away and stand well clear – just in case.

By Nettlestone Point, is Seaview, where there is the famous Seaview Yacht Club and, in season, many small-craft moorings. At one time a harbour existed nearby, and Sir John Oglander, the well known deputy governor of Isle of Wight wrote of it: '... they had made a good harbour by casting up of ye beach on both sydes of Nettlestone Point a mile into the sea, to be sene at this daye, and by tradition and some records have I also sene that you might have had at Barneslye inhabitants theyre, your choyce of 20 good Shipmaystors that woold undertake to carry you to any parte you desired.' There is hardly a sign of the totally silted-up acreage that was Barnsley Harbour, and its position is shown only by place names.

To the east, Bembridge Harbour (or is it Brading Parva or indeed Bradbury Magna?) prompts us that until recently big cargo-carrying ships used to navigate that far. Further back, in time, the Danes used the haven before going for King Alfred in 897 AD. The Romans also used the place, and a villa was dug up at Yarbridge in 1830.

In calm, settled weather, the nearby bays of Seagrove and Priory are very pleasant picnic spots, either ashore or at anchor. Priory Bay lies very close to St Helen's Fort and the entrance to Bembridge. It is well recommended as a secure anchorage for a pleasant Sunday afternoon, and is much used by the Bembridge locals when in search of a quiet sunny snooze.

The weather shore of St Helen's has been a boon and a blessing to sailors (whether fighting, fishing or cruising men) for centuries. St Helen's Road is just seaward of St Helen's Fort or Patch, and both are close in to the shore. In the days when the anchorage was used by the professionals, the island possessed a famous spring of water that was much sought after by outward-bounders because of what were called its excellent keeping qualities. Indeed, for centuries, our fighting fleets used almost exclusively to water here.

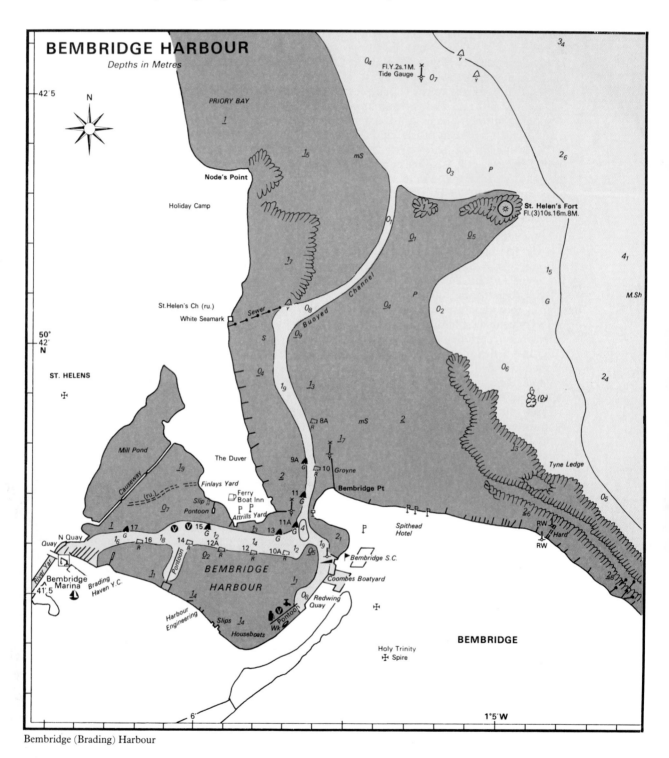

Bembridge (Brading) Harbour

Directions

Bembridge is approached straight from No Man's Land Fort or from St Helen's Road, via St Helen's Patch, leaving St Helen's Fort itself to port. The Bembridge tide-gauge light beacon is situate about three cables northwest of the not particularly elegant or distinguished fort. Anchoring is not permitted within a cable of the fort.

The actual entrance to Bembridge shows up clearly as a gap between heavily wooded shoresides. With St Helen's Fort in your sights, the Bembridge tide gauge and channel buoys stand out very clearly. I was not able to identify the yellow buoys that the Admiralty chart shows to be in the area. However, I did find many others that were not marked; indeed, the whole area round Bembridge is positively littered with yellow buoys. Although much more substantial than the usual kind of racing buoys, they are in fact precisely that; and there is available locally an excellent chart with comprehensive details.

The approach and entrance to Bembridge are both so good (naturally so as well as being excellently marked by the harbour authority) that it is a joy to go in. Special mention must be made of what is one of the most impressive landmarks I have ever seen. It is the legendary White Holy Stone, known as St Helen's seamark, just off Nodes Point, that has done local seamen service of one kind or another over the centuries. Three large houses and this massive white pillar (that looks from time to time like a rocket on a launch pad) of St Helen's church stand to starboard upon entering and are unmistakable. So, happily is the channel buoyage. The buoys are well maintained and clearly marked.

Bembridge's famous bar is supposed to be situate between red *Nos 6 and 8*; and the tide gauge at the entrance indicates the depth of water in this vicinity. (It is worth noting that it is said by those who should know, that this gauge under-reads by approximately 18 inches.) I tried four or five times to locate the actual position of the bar, but in the end concluded that it is a long and wide affair that exists on and off from red *No. 4* onwards. Indeed, it is worth taking care all along that stretch, especially so if there is wind against tide for it can be a very sloppy spot, with the chop easily reaching a top to bottom of 6ft. This can be particularly unpleasant between reds *8* and *10* with an easterly wind; and such conditions are not at all favourable for trying to avoid the bar on a hit-or-miss basis.

Not to be overlooked, though certainly never marking gold nor oil.

The *Bembridge* beacon and tide gauge is often occupied by harbingers that look more sinister than they really are.

The harbour

Bembridge, or, as it is still referred to in some places, charts and books, Brading Haven, is unique in so far as it is the only harbour on the Isle of Wight that does not face the north from its harbour mouth. Actually, it only just squeezes into the Solent in any case, really creeping more towards the English Channel and its open waters. However, Southsea is only six miles away; hardly any further than Ryde as the crow cruises, but when compared in terms of a shoreside experience, more than light years distant. Like its river's namesake across the island, Yarmouth, it is a most convenient point of departure for a round-the-island run or Channel crossing. Alker Tripp recalls some history:

'That broad level, joined as it formerly was to the present inlet, was all a part of Brading Harbour. It is said that, as late as the reign of Charles II, the harbour extended to Brading High Street, and that ships used to anchor beside the old houses there. A regular expanse of inland water existed when the Danes entered in 896 and King Alfred's ships surprised them. Brading, with its harbour, grew to considerable importance in the centuries that followed; and Sir John Oglander described it, in the reign of Charles I, as "formerly ye only towne for receypt of strangors that came by shippinge." "Ride and Cows", he said, were "no then knowen", whereas Brading was (by his account) "ye awntientest towne in owre Island". As a port it once contained Ryde, Sandown, and Shanklin in its boundaries.'

BEMBRIDGE HARBOUR

General Manager M. H. Coombes, Harbour Office, Bembridge, Isle of Wight ☎ (0983) 872828
The harbour authority publishes a small brochure with a map of the harbour inside:

'The Bembridge Harbour Improvement Co. Ltd., has marina berths at Bembridge Marina with accommodation for visiting yachts with draughts of up to 1·83m (6ft) at LWS. Visitors enquiries to Mr. R. Green, Berthing Master, ☎ (0983) 874436. Multihulls may be beached just inside the entrance north of the Bembridge Sailing Club. Swinging moorings are available at various yards and Bembridge Boatyard, Embankment Road, Bembridge, ☎ (0983) 872423 also has pontoon berths.

Entrance obviously depends upon tide state and draught of vessel. The Tide Gauge can be relied upon and the channel is well buoyed but not lighted. On springs and medium tides vessels of up to 1·83m (6ft) draught can enter 3 hours before and 2 hours after HW but on tides 4m, depth over the bar between Nos 6 & 8 buoys sometimes does not exceed 1·52m (5ft). On such days the tide gauge should be carefully observed. On high Springs depth over the bar exceeds 3m (10ft). From No. 10 buoy to the Marina there is a minimum depth of 1m (3ft) at LWS. Visitors berths are available at Bembridge Marina but it is advisable to contact the Berthing Master (0983) 874436 at busy weekends. Anchoring in the approach channel or in the Harbour is prohibited and the speed limit is 6 knots.'

The Bembridge launch can be called on VHF Ch 16, with the sign 'BHL'. Access to the harbour for a 3ft boat is 3 hours before and 2½ after HW. On a 3·6m neap tide, sometimes with high pressure there is no more than 5ft on the bar. Most of Bembridge Haven dries out, and there is only 1ft over the bar, at the biggest low water springs.

The entrance is bad when the wind is in the east. Norman, the harbour boatman, and Bembridge enthusiast, spends many a Sunday afternoon in the entrance channel in his launch, waiting for visiting yachts to leave. Often, four or five will need to be plucked off, having got the wind and the channel the wrong way round.

Quitting Bembridge at sunrise and returning at sunset takes you straight into the rays of the sun both ways, making pilotage quite tricky for a stranger.

There is a deep-water mooring near the HQ of Bembridge Sailing Club, placed by the harbour authorities for the use of deep-draught visiting vessels. Nearby, Attrill's Boatyard maintain their major mooring, also in deep water, indicated by a clearly marked red buoy. There is a splendid drying patch of clean hard sand just inside the entrance. It is an ideal spot for drying out, for it is well protected and has a hull-kindly gentle slope.

There is no petrol to be had in Bembridge over the weekend, and, in any case, the nearest garage is a good walk up the steepish hill past the village shopping centre. Diesel is available from Spinnaker Chandlery in small quantities by the can, and from Attrill's Boatyard, but not after noon over the weekends because you cannot count on being able to get them to come out. The nearest continuing supply of fuel is at the Tesco terminal at Ryde. Bembridge also suffers from the lack of a laundrette. But Spinnaker Chandlery is a splendid combination of all that is best in this world and the old one; and there is little that the sparring partnership of father and son cannot offer you, or obtain without delaying you for days or it costing you an arm and a leg.

Bembridge Harbour has some pleasing drying-out beaches, and the old Spithead Hotel is a magnificent sight.

Sadly, there is no easy public boat landing on the southeast side, since the glorious Royal Spithead Hotel is worthy of close inspection. It really does deserve refurbishing and rebuilding in parts. It is a monument that should not be lost, but at the moment is in need of care, protection and preservation. With the removal of the ugly excrescences that are currently attached to its facade, it would provide a splendid flagship of an hotel for its little corner of the world. Many people use the private club access pontoons that are nearby.

There is, however, a line of pontoons known as Fisherman's Wharf and owned by the harbour on the south side. It has a special merit in so far as it is close to the HQ of one Captain Stan. He factors the fish for the local fishermen, and sells it retail from his nearly-but-not-quite bottomless vessel on the pontoon. It is also close to the visitors' pontoons.

Bembridge

Tradition has it that, as late as the time of Charles II, Bembridge Harbour extended to Brading High Street, explaining, of course, the frequent references to Bembridge Harbour as Brading Haven.

Indeed, until recent times, the harbour went inland to the westward making a vast inland sea. It was towards the end of the 19th century that it became inhibited and impounded as it were in its contemporary discipline. The second causeway dyke isolated acres of the hinterland from the open sea. Brading Port, or the Kinge's Towne of Bradynge, thus became a really high and dry community.

An inspection of the OS maps will show that the River Yar (the second – or first as the case may be) almost divides this end into another island, just as much as does the western version.

Various companies were formed or floated decades back with the intention of creating the embankment. Initially, nothing went well, but in the end, after tragedies and bankruptcies, the work was completed. The present Bembridge Harbour Improvement Company Ltd has already created the marina and is now in the process of developing 'yachtsmen's residences' with associated berths.

Since Bembridge has many associations with seafaring of all kinds and with those to do with the smugglers for whom it was once a favourite haunt, it is a prime candidate for a Museum of the Sea. Martin Woodward is the proprietor of the six-gallery museum. A professional diver, specialising in previously uncharted wrecks, he has acquired most of the museum exhibits himself. There are all kinds of artefacts: pirate gold with pieces of eight; beautiful brass work; an exhibition of diving equipment; navigators' instruments; and the story of discovery of the submarine HMS *Swordfish*, complete with underwater pictures. Martin also runs the caffs across the street, one of which is called the Square Rigger.

This is an extract from a caption to one of his old pictures of Brading and Bembridge:

'Bembridge Foreland and the Brading Haven 1850. The fresh south westerly breeze depicts the fine sheltered waters known to seamen as St Helen's Roads. It is probably the safest and certainly the most historic anchorage on the south coast. It has afforded shipping shelter from the prevailing south westerly Atlantic weather for centuries. With Portsmouth nearby, the Royal Navy used its waters for repair and lay-up of their men of war. It was the scene of the mutiny at Spithead 1797. The seamark which is in fact the ruin of the old St Helen's Church was largely dismantled by seamen who used its stone to scour the wooden decks. From this, the term 'to holy stone the decks' was born. Suffice to say, the point above the sea-mark is called Horestone Point.' (Now called Nodes Point.)

Alker Tripp had a veritable soft spot for Spithead, its history and its men. Here he is on his hobby horse:

'The earliest history of Spithead is lost in the far past; but we hear of the roadstead in AD 296, when the fleet of Allectus was anchored here. Fleet after fleet followed, type after type, rig after rig.

The Jutes and the Saxons who displaced the Romans from the Isle of Wight possibly preferred the inlets and havens for their long-boats, and the Danes who harried them in turn probably did the same. The Danish pirates used the island as a base, and "lived at discretion, no force being able to withstand them." Then, in course of years, came the threat to England from Normandy, and Harold assembled a great fleet here to resist the coming of William.

King John assembled a fleet at Portsmouth and Spithead in 1205, for an expedition to France which, in fact, proved abortive. Amazingly picturesque the roadstead must have been with the tall fleets at anchor or making sail. From Spithead they sailed for the wars, trim and stately, and they returned to it again shot-battered, with their battle-scars and their prizes. Spithead was occupied by Blake's ships in the days of the Parliament; then the fleets of Torrington, Anson, and Hawke lay successively in the roadstead. Wolfe's expedition to North America was fitted out at Portsmouth, and the dead general was brought back here, his body being landed at Portsmouth, to the sound of minute guns from the fleet at Spithead; and HMS Invincible sank here while preparing for the St Lawrence River in 1758.

Ships just returned from long commissions were always a great contrast to the sprucely painted Home Fleet. The weather-worn vessel would be surrounded with "Jews and women" almost before she had come to anchor. Discipline for the while was relaxed; a first-rate (Mr. Masefield tells us) might have as many as 500 women aboard at the same time. Drink – despite every precaution – was smuggled on board, and the sailors and women "drank and quarrelled among the guns."

The nation in peace-time has always been apt to forget the Navy; and in the reign of Charles I, when Buckingham's expedition to Spain was fitted out, the flagship was the old Ark Royal, which had fought the Armada forty years before, and some ships were even wearing the same sails as they had in that year. The crews were equally neglected; the food was bad and pay uncertain. The whole fleet was in a state of sickness and mutiny. But Buckingham was not the man to share the hardships of the fleet; he held himself completely aloof, having reserved to himself a special transport and kitchen.

Under the Commonwealth everything was changed, and the Navy was really given due regard; more than half the annual revenue was spent upon it, and Blake – who believed in having a happy lower deck – saw that good pay was given. But the change hardly outlived the Restoration; pay again became uncertain and conditions wretched.

As years went on, moreover, the ships were filled with pressed men – men who had been earning good money elsewhere, and had no wish to be thrust under the grim discipline of the Navy, with bad food and uncertain pay.

Things came to a head in 1797. The sailors seem clearly to have been anxious to submit their grievances, in an orderly and respectful manner, to the authorities. But the Government was both dilatory and unsympathetic, and the mutiny at Spithead resulted – with scenes of bloodshed and violence. Lord Howe, the victor of the Glorious First of June, was appointed to settle matters and was given powers little short of absolute. Trusted as he was throughout the fleet, he effected a settlement based upon reason and not upon coercion, feeling no doubt that the sailors, though wrong, had been greatly wronged also.'

Leaving Bembridge astern and crossing to Portsmouth and experiencing the delights of Spithead can bring a flat-calm experience, but with a bright breeze it can make for a really lumpy trip. I am not alone in this opinion either. Alker Tripp again: 'Spithead is lake-like when in quiet mood. But with a strong breeze, it becomes quite an awkward seaway for smaller craft; its waves are much more disconcerting to a small yacht than the seas outside, which – though so very much larger – are less steep and sudden.'

Whenever I have made the crossing, it has been wind against tide, bringing up a short sharp sea that has been on the beam all the way; and if there is one thing that makes me irritable and over anxious it is a beam sea. Turning to starboard also has its riddles.

Inside the wide expanse of the entrance to Bembridge Harbour is the outstanding marker from which Holy Stone is said to get its name.

Bembridge Ledge

This rocky foreland and its associated rocks all make for an infamous spot; one that catches unawares both locals and strangers alike. The frequent founderings are a cause of considerable speculation in Bembridge Harbour; for no one seems able to work out how or why otherwise perfectly capable skippers decide (or manage) to go inside the cardinal marker and come aground, even losing their vessels. The area is safe in the main, its hazards are well promulgated, and its dangers are supposed to be well known – and certainly should be to any skipper who no more than scans the charts. (There is a similar catch-all off the North Foreland: the Longnose. Most years, two or three craft get caught on the outcrop, in spite of the dangers being well marked by not one but two buoys.)

On the Bembridge Ledge, the Dicky Dawes' Rocks are named after a local smuggler who was well known to the revenue men. On one occasion, when he was in danger of being overhauled by a revenue cutter he 'went about' and evaded capture by exploiting his own (very local) knowledge to run through a deep gut within the ledge; a practice denied to the revenue cutters sailing close-hauled.

It is said that Dicky Dawes used to sink his contraband in the holes of these rocks, biding his time for their unseen recovery. Risks were, of course, considerable, and the penalty could be watching the revenue men saw your boat in half. Even just after the turn of the last century, when the halcyon days of smuggling were coming to an end, it was estimated that some 10,000 barrels of spirit were illicitly brought ashore for 're-export' to Southsea.

I am convinced that there is some strange and perhaps beautiful legend attached to the nearby, smaller Ethel Ledge, but so far my questions have been received with blank looks; I have been unable to uncover its (or her) derivation.

St Helen's Fort is the largest landmark in the vicinity of the approach to Bembridge.

Then round the back, the outside or the seaside

For the best study of this region of the island, what the navigator really needs is a collection of large-scale Ordnance Survey maps, geological and geographical surveys, as well as all the tourist and townie guides that can be acquired; for there is no harbour, haven, port or marina until Yarmouth is reached. Nor is there any chance of being able to anchor in any serious way, except in fine and settled weather. Under such pleasant summer conditions, cruising becomes mere holidaymaking, with skipper and crew alike transmogrified into happily wide-eyed sightseers, intent upon enjoying the varied spectacles that such a perception of the Isle of Wight offers in abundance.

At the very tip of Bembridge Ledge, the first and quite unmistakable landmark is the Foreland, with its intriguing ancillaries Long Ledge, Black Rock Ledge and the Run.

Inshore of the *West Princessa* cardinal, marking the Princessa Shoal, there is plenty of water to permit a close inspection of Whitecliff Bay. In good weather, it offers a calm anchorage; and the whole might well be almost an SSLPP (a Site of Special Lobster Pot Preservation). Its associated ledge reaches far out to the east, so it is necessary to take a wide sweep.

Shag Rock should be watched out for; it stands at the north end of the bay, where the cliffs are about 30 metres. Being very close in, it proffers no hazard except to those who are searching out the minutiae of nooks, niches and crannies that thereabouts abound. One interesting feature is known as the Nostrils.

Steep and gaunt, the great cliffs of Culver must be the most impressive sight in the area. They are filled with chinks, cracks and other eccentricities formed by the interface of harsh flint with soft chalk, a conjunction that frequently causes the cliff to crumble and fall. Nearby and high above, the Earl of Yarborough's monument stands out most conspicuously; while below there are the remains of the wreck of the old tug *Harry Sharman*.

Sandown Bay, with Shanklin, makes for one great tourist and entertainment expanse; yet still unspoiled and quite grand. Sandown featured in Domesday as Sande. After Sandown Pier, there are two rocky outposts to watch for: Horse and Yellow Ledge.

Round the corner, after Church Rocks, Monks Bay, and Horeshoe Bay come Wheelers Bay and Ventnor with its eponymous pier and bay. Ventnor, another seaside resort, nestles under the everlasting arms and protection of Saint Boniface Down. Then come three coves (Castle, Steephill and Sir Richard's) before Woody Point and Woody Bay. Next are Binnel Point, Binnel Bay, Puckaster Cove and Reeth Bay. These areas are well encumbered with natural nasties and fabricated detritus. They are to be well avoided. For those with a bent for closer exploration, I can do no better than recommend *Wight Hazards* by Peter Bruce.

Perhaps the biggest, most famous Point is St Catherine's. The beginnings of the powerful tide race and overfalls associated with St Catherine's can be felt as far to the east as Dunnose. They create a most uncomfortable stretch of water; one not wise to encounter when the wind is against the tide, especially on the ebb. Nearer to the Atherfield Ledges, the worst of the race and broken water is associated with the flood.

It is a matter of personal choice whether to try to avoid St Catherine's excesses by going right inside (which requires some courage and a great deal of local knowledge); right outside, which means a long haul if it is to be worthwhile; or to sweat it out, which can not only be extremely uncomfortable, but also dangerous. I have always tried to ensure I navigate round the Point with neaps and settled weather in my favour.

Well inshore from the conspicuous white lighthouse of St Catherine's is Niton; today, pre-eminent as the HQ of BT's Maritime Radio Service. At one time, it was notorious for its smugglers who used to row across to Cherbourg in galleys equipped with six – which, believe it or not, could outrun a sailing vessel to windward. Legend has it that some of the sailors used to go to great lengths to disguise their smuggled tobacco so that it looked like the ship's genuine rigging.

There is a spectacular view of the cliff and its undercliff which slipped and crumbled. Perched on the top, the tower was built by Walter de Gadeton in the 14th century as a religious peace offering, after he had his way with barrels of wine taken illegally from a wreck belonging to the church – one that could have been on its way to the Abbot of Quarr. It was furnished complete as an oratory and light beacon and rebuilt in 1811 for the Tsar's visit. There is no danger that you will confuse it with the real thing, the lighthouse built in 1840.

The octagonal tower with the conical roof is known as the Pepperpot. A light built later, though never used as it was built too high to be of use in fogs, is known as the Mustardpot. Just round the corner, after Rocken End and Watershoot Bay, come Chale Bay and Blackgang Chine.

The well marked ledges off Atherfield stretch out for about a mile off Atherfield Point. The low earth cliffs of Brook and Atherfield are impressive when close to, but when seen from any seaward distance, they are quite overcome by the splendour of the full island downs towering behind them. Atherfield Point with its ledges and fishing cove are to be avoided without local knowledge or piloted assistance.

The next major places of interest are Freshwater Bay and the Needles, but before they are reached there are some pleasingly characteristic sights of this side of the island to be observed: Brightstone Bay and Chilton Chine, Brook Bay and Compton Bay. There are also rocky-hazard items to be avoided: Brook Ledges, Hanover Point (and its associated Fossil Forest), Hardman Rock, and the intriguingly and pleasingly named Priscilla and Thimble Rocks.

Finally, we reach Freshwater Bay. On its western side, just beneath the Redoubt, are what are known as the Freshwater Caves; and at the eastern side are the Arched Rock, Stag Rock and Mermaid Rock which are all part of a long shelf of rocks. It seems likely that they once formed part of the main cliff, and, as token of that claim, there is still to be found a small patch of sea grass clinging to the top of the Mermaid. It is said that the Stag Rock got its name, many years ago, from a stag that was being pursued by hounds. No doubt as one between the devil and the deep blue sea it leapt for the rock from the cliff's edge, which was at that time less worn and consequently closer. Today it would be something of a gambado.

Freshwater Bay is unique on the island: a small-is-beautiful experience, where the bay was at one time no bay at all, with the cliffs showing a united facade simple to the sea. This former high rise is the face that now makes up the previously mentioned rocks, which, with rough weather, throw up ominous breakers, spume, surf and spray. An inhospitable spot at the worst of times, it is an idyllic spot at the best, with its waters being as turquoise clear as any off Cornwall.

Just to the west of Freshwater is Watcombe Bay with more caves. Neptune's is 200ft deep and nearby Bar is 90ft. Frenchman's Hole is so called because a fugitive Frenchman is supposed to have tried to find a secure billet there, but managed only to conceal himself for so long that in the end he starved himself to death.

Not far away are the strangely titled Lord Holme's Parlour and/or Kitchen and/or Cellar. Tradition says that the noble lord and gallant admiral used to entertain his guests in the first, while their feasts were prepared in the second and the wine kept in the third. Roe Hall towers a good 350ft above the nearby uniquely shaped masses of chalkstone known individually as Wedge Rock and Old Pepper Rock; while Main Bench is the name given to the by no means modest cliffs at the western extremity of this outcrop.

However, it is a tribute to another Lord that stands highest and most proud in this stretch. Nearly 40ft tall in Cornish granite, it is the Tennyson Cross, dating from 1897. It stands by what used to be known as High Down, 'the ridge of a noble down', and is now entitled Tennyson Down. The inscription reads, 'In memory of Alfred, Lord Tennyson this cross is raised, a beacon to sailors, by the people of Freshwater and other friends in England and America.'

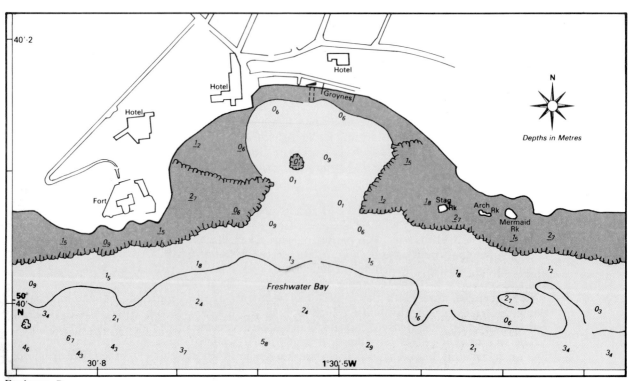

Freshwater Bay

In 1927, the late Lord Tennyson presented 155 acres of the down around the cross to the National Trust in memory of the poet laureate who, in his later years, used to make a daily pilgrimage to the spot, declaring the air on the downs to be worth sixpence a pint. In the landward hollow below is Farringford, his home. 'Round and round the spicy downs the yellow Lotosdust is blown... Live and lie reclined On the hills like Gods together, careless of mankind.'

Freshwater has for a long time been a place of pilgrimage, but was, of course, at its height in victorious Victorian and heady Edwardian days. Anne Thackeray, the daughter of the novelist, wrote, 'Everybody at Freshwater is either a genius, or a poet, or a painter or peculiar in some way.' After one of Tennyson's private readings of his poetry, she described the experience as 'a sort of mystical incantation.'

However, Tennyson was not the only writer who drooled over parts of the island. J. B. Priestly had a thing about Godshill, considering it to possess romantic scenery. Nearby, in 755 AD, St Boniface landed in the tiny cove now known as Monk's Bay; and 'maidens' used to dress his well on Feast Days.

Moving along, pretty little Bonchurch was something of a spellbinder to all sorts of scribblers: it was holiday host to Dickens; Keats, whose cliff-top abode was at close-by Shanklin, used to visit the place regularly, calling it Primrose Village. Alfred Noyes lived here for some time. Although he is best known for his highwayman curiosity (no doubt inspired by nefarious various locals), he also coined the following sea-based couplet:

'Apes and ivory, skulls and roses, in junks of old Hong-Kong,
Gliding over a sea of dreams to a haunted shore of song.'

Perhaps not exactly island based, but redolent of native atmosphere nevertheless.

Perhaps the most notorious of Bonchurch's clutch of writers was H. de Vere Stacpoole, whose (infamous) novel *The Blue Lagoon* was, it is said, inspired by its famous mini lake. He also wrote, 'Bonchurch's pond never fails to inspire me: it is an eternal source of romance and imagination. The whole area teems with romance. It is not difficult to close one's eyes of a summer evening and see fairy banquets in the garden.'

One who would see almost everything but fairy banquets at the bottom of his garden was born and buried there: Algernon Charles Swinburne. His lush mush and vexed sex must have been as much anathema to his neighbours as it was to Queen Victoria. One can imagine her cringing at Osborne as the air waves bore across such lines as:

'I will go back to the great sweet mother,
Mother and lover of men, the sea.
I will go down to her, I and no other,
Close with her, kiss her and mix her with me.'

Or indeed, these lines, even more likely to disturb, perturb and generally upset; one of his most famous and often quoted aspirations:

'Change in a trice
The lilies and languors of virtue
For the raptures and roses of vice.'

However, in *The Garden of Proserpine*, he turns his back on Baudelaire and Huysmans for a turn with Tennyson:

'From too much love of living,
From hope and fear set free,
We thank with brief thanksgiving,
Whatever gods there may be
That no life lives for ever;
That dead men rise up never;
That even the weariest river
Winds somewhere safe to the sea.'

Let us hope that he and his fellow languishing poets found their secure and sure rest.

The cliffs are host to swarms of seabirds: guillemots, puffins, razorbills and the good old herring gull. The best time to view the birds is about May, in springtime when a young bird's fancy turns to brideing and breeding.

Last before the Needles comes Scratchell's Bay. In calm and settled weather this makes an ideal spot for anchoring off and picnicking ashore – as witness the name of the eastern end, Sun Corner. However, there is the off-lying St Anthony's Rock, named after the wreck of the treasure ship, which dries to over half a metre. (There are others as well, for more detail, please see *Wight Hazards* by Peter Bruce). I would advise a LWS reconnoiter, standing safely off, before attempting any onshore onslaught; especially since Scratchell's Bay is now often celebrated for a particularly bizarre incident that occurred there over 200 years ago. There is an entry in the Lymington parish register dated May 20th, 1736 that reads as follows: 'Samuel Baldwyn, Esq., was immersed without the Needles, in Scratchell's Bay, sans ceremonie.' The tale is that the said Samuel Baldwyn's wife had threatened to dance on his grave, so, in order to thwart her worst wishes, he put a strict ordinance in his will that he was to be thrown into the sea. There are tales of moaning groans at very low tides, and some claim sightings of ghosts!

Cowper also has a word: 'In Scratchells Bay I have anchored, but I do not recommend it to others. Off Sun Corner, the angle of the cliff at the S. end of Scratchells Bay, lies Pepper Rock, which never or seldom covers. Off the Needles, in a N.W. by N. direction, distant about half a cable, there are two dangerous rocks. The Goose Rock, nearest in, dries, but the outer rock has only 6ft. on it.'

The Needles

The Needles consist of three quite separate isolated risers of chalk, solidly sombre at most times; but occasionally chocolate-boxish when their white heights show brilliantly against a turquoise sky, standing as gracious as any monarch's monument. My recurrent memories are of majestic grey chalk against looming grey clouds with the wind against the tide; and *Valcon* performing a slow dance of bows against short breakers to the rhythm and blues of the Shingles, as the voices of drowned sailors and deserted mermen growl and grumble from the bowels of the deep.

At one time, before the River Solent forced its way through to create the Island of Wight, the Needles formed one end of a long track of chalk ridge that ended with what is now known as Old Harry, by Swanage and Poole.

Pictures dating from the middle of the 18th century show a fourth, extremely slim riser, at about 120ft high. It fell in 1764, with a resounding noise that was heard all over the island. Its thin finger, known locally and variously as Cleopatra's Needle, Lot's Wife or the Thin Man, must have been the prime cause for their being named Needles since the rest much more resemble trunks, stumps or teeth. The fallen angel used to stand between the first and second from the shore. On the remaining proud peaks you can see cormorants, airily drying out. They are known locally by the fetching name of Isle of Wight Parsons.

It is not without significance that Tennyson frequently passed within singing distance of the Shingles, just around the corner, when being ferried from Lymington to Wight. It is now common knowledge (except to the inhabitants of Salcombe in South Devon, who have their own territorial claim) that it was on one of these ferry journeys back to his home on the island that he composed the famous lines *On Crossing the Bar*. I believe it equally likely that the strange sounds that emerge from this underwater bank of stones gave rise to another of his famous water poems, *The Kraken*.

> Below the thunders of the upper deep;
> Far, far beneath in the abysmal sea,
> His ancient, dreamless, uninvaded sleep
> The Kraken sleepeth: faintest sunlights flee
> About his shadowy sides: above him swell
> Huge sponges of millennial growth and height;
> And far away into the sickly light,
> From many a wondrous grot and secret cell
> Unnumbered and enormous polypi°
> Winnow with giant arms the slumbering green.
> There hath he lain for ages and will lie
> Battening upon huge seaworms in his sleep,
> Until the latter fire shall heat the deep;
> Then once by man and angels to be seen,
> In roaring he shall rise and on the surface die.

However, it is on quite a different note, from another of his works, that we can now quit the island:

> 'Surely, surely, slumber is more sweet than toil, the shore
> Than labour in the deep mid-ocean, wind and wave and oar;
> Oh rest ye, brother mariners, we will not wander more.'

But, as so often, the last word must go to Shakespeare: 'Be not afeard: The isle is full of noises, Sounds and sweet airs that give delight and hurt not.'

Appendix

I. CHARTS

Admiralty

Chart	Title	Scale
394	The Solent – Eastern Part	20,000
1905	Southampton Water and approaches	20,000
2021	Harbours and anchorages in the West Solent	
	Yarmouth	3,000
	Freshwater Bay	5,000
	Lymington	5,000
	Alum Bay	10,000
	Beaulieu River	10,000
	Newtown River	12,500
	River Yar	12,500
	Approaches to Keyhaven	7,500
2022	Harbours and anchorages in the East Solent	
	Hillhead Harbour	3,000
	Bembridge Harbour	5,000
	Entrance to River Hamble	5,000
	Ashlett Creek	10,000
	Wootton Creek	10,000
	Sandown Bay	20,000
	Bursledon to Botley	25,000
2040	The Solent – Western Part	20,000
2041	Port of Southampton	10,000
2050	Eastern approaches to the Solent	75,000
2625	Approaches to Portsmouth	7,500
2631	Portsmouth Harbour	7,500
2793	Cowes Harbour and River Medina	3,500
	Folly Point to Newport	10,000
3418	Langstone and Chichester Harbours	20,000

Imray

C3	Isle of Wight	52,000
	Plans Southampton Water, Hamble River, Lymington, Bembridge	
C9	Isle of Wight to Beachy Head	112,000
	Plans Newhaven, Shoreham, Littlehampton, Brighton, Portsmouth	
C15	The Solent	
	Plans River Hamble, River Itchen, Yarmouth, Lymington, Beaulieu, Wootton Creek, Newtown River, Cowes, Bembridge, Hythe Marina Village	35,200
Y33	Langstone and Chichester Harbour	22,000
	Plans Northney Marina, Emsworth Yacht Harbour, Chichester Yacht Basin and Birdham Pool	

II. USEFUL ADDRESSES

ROYAL YACHTING ASSOCIATION

The RYA is now sited not far from the Solent area:
Royal Yachting Association, RYA House, Romsey Road, Eastleigh, Hampshire SO5 4YA.
☎ Southampton (0703) 629962

SOLENT YACHT CLUBS

There are many yacht clubs in the Solent area. The following is a list of the main ones.

Beaulieu River Sailing Club
Needs Ore Point, Beaulieu, Hants.

Bembridge Sailing Club
Embankment Road, Bembridge,
Isle of Wight PO35 5NR
☎ Isle of Wight (0983) 872686 (Clubhouse)

Brading Haven Yacht Club
Embankment Road, Bembridge,
Isle of Wight PO35 5NS
☎ (0983) 872289

Civil Service Sailing Club
Portsmouth Group, The Sailing Centre,
Weevil Lane, Gosport, Hants PO12 1AZ

Cowes Corinthian Yacht Club
39 Birmingham Road, Cowes,
Isle of Wight PO31 7BH
☎ Isle of Wight (0983) 292405/296333 (Secretary),
☎ Isle of Wight (0983) 293526 (Members)

Eastney Cruising Association
Fort Point, Ferry Road,
Eastney, Southsea, Hants PO4 9LY
☎ Office Portsmouth (0705) 734103
☎ Members Portsmouth (0705) 827396

Fareham Sailing & Motor Boat Club
The Boathouse, Lower Quay,
Fareham, Hants PO16 0RA

Gurnard Sailing Club
Shore Road, Gurnard, Isle of Wight PO31 8LD
☎ Isle of Wight (0983) 295169

Hamble River Sailing Club
The Ferry Hard, The Green,
Hamble, Southampton SO3 5JB
☎ Southampton (0703) 456201

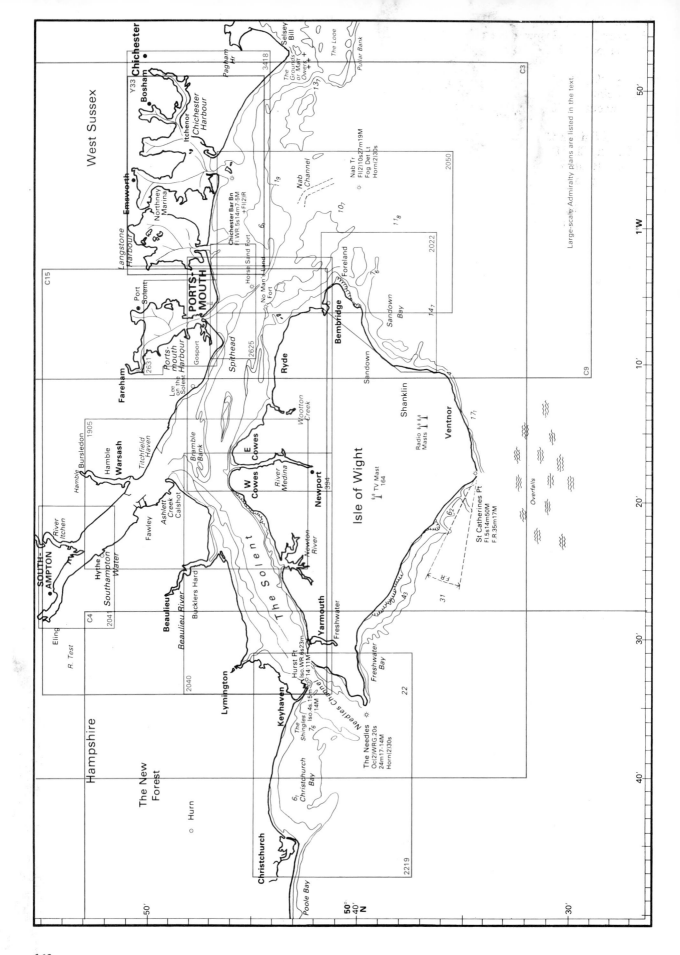

The map/chart contains the following labels:

Hampshire

West Sussex

Selsey Bill

The Looe

Chichester
Bosham
Y33
Pagham Hr
3418

Itchenor
Chichester Harbour

Emsworth

Northney Marina
Langstone Harbour

The Grounds or Malt Owers
13₇

PORTS-MOUTH
Chichester Bar Bn
Fl.WR.5s14m7.5M
+Fl(2)IR

11₉

Nab Channel

Nab Tr
Fl(2)10s27m19M
Fog Det Lt
Horn(2)30s
2050

10₇

11₈

Port Solent

C15

Horse Sand Fort

No Man's Land Fort

Fareham

2022

Portsmouth Harbour
2631

Gosport

Spithead

2625

Lee on the Solent

Ryde

Bembridge

Foreland

6

14₇

C9

Sandown Bay

Sandown

Wootton Creek

Shanklin

Ventnor

17₁

Bramble Bank

Hamble Bursledon
1905

Hamble
Warsash

Titchfield Haven

Radio Masts

Isle of Wight

W E
Cowes

W Cowes

River Medina

Newport
394

TV Mast
164

River Itchen

SOUTH-AMPTON

Ashlett Creek
Calshot

Fawley

Hythe
Southampton Water

Newtown River

St Catherines Pt
Fl.5s14m50M
F.R.35m17M

6₂

F.R

31

4₃

The New Forest

R. Test

Eling

C4
2041

Beaulieu
Beaulieu River

Bucklers Hard

Yarmouth

Freshwater

The Solent

Lymington
2040

Overfalls

Hurst Pt
Iso.WR.6s23m
14 11M
14M

Keyhaven

Freshwater Bay

22

Needles Channel

The Shingles

The Needles
Oc(2)WRG.20s
24m17-14M
Horn(2)30s

7₆

Christchurch

Christchurch Bay
6₁

Hurn

Poole Bay

2219

50° 40′ N

50′

1°W

50′

10′

20′

30′

40′

30′

Large-scale Admiralty plans are listed in the text.

162

Hardway Sailing Club
103 Priory Road, Gosport, Hants PO12 4LF
☎ Portsmouth (0705) 581875

Hayling Island Sailing Club
Sandy Point, Hayling Island, Hants PO11 9SL
☎ Portsmouth (0705) 463115

Hill Head Sailing Club
The Haven, Cliff Road, Hill Head,
Fareham, Hants PO14 3JT
☎ Stubbington (0329) 664843

Hurst Castle Sailing Club
The Clubhouse, Keyhaven,
Lymington, Hants SO41 0TP

Island Sailing Club
70 High Street, Cowes, Isle of Wight PO31 7RE
☎ Isle of Wight (0983) 296911

Keyhaven Yacht Club
The Clubhouse, Keyhaven,
Lymington, Hants SO41 0TR
☎ Lymington (0590) 43253

Lee-on-the-Solent Sailing Club
46, Marine Parade East,
Lee-on-the-Solent, Hants PO13 9BW
☎ Lee-on-the-Solent (0705) 550317 (Members)
Except Tuesday morning, phone calls will be
answered during normal licensing hours.

Lymington Town Sailing Club Ltd
Bath House, Bath Road,
Lymington, Hants SO41 9SE
☎ (0590) 672096

Medina Mariners' Association
c/o Folly Harbour Office,
Whippingham, Isle of Wight PO32 6NB
☎ Isle of Wight (0983) 297815

Netley Sailing Club (A.S.A.)
Adjoining Royal Victoria Country Park,
Netley Abbey, Southampton SO3 5GA
☎ Southampton (0703) 454272

Portchester Sailing Club
The Old Vicarage, Waterside Lane,
Porchester, Hants PO16 9QN
☎ Cosham (0705) 376375

Portsmouth Sailing Club
21 Bath Square, Old Portsmouth, Hants PO1 2JL
☎ Portsmouth (0705) 820596

Royal Air Force Yacht Club
Riverside House, Hamble, Southampton SO3 5HD
☎ Southampton (0703) 453278

Royal Corinthian Yacht Club
Castle Rock, The Parade,
Cowes, Isle of Wight PO31 7QU
☎ Isle of Wight (0983) 292608

Royal London Yacht Club
The Parade, Cowes, Isle of Wight PO31 7QS
☎ Isle of Wight (0983) 292949

Royal Lymington Yacht Club
Bath Road, Lymington, Hants SO41 9SE
☎ (0590) 672677

Royal Naval Club and Royal Albert Yacht Club
17 Pembroke Road, Portsmouth PO1 2NT
☎ Portsmouth (0705) 824491

Royal Naval Sailing Association
c/o RNC and RAYC, 17 Pembroke Road,
Old Portsmouth, PO1 2NT
☎ Portsmouth (0705) 823524 & 822351, Ext. 23701

Royal Solent Yacht Club
Yarmouth, Isle of Wight, PO4 0NS
☎ Isle of Wight (0983) 760256 (Office)
☎ Isle of Wight (0983) 760239 (Members)

Royal Southampton Yacht Club
1 Channel Way, Ocean Village,
Southampton SO1 1XE
☎ Southampton (0703) 223352

Royal Southern Yacht Club
Hamble, Southampton SO3 5HB
☎ Southampton (0703) 452179

Royal Yacht Squadron
The Castle, Cowes, Isle of Wight PO31 7QT
☎ Isle of Wight (0983) 292191

Royal Victoria Yacht Club
91 Fishbourne Lane,
Ryde, Isle of Wight PO33 4EU
☎ Isle of Wight (0983) 882325

Sea View Yacht Club
The Esplanade, Seaview, Isle of Wight PO34 5HB
☎ Isle of Wight (0983) 613118

Stokes Bay Sailing Club
The Promenade, Stokes Bay, Alverstoke,
Gosport, Hants PO12 2AU
☎ Portsmouth (0705) 581513

Warsash Sailing Club
Shore House, Shore Road,
Warsash, Southampton SO3 6FS
☎ Locks Heath (0489) 83575 & 6651 (Quay House)

Yarmouth Sailing Club
Bridge Road, Yarmouth, Isle of Wight, PO41 0NL
☎ Isle of Wight (0983) 760270

HARBOURMASTERS

Beaulieu River and Buckler's Hard Yacht Harbour
Harbourmaster W. H. J. Grindey
Bucklers Hard, Beaulieu,
Brockenhurst, Hants SO4 7XB
☎ Lymington (0590) 63200 and 6323

Bembridge Harbour
General manager M. H. Coombes
Harbour Office, Bembridge, Isle of Wight
☎ Isle of Wight (0983) 872828

Chichester Harbour
Harbourmaster Captain J. A. H. Whitney
The Harbour Office, Itchenor,
Chichester, West Sussex PO20 7AW
☎ Chichester (0243) 512301

Cowes Harbour
Harbourmaster Captain H. N. J. Wrigley
Town Quays, Cowes, Isle of Wight
☎ Isle of Wight (0983) 293952

Hamble River
Harbourmaster Captain C. J. Nichol, O.B.E.
Harbourmaster's Office, Shore Road, Warsash.
☎ Locks Heath (048 95) 6387.

Keyhaven
River warden Tom Holt, Esq.,
River Warden's Office, The Quay,
Keyhaven, Nr. Lymington.
☎ Lymington (0590) 645695

Langstone Harbour
Harbourmaster H. J. Owen, Esq.,
☎ Portsmouth (0705)463419

Lymington River
Harbourmaster F. Woodford
Harbourmaster's Office, Bath Road, Lymington.
☎ Lymington (0590) 672014

Newtown River
Controlled by the National Trust
Harbourmaster Captain Abernethy,
Hollis Cottage, Newtown, Nr Newport,
Isle of Wight, PO30 4PA.
☎ Isle of Wight (0983) 78424

Newport Harbour
Controlled by Medina Borough Council
Harbourmaster W. G. Pritchett
Town Quay, Newport.
☎ Isle of Wight (0983) 525994 & 520000 Ext. 2144

Yarmouth Harbour
Harbourmaster Captain N. W. Hunt, The Quay,
Yarmouth, Isle of Wight, PO41 0NT.
☎ Isle of Wight (0983) 760321

Wootton Creek
Wootton Creek Fairways Association,
Hon. Sec. R. W. Perraton Esq.,
The Moorings, Sloop Lane,
Wootton Bridge, Nr Ryde, Isle of Wight.
☎ Isle of Wight (0983) 882763

III. BEAUFORT SCALE

Beaufort No.	Description of wind	Velocity in knots	Velocity in mph	Velocity in km/h	Sea state code	Sea state term	Sea criterion	Wave height in metres	Land observations
0	Calm	<1	<1	<1	0	Calm glassy	Like a mirror.	0	Calm, smoke rises vertically
1	Light air	1–3	1–3	1–5	1	Calm rippled	Ripples.	0–0·1	Direction of wind shown by smoke drift but not by wind vanes.
2	Light breeze	4–6	4–7	6–11	2	Smooth wavelets	Small wavelets.	0·1–0·5	Wind felt on face, leaves rustle, ordinary vanes moved by wind.
3	Gentle breeze	7–10	8–12	12–19	3	Slight	Large wavelets.	0·5–1·25	Leaves and small twigs in constant motion, wind extends light flag.
4	Moderate breeze	11–16	13–18	20–28	4	Moderate	Small waves, breaking.	1·25–2·5	Raises dust and loose paper, small branches are moved.
5	Fresh breeze	17–21	19–24	29–38	5	Rough	Moderate waves, foam.	2·5–4	Small trees in leaf begin to sway, crested wavelets form on inland waters.
6	Strong breeze	22–27	25–31	39–49			Large waves, foam and spray.		Large branches in motion, whistling heard in telegraph wires, umbrellas difficult.
7	Near gale	28–33	32–38	50–61	6	Very rough	Sea heaps up, foam in streaks.	4–6	Whole trees in motion, inconvenience felt walking.
8	Gale	34–40	39–46	62–74			Higher longer waves, foam in streaks.		Breaks twigs off trees, generally impedes progress.
9	Strong gale	41–47	47–54	75–88	7	High	High waves, dense streaks of foam, spray impairs visibility.	6–9	Slight structural damage occurs (chimney pots and slates removed).
10	Storm	48–55	55–63	89–102	8	Very high	Very high tumbling waves, surface white with foam, visibility affected.	9–14	Seldom experienced inland, trees uprooted, considerable structural damage occurs.
11	Violent storm	56–63	64–72	103–117	9	Phenomenal	Exceptionally high waves, sea covered in foam, visibility affected.	>14	Very rarely experienced, accompanied by widespread damage.
12	Hurricane	>63	>72	>118			Air filled with spray and foam, visibility very severely affected.		

IV. CONVERSION TABLES

metres–feet

m	ft/	ft
0·3	1	3·3
0·6	2	6·6
0·9	3	9·8
1·2	4	13·1
1·5	5	16·4
1·8	6	19·7
2·1	7	23·0
2·4	8	26·2
2·7	9	29·5
3·0	10	32·8
6·1	20	65·6
9·1	30	98·4
12·2	40	131·2
15·2	50	164·0
30·5	100	328·1

centimetres–inches

cm	in/cm	in
2·5	1	0·4
5·1	2	0·8
7·6	3	1·2
10·2	4	1·6
12·7	5	2·0
15·2	6	2·4
17·8	7	2·8
20·3	8	3·1
22·9	9	3·5
25·4	10	3·9
50·8	20	7·9
76·2	30	11·8
101·6	40	15·7
127·0	50	19·7
254·0	100	39·4

metres–fathoms–feet

m	fathoms	ft
0·9	0·5	3
1·8	1	6
3·7	2	12
5·5	3	18
7·3	4	24
9·1	5	30
11·0	6	36
12·8	7	42
14·6	8	48
16·5	9	54
18·3	10	60
36·6	20	120
54·9	30	180
73·2	40	240
91·4	50	300

kilometres–statute miles

km	M/km	M
1·6	1	0·6
3·2	2	1·2
4·8	3	1·9
6·4	4	2·5
8·0	5	3·1
9·7	6	3·7
11·3	7	4·3
12·9	8	5·0
14·5	9	5·6
16·1	10	6·2
32·2	20	12·4
48·3	30	18·6
64·4	40	24·9
80·5	50	31·1
120·7	75	46·6
160·9	100	62·1
402·3	250	155·3
804·7	500	310·7
1609·3	1000	621·4

kilograms–pounds

kg	lb/kg	lb
0·5	1	2·2
0·9	2	4·4
1·4	3	6·6
1·8	4	8·8
2·3	5	11·0
2·7	6	13·2
3·2	7	15·4
3·6	8	17·6
4·1	9	19·8
4·5	10	22·0
9·1	20	44·1
13·6	30	66·1
18·1	40	88·2
22·7	50	110·2
34·0	75	165·3
45·4	100	220·5
113·4	250	551·2
226·8	500	1102·3
453·6	1000	2204·6

litres–gallons

l	gal/l	gal
4·5	1	0·2
9·1	2	0·4
13·6	3	0·7
18·2	4	0·9
22·7	5	1·1
27·3	6	1·3
31·8	7	1·5
36·4	8	1·8
40·9	9	2·0
45·5	10	2·2
90·9	20	4·4
136·4	30	6·6
181·8	40	8·8
227·3	50	11·0
341·0	75	16·5
454·6	100	22·0
1136·5	250	55·0
2273·0	500	110·0
4546·1	1000	220·0

Index